D1077593

KENYA

FODOR'S TRAVEL PUBLICATIONS

are compiled, researched, and edited by an international team of travel writers, field correspondents, and editors. The series, which now almost covers the globe, was founded by Eugene Fodor in 1936.

OFFICES
New York & London

Fodor's Kenya

Area Editor: Pamela Carson
Editorial Contributors: John Eames, Hilary Hughes, John Mayor, Ian Slack
Executive Editor: Richard Moore
Assistant Editors: Thomas Cussans, Margaret Sinclair
Illustrations: David Canright, Beryl Sanders
Maps and Plans: Brian Stimson, Swanston Graphics, Bryan Woodfield
Photographs: Photobank, Scenario Features (Nairobi)

SPECIAL SALES

Fodor's Travel Publications are available at special discounts for bulk purchases (100 copies or more) for sales promotions or premiums. Special editions, including personalized covers, excerpts of existing guides, and corporate imprints, can be created in large quantities for special needs. For more information, write to Special Marketing, Fodor's Travel Publications, 201 East 50th Street, New York, NY 10022.

FODOR'S
KENYA

FODOR'S TRAVEL PUBLICATIONS, INC.
New York & London

Copyright © 1987 by Fodor's Travel Publications, Inc.

All rights reserved under International and Pan-American Copyright Conventions. Published in the United States by Fodor's Travel Publications, Inc., a subsidiary of Random House, Inc., New York, and simultaneously in Canada by Random House of Canada Limited, Toronto. Distributed by Random House, Inc., New York.

No maps, illustrations, or other portions of this book may be reproduced in any form without written permission from the publisher.

ISBN 0-679-01378-4
ISBN 0-340-40011-0   (Hodder & Stoughton)

The following Fodor's guides are currently available; most are also published in a British edition by Hodder & Stoughton.

Country and Area Guides

Australia, New Zealand
  & the South Pacific
Austria
Bahamas
Belgium & Luxembourg
Bermuda
Brazil
Canada
Canada's Maritime
  Provinces
Caribbean
Central America
Eastern Europe
Egypt
Europe
France
Germany
Great Britain
Greece
Holland
Hungary
India, Nepal & Sri Lanka
Ireland
Israel
Italy
Japan
Jordan & the Holy Land
Kenya
Korea
Loire Valley
Mexico
New Zealand
North Africa
People's Republic
  of China
Portugal
Province of Quebec
Scandinavia
Scotland
South America
South Pacific
Southeast Asia
Soviet Union
Spain
Sweden
Switzerland
Turkey
Yugoslavia

City Guides

Amsterdam
Beijing, Guangzhou,
  Shanghai
Boston
Chicago
Dallas & Fort Worth
Florence & Venice
Greater Miami & the
  Gold Coast
Hong Kong
Houston & Galveston
Lisbon
London
Los Angeles
Madrid
Mexico City &
  Acapulco
Munich
New Orleans
New York City
Paris
Philadelphia
Rome
San Diego
San Francisco
Singapore
Stockholm, Copenhagen,
  Oslo, Helsinki &
  Reykjavik
Sydney
Tokyo
Toronto
Vienna
Washington, D.C.

U.S.A. Guides

Alaska
Arizona
Atlantic City & the
  New Jersey Shore
California
Cape Cod
Chesapeake
Colorado
Far West
Florida
Hawaii
I–10: California to Florida
I–55: Chicago to
  New Orleans
I–75: Michigan to Florida
I–80: San Francisco to
  New York
I–95: Maine to Miami

New England
New Mexico
New York State
Pacific North Coast
South
Texas
U.S.A.
Virginia
Williamsburg, Jamestown
  & Yorktown

Budget Travel

American Cities (30)
Britain
Canada
Caribbean
Europe
France
Germany
Hawaii
Italy
Japan
London
Mexico
Spain

Fun Guides

Acapulco
Bahamas
Las Vegas
London
Maui
Montreal
New Orleans
New York City
The Orlando Area
Paris
Puerto Rico
Rio
Riviera
St. Martin/Sint Maarten
San Francisco
Waikiki

Special-Interest Guides

The Bed & Breakfast Guide
Selected Hotels of Europe
Ski Resorts of North
  America
Views to Dine by around
  the World

MANUFACTURED IN THE UNITED STATES OF AMERICA   10 9 8 7 6 5 4 3 2 1

CONTENTS

v

NATIONAL PARKS AND GAME RESERVES

Marine National Parks

Mountain National Parks

FOREWORD

To the popular imagination, nourished by Hemingway and countless movies shot with Kilimanjaro as a backdrop, Kenya *is* Africa. The thrills of archetypal safaris, with rhinos, buffalos and hyenas crowding to an evening waterhole or lions and cheetahs stalking a passing Land Rover, vie with miles of relaxed beaches, protected by an endless coral reef. Out of a history of Great White Hunters—among whom Teddy Roosevelt looms bear-large—has grown a romantic appeal which inexorably draws the modern traveler in search of change from the usual vacation destination.

Nor will Kenya disappoint those expectations. Although the country is suffering from many of the ills that are besetting a large part of Africa—food shortages and economic difficulties—a visit there is still an adventure worth while undertaking.

This recent addition to our series is organized slightly differently from our other books. The early chapters cover information to help you plan your trip, followed by a brief look at Kenyan history and details of some of the animals and birds that you are likely to see in the National Parks. Then come eight chapters which breakdown the country into areas, including the two main cities, Nairobi and Mombasa, with a certain amount of practical information. The final section of the Guide covers the National Parks more fully, including the Marine Parks and the Mountain Parks, with Park Data, outlining some of the useful information to help with visits to these fascinating areas.

We would like to thank the many people who have helped us during the preparation of this edition. Ms. Wangui M. Karanja, Tourist Officer of the Kenya Tourist Office in London and her staff; Mr. Ndavi, Information Attaché of the Kenya High Commission in London and his staff; Mr. J.M. Gitau, Deputy Secretary of the Ministry of Tourism in Nairobi for his interest and assistance; and many experts and friends for putting their knowledge at our disposal. Among them we would like to thank especially Pamela Carson for her invaluable help and advice.

All prices quoted in this Guide are based on those available to us at the time of writing, mid 1986. Given the uncertain economic climate and the considerable volatility of current costs in Kenya, it is inevitable that changes will have taken place by the time this book becomes available. We trust, therefore, that you will take prices quoted as indicators only, and will double-check to be sure of the latest figures.

We really do welcome letters, telling us of your experiences or correcting any errors that may have crept into the Guide. Such letters help us to improve our coverage, and also give us that essential "consumer's eye view," which is so helpful to all compilers of travel guides.

Our addresses are —
in the U.S.: Fodor's Travel Publications, 201 East 50th Street, New York, NY 10022.
in Europe: Fodor's Travel Publications, 9-10 Market Place, London W1.

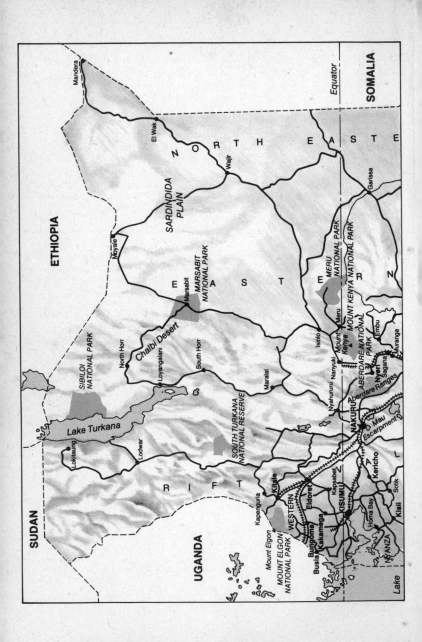

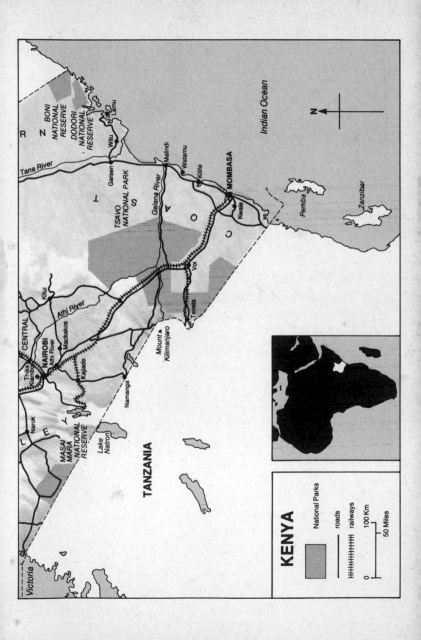

LANGUAGE/30

For the Business or Vacationing International Traveler

In 30 languages! A basic language course on 2 cassettes and a phrase book . . . Only $14.95 ea. + shipping

Nothing flatters people more than to hear visitors try to speak their language and LANGUAGE/30, used by thousands of satisfied travelers, gets you speaking the basics quickly and easily. Each LANGUAGE/30 course offers:

- approximately 1½ hours of guided practice in greetings, asking questions and general conversation
- special section on social customs and etiquette

Order yours today. Languages available: YIDDISH (available fall '86)

ARABIC	INDONESIAN	PORTUGUESE
CHINESE	IRISH	VIETNAMESE
DANISH	ITALIAN	RUSSIAN
DUTCH	TURKISH	SERBO-CROATIAN
FINNISH	JAPANESE	SPANISH
FRENCH	KOREAN	SWAHILI
GERMAN	LATIN	SWEDISH
GREEK	NORWEGIAN	TAGALOG
HEBREW	PERSIAN	THAI
HINDI	POLISH	

To order send $14.95 per course + shipping $2.00 1st course, $1 ea. add. course. In Canada $3 1st course, $2.00 ea. add. course. NY and CA residents add state sales tax. Outside USA and Canada $14.95 (U.S.) + air mail shipping: $8 for 1st course, $5 ea. add. course. MasterCard, VISA and Am. Express card users give brand, account number (all digits), expiration date and signature.
SEND TO: FODOR'S, Dept. LC 760, 2 Park Ave., NY 10016-5677, USA.

FACTS AT YOUR FINGERTIPS

PLANNING YOUR TRIP. Naturally, what your visit to Kenya will cost entirely depends on what kind of trip you are contemplating—on your choice of safari, the degree of comfort you want and so on. There is a huge range of possibilities but, whatever trip you like the sound of, remember that there is one factor that you should always keep in mind—namely that a large chunk of your outlay will be spent on simply getting you to Kenya and back. For this very reason it would be well to study as many of the available tour programs as you can. They vary tremendously in their coverage, and can include either coast resort or safari, or a combination of the two.

Living costs in Kenya are fairly reasonable, though—as with most major vacation destinations—they vary considerably with the season. While accommodations in Nairobi and Mombasa compare very favorably with U.S. and European prices, the safari lodges tend to be costlier, due to their remoteness from centers of supply.

One of the other factors which can be significant when planning a Kenya trip is that many of the attractions of the country are best experienced in a group, even a small one of, say, four or six. This will also help spread the outlay a bit.

SOURCES OF INFORMATION. The Kenya Tourist Offices or Diplomatic Missions abroad, which can give you any information you might need over and above that supplied by your tour operator, are—
Kenya Tourist Offices—U.S.—East: 424 Madison Ave., New York, NY 10017 (212–486–1300). **West:** Doheny Plaza, Suite 111–112, 9100 Wilshire Blvd., Los Angeles, CA 90212 (213–274–6635). **U.K.:** 13 New Burlington St., London W.1 (01–839 4477/8).
Kenya Diplomatic Missions—Canada: Gillia Building, Suite 600, 141 Laurier Ave., West Ottawa, Ont. K1P 5J3. **U.K:** 45 Portland Place, London W1N 4AS (01–636 2371/5). **U.S.:** 2249 R St. NW, Washington D.C. 20008 (202–387 –6101/2/3/4).

TOUR OPERATORS. Africa specialist firms tend to come and go, but the following are a few of those which have stayed the course, and have Kenya programs that cover both safari trips and coastal holidays.

In North America. Abercrombie & Kent, 1420 Kensington Rd., Suite 111, Oak Brook, IL 60521 (312–954–2944).
Four Winds Travel Inc., 175 5th Ave., New York, N.Y. 10010 (212–505–0901).

1

East Africa Travel Consultants Inc., 574 Parliament St., (Cabbagetown), Toronto, Ont. M4X 1P8 (416–967–0067).

KLR International Inc., 1560 Broadway, New York, NY 10036 (212–869–2850).

Lindblad Travel, PO Box 912, Westport, CT 06881 (800–243–5657).

Maupintour, 1515 St. Andrew's Drive, Lawrence, KS 66044 (913–843–1211).

Mountain Travel, 1398 Solano Ave., Albany, CA 94706 (415–527–8100).

Park East Tours, 1841 Broadway, New York, NY 10023 (800–223–6078, 212–765–4870).

Perry Mason Safaris, PO Box 1643, Darien, CT 06820 (203–838–3075).

Thorn Tree Safaris, 1352 Broadway, Hewlett, NY 11557 (516–826–8776).

United Touring International, 1315 Walnut St., Suite 1704, Philadelphia, PA 19107 (215–545–1355).

In the U.K. Abercrombie and Kent, 42 Sloane St., London S.W.1 (tel. 01–235 9761–4).

Hayes and Jarvis, 6 Harriet St., London S.W.1 (tel. 01–235 3648).

Kuoni Travel, 33 Maddox St., London W.1 (for personal callers only); Kuoni House, Dorking, Surrey (tel. 0306 885044).

Rankin Kuhn, 13–17 New Burlington Place, London W.1 (tel. 01–439 4120).

Sovereign Holidays, P.O. Box 410, West London Terminal, Cromwell Rd., London S.W.7 (tel. 01–370 4545).

Speedbird Worldwide, 152 King St., London W.6 (tel. 01–741 8041).

Swan Hellenic, 77 New Oxford St., London W.C.1 (tel. 01–831 1616).

Tracks Africa Ltd., 12 Abingdon Rd., London W.8 (tel. 01–937 3028).

 WHEN TO GO. The tourist year divides up into high, middle and low seasons, but the interpretation of the precise periods these cover seems to vary between one tour operator or hotelier to the other. One of the leading safari firms, which knows the country and the U.S. trade better than most, sets it out as follows:

High—December 1 to March 31 and June 1 to August 31; *Low*—April 1 to May 31 and September 1 to November 31; the rest is *Middle* season. The weather at any time in the year is fine, if intermittently fine at the coast and in the highlands during "the long rains" (April to June) and the "short rains" (October to November).

The seasons make virtually no difference at all to the safari in the arid Lake Turkana area. In fact, the impact of the rains up there, such as they are, is the odd flash-flood along the myriad of normally dry sand rivers or *luggas* and the occasional wild-flower blooming in the desert. The roads—mostly sand tracks—are sometimes washed out and impassable in the fringe areas of the desert, around Samburu or up the coast from Malindi to Lamu. But usually there's no real problem for a northern Kenya safari in the low season, particularly if you go by four-wheel drive vehicle or camel.

Elsewhere in the country, the rains can make a mess of the roads—in the highland areas, for instance, over the Aberdares, around Mount Kenya and in parts of Masailand. Sometimes the roads are closed for a while in the mountain parks. But apart from the odd day now and then, the tracks in the 8,000 square miles of Tsavo are passable.

At the coast the character of the rains is a downpour followed by a break in the clouds for a long, bright interval. It's seldom overcast and miserable all day anywhere in the country, apart from the higher sections of the highlands.

For many resident "shag-bags" (a local colloquialism for persistent safari-types) the low or rainy season is actually preferred. The country is more spectacular, vivid green and flowering, with dramatic skies for a backdrop to the photographs. It's also the affordable season, with most of the tour operators and hotels offering rates geared to tick-over rather than profit.

In the high season, it's more or less twelve hours of daily sunshine—but it's an expensive time and often difficult to find a bed, especially in the safari lodges and camps.

Another factor in deciding when to make the trip is the incidence of the animal mass migrations. The most photogenic of these, with up to two million plains game on the move, is in the Masai Mara anywhere from mid-August to the end of September.

 SEASONAL EVENTS. There is not much in the way of regular annual happenings—apart from the Agricultural Shows, in particular the Nairobi International in September. The big sports annual is the Safari Rally at Easter, and there are a number of regular fishing festivals at the coast between November and January.

Public Holidays. New Year's Day; May 1 (Labor Day); June 1 (Madaraka Day, the anniversary of Kenya's self-government); October 20 (Kenyatta Day); December 12 (Jamhuri or National Independence Day); Christmas Day and Boxing Day; Easter (Good Friday and Easter Monday); Idd ul Fitr, the Moslem holiday, a moveable feast at the first sighting of the new moon after Ramadhan.

 MONEY. Kenya shillings and cents are worked on the decimal system—100 cents equals one shilling, written Shs.1/-. Coins are copper—five cents and ten cents; silver—50 cents, and one shilling; notes—Shs. 5/-, 10/-, 20/- (still called a pound), 50/- and 100/-.

The rate of exchange varies daily, of course, but was approximately Shs. 13/- to the U.S. dollar and around Shs. 24/- to the pound sterling as we went to press, mid 1986.

The national banking authority is The Central Bank of Kenya, Harambee Avenue, P.O. Box 30463, Nairobi. There are two major government-owned commercial banks and a number of sectoral development banks. Of the foreign banks operating in Kenya, most are British-based with others headquartered in the United States, the Netherlands, India and one or two of the Arab states.

If you are intending to use **credit cards,** check with the issuing agency on their validity in Kenya. American Express, Diners and Visa cards are acceptable to a limited extent in a country not yet won over to plastic credit.

Travelers' checks can be cashed at banks and hotels and also at lodges on safari, and a receipt should be obtained. On departure from Kenya this receipt will have to be shown to the cashier at the airport bank before any surplus Kenya cash can be converted into overseas currency. When cashing travelers' checks you will be required to show your passport.

 TRAVEL DOCUMENTS. Generally there is a delay in getting a passport, so give it priority in your plans. **U.S. residents** may apply in person to U.S. Passport Agency Offices, at selected Post Offices and county courthouses. They will need 1) proof of citizenship, such as a birth certificate; 2) two identical photographs, in either black and white or color, two inches square, on nonglossy paper and taken within the past six months; 3) $35 for the passport itself plus a $7 processing fee if applying in person (no processing fee when applying by mail) for those 18 years and older, or if under 18, $20 for the passport plus a $7 processing fee if applying in person (again, no extra fee when applying by mail). Adult passports are valid for ten years, others for five years; 4) proof of identity such as a driver's license, previous passport, any governmental ID card, or a copy of an income tax return. When you receive your passport write down its number, date and place of issue separately; if it is later lost or stolen, notify either the nearest American Consul or the Passport Office, Department of State, Washington, DC 20524, as well as the local police.

British subjects. Passport forms are obtainable from your travel agent or local head post office. The application should be sent to the Passport Office for your area (as indicated on the guidance form) or taken personally to the issuing post office. Apply at least five weeks before the passport is required. The regional Passport Offices are located in London, Liverpool, Peterborough, Glasgow and Newport (Gwent). The application must be countersigned by your bank manager or by a solicitor, barrister, doctor, clergyman or Justice of the Peace who knows you personally. You will need two photos. The fee is £15.

U.K. passports in the "C" or "D" series (those issued by United Kingdom Consular and High Commission posts overseas) or passports issued in Dependent Territories must carry the mention "Holder has the right of abode in the U.K.," or "Holder is entitled to (re)admission to the U.K."

Visas. U.S. citizens visiting Kenya require visas. Contact your nearest Kenyan consulate or embassy for details. Canadian and British citizens do not require visas. Note, however, that *any* traveler, regardless of nationality, must have a visa to enter Kenya if they have also visited the Republic of South Africa.

Health Documents. No vaccination certificates are required, unless you arrive from areas infected with yellow fever or cholera. (See also *Health* below).

 WHAT TO TAKE. The essential documents, of course —passport with valid visa (for U.S. citizens), tickets, travelers' checks, credit cards and driving licence, whether you plan to drive or not.

Don't overload yourself; you can usually get things washed and pressed fairly swiftly in Kenya unless you're on one of those frantic whistle-stop tours. So one largish suitcase, which could be left in the base hotel, and a zip-pocketed carrying bag for the short safaris.

Lightweight, drip-dry casual wear—not necessarily the Hollywood-style khaki-greens, festooned with epaulets, button-down pockets and slots for rifle shells—just the things you'd feel comfortable in on a summer's day at home. And not too gaudy; better to blend into the bush and not alarm the wildlife. So, say, three sets of jeans or slacks or coulottes; shirts; shirt-blouses, light underwear and socks—plus light ankle boots, sneakers or flat shoes, maybe a scarf and a sun-hat of some sort. But not the one with the plastic leopard-skin band or you'll raise a few grins among the locals tourist-spotting at the Thorn Tree cafe.

For the Kenya highlands—if you're going to the forest lodges, for instance— you'll need a heavier set of clothes: wool or cord slacks and thick sweaters. It can get perishing cold at night, even in Nairobi.

You'll need sports clothes, depending on what you plan to do—swim, fish, play golf, climb mountains or whatever—and perhaps one smart outfit (tie and jacket for the men) for dining out in the two towns or even in the lodges. Nightwear is optional.

Generally no-one is too fussed about what you wear, unlike some other countries in Africa. In Kenya, it's all that much more casual so long as the appearance is not outrageous or indecent. At the coast, neither the Moslem citizens nor the African administration is wildly excited about tourists going stark naked on the beaches. The minimal bikini is requested, plus some sort of further cover in the population centers outside the hotels. The traditional coast casuals are ideal—sarongs *(kikois),* cotton tunic shirts and kaftans *(kitenges* and *kangas)* and white flowing, neck-to-toe elegance called the *kanzu.* At the classier beach hotels, it's worth dressing up in the evenings for a dinner-dance or disco.

Take all the toiletries and cosmetics you'll need since they're generally expensive in Kenya. Also any special prescription medicines, oils and lotions, and a pair of good sun-glasses.

Cameras, of course; maybe binoculars (for bird-watchers); any sports gear you plan to use (guns excepted); plus whatever small items like a battery shaver, hairdryer and—if you're American—a voltage converter up from 110 to 220v.

HEALTH. The sun is probably the most serious health hazard. It's deceptively powerful directly overhead around the equator and light skins must be exposed gradually. At the coast, the drill is to start the sunbathing in the early morning and late afternoon, extending the exposure time each day as the skin begins to tan. Lotions and oil, protection for the eyes and head—also the back when goggling—are recommended. So are extra vitamins, particularly vitamin A.

Malaria is endemic in Kenya. Most of the highland areas are free of it, but the popular game parks and the coastal areas are malarial risks. Visitors to such areas are advised to take anti-malarial drugs prophylactically—two weeks before leaving for Kenya, continued in Kenya and then for another four weeks on return home. There are several kinds of tablet on the market, some to be taken daily, some weekly. There also are several precautions to take while in Kenya—all of them directed at the villain of the piece, the mosquito. Keep yourself well-covered after dark, where clothing is concerned; make sure, if you are not in an airconditioned room, that the window or bed netting is secure; use an aerosol insect spray in your bedroom; use an insect repellent on your skin— and make sure you have a good one; take your pills regularly up to 4 weeks after you leave the area. Remember the vital thing—malaria can be a killer.

Swimming inland, in slow-moving rivers or the edge of lakes, carries the risk of bilharzia or schistosomiasis, a snail-borne bug that gets into the human body through the skin and attacks the liver. The result is lassitude, which until recently couldn't be treated effectively.

Altitude can be a problem for some people in Nairobi and the highlands. It generally takes a couple of days to get acclimatized and get over a tendency to zonk out in the middle of the day. Up on the mountains, above 3,000 meters (10,000 ft.), there is a risk of pulmonary oedema, a capricious suffusion of the lungs which might bring down an athlete and leave a habitual smoker to go on up to the summit.

Tap water in Nairobi is supposed to be drinkable, and may well be for anyone but new arrivals who are going to get "the runs" anyway from a change of diet and surroundings. Anywhere else the water should be boiled unless it's been drawn from ice-cold mountain streams. Overall, the advice is that the visitor should bank on a mildly upset stomach sometime during the safari and so should bring along some mild antidote.

At the coast, swimming is almost entirely without hazard in the inshore waters. The sharks can't get in except where the fringing reef is broken opposite river outlets. There are some minor pests on the reef itself, like a colorful feathery thing with poisonous spine called by various names including "dragonfish." The worst of them is a "stone-fish" which camouflages itself as a lump of coral and delivers a paralysing dose of poison. It doesn't happen often, but when somebody does step on the brute they're in need of immediate medical attention.

AIDS. Most readers will be familiar with this deadly virus, which has already killed tens of thousands, and infected hundreds of thousands, in the West. Visitors to Kenya should be warned that AIDS has reached even more horrifying dimensions in Central and East Africa. Statistics vary on the extent of infection, but most agree that a majority of prostitutes in major cities are infected; in some tribal areas infection is reputed to be almost 100%. Doctors speculate that in some African countries the infection rate may be 30% of the *total* population.

AIDS remains something of a mystery to the medical profession, and matters are not helped any by the fact that African health authorities—perhaps fearing international embarrassment or a drop-off in tourism or business travel—have been less than forthcoming in supplying information about the spread of the disease in their countries. What statistics are available are almost certainly more optimistic than is warranted. AIDS is what is known in medicine as a lenti-virus; it can take years for the symptoms of such a virus to manifest themselves. Thus, for every person showing symptoms of the disease, there are many more who have been exposed to it. It is presumed they are all carriers. Infection with the AIDS virus appears to be permanent, and no one has ever recovered from the disease once full symptoms are diagnosed. Doctors believe that only a minority of those infected get "full-blown" AIDS. But remember that AIDS is a young disease, and whatever manifestation you see of it anywhere in the world is likely to be only the tip of the iceberg.

AIDS is communicable in two ways: vertically (babies born with AIDS through infected parents) and horizontally. Horizontal transmission tends to involve the passage of bodily fluids from an AIDS carrier to another person. The major risks here are sexual intercourse, infection by contaminated syringes and blood transfusions. It should be strongly stressed, however, that, despite the fact that AIDS has been transmitted primarily through homosexuality in the West, heterosexuals are also at risk, especially in Africa. It has long been known that men could pass the disease to women; it has recently been established that women can pass it to men. You should forget any ideas you may have about AIDS being a "homosexual disease." Promiscuous homosexuality is far, far less widespread in Africa than it is in the West, and women are dying of the disease in Africa at the same rate as men. Kenya is full of sexual temptations: singles' bars are many and brothels are affordable. But Western doctors, when consulted by prospective travelers to Kenya inquiring about safety, always recommend: "*Just don't do it.*" Intercourse of any kind, under any circumstances and with any precautions, will always leave you at risk for AIDS.

A word should be said about the lesser horizontal-transmission risks. Never inject yourself, or allow yourself to be injected, with an unsterilized needle. Avoid unnecessary transfusions of blood not tested for AIDS. Western hospitals are now able to screen blood samples for the virus; such facilities are rare in Africa. If you are, or expect to be, in need of a transfusion, try to consult your embassy.

Finally, there is no reason for fear of AIDS to keep you from going to Kenya. It is almost certain that the virus is *not* transmissible through insect bites, saliva, toilet seats, doorknobs, linen or any of the the objects which could transmit the virus through "casual contact," as it is called in Europe and America.

Medical Services. Overall, these are better in Kenya than in most other African countries. There are one or two good hospitals in Nairobi and at the coast; a few specialist physicians and surgeons—one or two with international reputations—and some fine dentists and opticians. Allow somewhere in the region of $20 for a consultation.

Most medicines are available in the country, but visitors are advised either to bring special prescriptions with them, or at least a note of what they are. This applies also to spectacles. Medicines are generally expensive, from 50 to 100% more than they would cost in Europe and the U.S.

Medical Insurance. Cover can be bought locally at a reasonable cost, and there is an *International Association for Medical Assistance to Travelers* (IAMAT) with offices in the U.S. (736 Center St., Lewiston, N.Y. 14092, tel. 716–754 4883), Canada (1268 St. Clair Ave. W., Toronto). Another option— and a supportive gesture—is to buy inexpensive insurance from the famous *Flying Doctor Service* in Kenya. Temporary membership valid for one month costs Shs. 35/-. In the event of a serious illness or accident on safari, the doctors will fly out from their headquarters at Wilson Airport and either treat the casualty themselves or fly him to hospital back in Nairobi.

Otherwise, an excellent source of medical insurance is *Europ Assistance Worldwide Service Inc.,* 1333 F St., NW, Washington, DC 20004 (800–821–2828).

Getting to Kenya

FROM THE STATES

BY PLANE. The cheapest way to get to Kenya from North America is probably to take a stand-by flight to London then to shop around for one of the travel agents or tour operators specializing in African destinations. This, naturally enough, will take a lot of time and not a little patience. The second-best scheme is to take a pre-packaged trip, with the airfare included. There are a lot of these available and the saving is considerable on what is one of the highest fares around. We outline some of the possibilities elsewhere in this section.

If you want to separate the air part of your trip from the rest and pay good money down, then there are three routes open to you.

1 Direct from New York by Pan Am. A long (16 hour) flight across the Atlantic to West Africa, with possible calls in Dakar, Accra and other cities before reaching Nairobi. Two flights a week, Monday and Thursday.

2 From the western seaboard of the U.S. it is possible to go via the Far East and/or Australasia to some stopover point in the East with connecting flights to Nairobi, routing through Bombay (via the Seychelles) or Karachi. This route

would be great fun if you take advantage of built-in stopovers, but you will have to be sure they apply on the flight you choose. Otherwise, it is a tiring prospect.

3 From North America via South America and Southern Africa. This is an interesting trip, stopping over in Rio, then on to Johannesburg, and on up directly to Nairobi. South African Airways also flies direct from New York to Johannesburg.

FROM EUROPE

BY PLANE. Since Kenya was a British domain until 1963, the flights are best out of London with nightly flights by either British Air or Kenya Airways. There are other European choices, with flights from most of the major capitals by national carriers. Some, such as KLM out of Amsterdam, have special offers from time to time. Aeroflot has a weekly flight, but it means going via Moscow and involves a long wait between planes; it is, however, quite cheap.

For some reason, the Europe–Kenya sector is among the most expensive in the world. According to season, a round-trip London–Nairobi flight will set you back between £450 and £550. Once again, we urge you to look into the package possibilities as the main way of minimizing the cost of the flight part of your trip.

BY CAR. Kenya can only be reached from the north and on a rough, uncertain route across the Sahara (in convoy); a ferry down the Nile as far as Juba; overland on sand tracks to the western shore of Lake Turkana in northern Kenya; then asphalt all the way to Nairobi. (At the time of writing—mid-86—the Cairo–Nairobi route had been rendered largely impassable as a result of conflicts in the Sudan). Organized overland trips are available out of London for the young and gregarious. Check the London *Times* small ads.

One company that organizes such treks is *World Tracks,* 12 Abingdon Rd., London W8 (tel. 01–937 3028/9/30). They have a 12 or 15 week trek from London, via Spain, North Africa, Chad, Cameroon, and Zaire.

Access from the south is possible now that the Kenya/Tanzania border is open again. Access from the west ought to be possible in the next few years, when a planned transcontinental highway is built.

 CUSTOMS. You can bring in all the personal effects you need, including cameras and any amount of film. Equipment like videos, radios, etc., might cause something of a hassle with the customs officer—but it's up to you. Anything can be left in bond until your departure. Don't think of bringing in any weapons unless you have permits from the Firearms Bureau of the Kenya Police. Game hunting in Kenya is banned, although some bird shooting is permitted on licence.

Other don'ts include drugs, unless they're obviously medicinal; pornography; pets and agricultural or horticultural materials. Finally don't tempt fate by bringing in too much jewelry or cash—use travelers' checks.

Currency Regulations. The Exchange Control Act is strict in Kenya—no import or export of Kenya shillings, and no attempting to deal outside the banks or hotels licensed to exchange foreign cash or travelers checks. There is no limit to the amount of hard currency that can be brought into the country, but it has to be declared on arrival with (possibly) evidence required on departure on how the money was changed. The equivalent of up to Shs. 4,000/- (about U.S. $250) can be taken out.

Visitors are also required to have in convertible foreign currency a sufficient sum for their own subsistence while in Kenya. The minimum sum in convertible foreign currency which must be shown to an Immigration Officer on request is an equivalent sum of U.S. $250. This does not apply to visitors on all-inclusive prepaid package tours.

Staying in Kenya

 HOTELS. Kenya can be done any which way as far as accommodation costs are concerned, from the low low level of the local population to the millionaire-style of palatial recreation centers like the Mount Kenya Safari Club. By U.S. and European standards, Nairobi and Mombasa hotels are reasonably priced, but out on safari prices tend to be higher because of the distances from the centers of supply. There are only a few luxury hotels (L) and (E), mainly corresponding to a normally expensive-comfortable hotel in Europe and the States—among them the Hilton, Inter-Continental, Mount Kenya Safari Club and Norfolk. Some of the beach hotels are also serviced to a reasonable international standard. The moderate hotels (M) are for people on a tightish budget but are perfectly adequate, often with a lot of atmosphere and character. Kenya's inexpensive hotels (I) are about as basic as you can get and are definitely for the adventurous. We should stress again that you will get a much better deal if your accommodations are included as part of a complete package deal.

Up-country there are a few swish international spots, slightly less prestigious accommodations though still ultra-comfortable, and simple country hotels air-conditioned and with character.

Tented camps, for many the best way to spend the night in the African bush, also run from the luxurious to simple and remote, such as the island camp in the middle of Lake Baringo. Another possibility are the self-help African-style cottages—*bandas*—comfortable, and with all basic amenities apart from food.

Normally full rates operate during the high season, roughly end-October to end-March. For the rest of the year there are cut-rate deals all over the country, especially on the coast during the long rains, April to June. In that "low season," tariffs could be cut below half the high-season rates.

Camping. There are serviced sites, at nominal costs, in most of the Parks. The form is to fix it with the warden at the park headquarters immediately on arrival. It may seem to be dangerous camping in the middle of a parkful of wild animals, but it isn't—providing everyone keeps to the rules (published in the park literature). Basically, the wildlife—with the exception of bugs—do their best to avoid contact with people.

Camping elsewhere in Kenya is entirely possible, and carries the usual risks—like human intrusion. The rule is to choose a site way out in the bush somewhere (*never* on a sand-river bed), well away from urban centers and villages.

There are a few established camp sites on the popular beaches, and nothing to stop anyone pitching a tent anywhere away from the hotels and residential beach plots. Complete gear for camping is available for hire in both Nairobi and Mombasa.

 RESTAURANTS. (See also *Food and Drink,* following.) The quality and price of food in restaurants vary enormously, but international-type meals at the main hotels and at city restaurants are not expensive by U.S. and European standards. Prices at a luxury Nairobi hotel might run, per person —U.S. $7 for a Continental breakfast, $14 for lunch, &FA20 for dinner, without wine. A super restaurant in Mombasa (say The Tamarind) might run up to $30 for a three-course dinner, without wine. These are likely to be the top range of prices, all others will grade downwards. $10 a head for a three-course dinner in a moderate restaurant, or $6 at an all-you-can-eat buffet.

Nairobi covers the waterfront as far as the range of cuisine is concerned. In its own way it mirrors any Western city, with the added inducement of a dash of African cuisine.

Most people on the coast eat at the hotels where the food ranges from adequate and edible, to abundant and first class—sometimes abundant only for a brief moment at the hotels favored by the German tours who tend to launch a fast and violent *blitzkrieg* on the lunch buffet as soon as the gong goes.

For the more adventurous, Mombasa and the coast—north and south—offer scores of small hotel cafés, rather scruffy diners, open shopfront delicatessens (African, Arab and Swahili), as well as stalls and individual enterprise with charcoal *jiko* stoves dispensing goat-meat kebabs and roast corn or casava. The equivalent of the sandwich is the *samosa,* a hot spicey envelope of papadum pastry and ground meat or vegetable filling. For dessert there is a vast range of Indian sweetmeats, ice cream, and delicious *halva.* And to finish, a chew and a spit of *betel* leaves, a long chew on a stimulant weed called *miraa,* or a cold lager. Better than anything, is perhaps one of about 30 exotic fruit juices.

In the area of international cuisine, restaurants along the coast are perhaps not always up to Nairobi standards, but they are good enough.

Up-country there are very few separate restaurants as such, apart from African and Asian basic eateries; but there is often excellent, reasonably-priced food in the small town hotels and in all the game lodges and tented camps.

All in all, the visitor to Kenya tends to be surprised by the quality of the food which—in restaurants or out in the bush on safari—is usually presented as a full English breakfast, a large and varied cold table for lunch, and Continental cuisine in three courses for dinner. Indeed, the food served at the safari lodges is usually of the most solid British variety, reminiscent of the kind of Victorian Sunday dinner which has almost vanished from Britain itself—a succulent roast, three vegetables and a heavy rich dessert.

Whichever cuisine you favor, Kenya will be able to satisfy the most Falstaffian appetite.

FOOD AND DRINK. Food in Kenya, like society, is stratified in three thick layers—African, Asian, and a sort of combination International and English.

African food is very simple and cheap. Frankly, most Western visitors are likely to find it unpleasant, though it can be worth trying a dish or two nonetheless. The staple food is maize milled into flour, the resultant mushy mixture—known as *posho*—then boiled. This is served in a few tourist restaurants with a beef stew called *ngali*. A posho hash with beans, potatoes and other vegetables is called *irio*, while the same thing, with the ingredients unmashed, is *githeri*. A steamed banana porridge called *matoke*, home-grown rice and a starchy pasta are also popular locally.

Asian food is a better bet, with a representative range of restaurants in Nairobi—Chinese, Korean, Indian and Middle Eastern. Of these, Indian restaurants are generally best, occasionally rising to gourmet standards.

The final category—international, albeit with a pronounced English bias—is mostly very good. Ingredients are excellent, and a wide range available. And, so long as they are not imported, prices are low. Fillet beef comes at around $2 a pound, as does "venison"—a haunch of impala or Thompson's gazelle—with just about everything else less expensive. This includes a range of superb pork products and excellent lamb and mutton.

Fresh-water fish, apart from farmed trout, are not all that good, however. The most common fishes are tilapia, black bass and Nile perch, all of which need a curry or Portugaise sauce to defeat the taste of muddy lake bottom. Seafish, on the other hand, is excellent, especially rock cod and parrot fish. Shellfish is usually available, though it is by no means abundant: look out for jumbo prawns, smallish crabs—these only occasionally available—spiny lobster and langoustine, of which only the tail is edible. For dedicated gourmets, the mini-oysters at Mida Creek above Mombasa are highly recommended. Returning to prawns for a moment, try an explosive dish called *prawns piri piri*. This is best with tiger prawns, magnificent monsters weighing anything up to a quarter-of-a-pound apiece. The piri piri butter in which they luxuriate, especially in a gourmet haven like the Tamarind restaurant in Mombasa, is made of butter, red chilies, garlic, lime juice and paprika, topped off with a little chili powder to ensure that the taste explosion will go off as planned.

Most fruit and vegetables are grown in Kenya, apart from such stubbornly temperate things as cherries. But avocados, asparagus, artichokes, young green beans, and, of the fruits, pineapple, mangoes, paw-paw (papaya), abound.

Drink. The most common drink is beer; principally good light lagers brewed locally and consumed in Germanic quantities. Nothing much else can be recommended, however. Spirits and wines—the latter always imported—are very expensive: even the house wine in an ordinary restaurant may cost above U.S. $12 a bottle. Nonetheless, all alcoholic drinks are price-controlled, albeit only loosely. Prices rise with the class of hotels, bars and restaurants. Drinking laws appear to range from the lax to the unobserved.

CLOSING TIMES. Business hours are anything from 8 A.M. to 5.30 P.M., with the general stores or Indian *dukas* staying open well into the evening and over most of the weekend. In Mombasa, trade may start as early as 7 A.M. with a long siesta break any time from 12.30 to 4.00 P.M. and then a re-opening until after dark. (Buying in the retail trade has a touch of the Persian market about it, with haggling possible in Nairobi and mandatory in Mombasa.)

Banking hours in Nairobi are from 9–2 Monday through Friday and on the first and last Saturdays of each month from 9–11, excluding national holidays. Airport banks are open until midnight every day.

SOUVENIRS. Shopping for souvenirs is one of the pleasures of travel to distant lands, and in Nairobi you will find an abundance of souvenirs for every taste. Gemstones and semi-precious stones such as tanzanite, tsavorite, malachite and verdite, amber and silver ornaments, baskets, hand-engraved crystal, batiks, sari silks, handprinted cotton material, beadwork, African carvings, art and jewelry are among the many items from which to choose. On various safari circuits to National Parks and Game Reserves, most lodges and hotels have gift shops.

One souvenir you will not be able to buy in Kenya is anything made from *any* part of *any* animal or bird, as this trade is banned by the government. You may be approaced in the street by sellers of "elephant hair and giraffe tail bracelets." Not only is this illegal, but the items are invariably plastic. They should always be refused.

On your return home, a bag of excellent Kenya coffee makes a welcome present for those left behind. Try the coffee shop on Mama Ngina St., or any supermarket, or the Duty-Free Shop at the Airport (where items must be paid for in foreign currency).

SECURITY. The fantasies about Africa are legion— from a spear in the back to a scorpion in your shoe. Although not so safe as it used to be, Kenya is still one of the more secure African countries and among the healthiest on earth. Many Europeans have lived there all their lives and wouldn't live anywhere else.

In Town. Crime is not insignificant, but the commonsense rules are the same as in most other strange places. Keep out of the dark back streets at night and out of the sleazier bars and dance dives. Many tour operators advise their clients to take a taxi when traveling around Nairobi rather than walking and we seriously endorse this. If you are going to one of the African dance halls, among the liveliest places around, then go in a group and, obviously, don't carry too much money or valuables around with you.

Muggings and bag-snatching happen, but there's a rather savage deterrent for it. Someone shouts "thief" and suddenly it's a Roman holiday, with the mob giving chase and meting out summary justice when they catch him.

Violent crime is not very common against tourists, including rape and sexual assault in a society which has fairly liberal access to sex. If you are accosted, it's more likely that the local villains are after your car or your property, not your body. Problem areas in this respect are deserted beaches and drunken, mixed-company parties.

Probably the commonest urban crime in Kenya is car theft, followed by house-breaking. For tourists, it's the "con" and the lifting of valuables left lying around.

In any threatening situation, the rule is not to panic nor make any sudden moves in attack or retreat. Keep quiet and do what you're told, within reason—basically apply commonsense.

Up-country. Theft is about the only real problem. Violent attack on tourists is still rare. Where it has happened is in the north of the country, when the Somali *shifta* gangs are around and tourists have been warned to stay out of the area. It has also happened in Masai country, but there has usually been some serious provocation. In general, the vast bush areas in Kenya amount to one great campsite and are entirely safe providing people stick to a few fundamental rules.

We will return to the problems of snakes and scorpions under our general treatment of safaris.

 TIPPING. It's legal in Kenya, unlike in some other African countries, and no-one is too proud to accept a reasonable tip. Give about what you'd give at home for decent service, like adding ten percent to the restaurant bill unless it's added already. In that case, slip the waiter a five or ten shilling note. The biggest tip will probably go to your tour driver if he's turned out to be helpful and responsive on the trip. Maybe as much as 250/- per passenger after a 12-day safari.

Other Largesse. Use your judgement, but as a rule don't give to beggars on the streets in towns. The authorities are trying to get rid of this embarrassment and the best deterrent is the sure knowledge that pan-handling doesn't pay. Parking boys—aggressive, unoccupied youngsters who "let you into" an empty parking bay—are also to be discouraged. The implied threat is that if you don't give them cash to look after the car while you're doing your business, there might be a scratch on the paint-work when you get back. It's a poker game they play and with the locals they generally lose out. In the country, if you break down or get bogged down, there'll almost certainly be a horde of youngsters around you in no more than a minute. They appear like phantoms out of a vast totally empty landscape. Choose the most likely of them, get them to push or go for mechanical help, then reward them with a few shillings each. Five shillings to a child out in the sticks is a minor bonanza.

 LANGUAGE. English is understood by most people in up-country Kenya, but not so much at the coast which is predominantly Moslem, speaking the Afro-Arab-Indian mix called Swahili. It's not a difficult language but not a very rich one, which is why it failed to make it as the national language in Parliament or in commerce or industry. English is taught in schools all over the country, so there is always someone who will understand what you're talking about, even in the remote bush.

 PHOTOGRAPHY. Those once-in-a-lifetime holiday films are vulnerable to the X-ray security machines on airports. Warning notices are displayed sometimes, and passengers are advised to remove film—or cameras with film in them—for a hand check. But many airport authorities will not allow hand inspection and insist that all luggage pass through the detection devices.

There are two steps you should follow. First, ask for a hand-inspection whenever you can. Second, buy one or more *Filmashield* lead-laminated bags, which are manufactured by the American SIMA Products Group, 4001 W. Devon Ave., Chicago, Ill. 60646. These will protect films from low-dosage X-rays, but should not be relied on against the more powerful machines. The bags are also available in Britain.

A point about snaps in Kenya itself. *Don't* photograph anyone without their consent, not even the simple tribesmen way out in the bush. Smile, wave your camera around, offer a few shillings, and that ought to do it. The Masai have got wise, by the way. They're looking for up to ten dollars a shot of their handsome profiles. But tell them to forget it—in American, they'll understand— and offer them ten shillings. Otherwise, go look for someone with less of an eye for the main chance.

 TIME. Kenya is three hours ahead of G.M.T. Unless there are single and double summer times in operation, noon in Nairobi is 9 A.M. in London; 4 A.M. in New York. On the equator there's almost exactly 12 hours of day and 12 hours of night with little variation throughout the year. Sun is up around 6.30 A.M., with a sudden nightfall after 6.30 P.M.

 MEASUREMENTS. These are loosely metric in Kenya —kilometers, kilograms, centigrade and so on. But old habits die hard and it's also so-many-miles and so-many- degrees-fahrenheit.

ELECTRICITY. Fluctuating around 220 volts, 50 cycles. Especially fluctuating in the generator-powered lodges.

GOLF. Kenya is renowned as a sporting nation, but mainly for its world beating athletes and the incomparable Safari Rally. So it comes as a surprise to many visitors that another sport flourishes in Kenya—the royal and ancient game of golf. Thirty courses scattered throughout the country offer a variety of challenges to any visiting golfer, any day of the year. Even in the rainy season, from March to May, the sun will normally shine every day for at least the duration of 18 holes of golf. Moreover, the golf is inexpensive. At the best clubs, even at the weekends, the green fees will be no more than $12 and the services of a well trained caddie for 18 holes will never cost more than $2. On the smaller courses, the green fees are as little as $2 on a weekday.

The standard of courses is set by the major clubs in the metropolitan area of Nairobi, especially the three championship courses at Muthaiga, Karen and Royal Nairobi. Then there is the option of two main safari circuits: "up country" to the cool of the highlands, or southeast to the tropical Indian Ocean. In either case, the best of Kenya's world famous wildlife parks may be taken in on the way.

Many Kenya tour operators offer packaged combination game and golfing safaris, covering most of the courses. The individual visitor merely requests a game at the course of his choice from the club secretary.

For further information contact club secretaries or captains at the following addresses and telephone numbers:

Muthaiga Golf Club, Box 41651, Nairobi (tel. Secretary—Nairobi 65214; Professional—Nairobi 65334); **Karen Country Club,** Box 24816, Nairobi (tel. Secretary—Karen 2223); **Royal Nairobi Golf Club,** Box 46221, Nairobi (tel. Secretary—Nairobi 27333); **Limuru Country Club,** Box 10, Limuru (tel. Secretary—Tigoni 351); **Sigona Golf Club,** Box 10, Kikuyu (tel. Manager—Kikuyu 2152); **Thika Sports Club,** Box 257, Thika (tel. Thika 21321); **Veterinary Laboratory Sports Club,** P.O. Kabete (tel. Nairobi 592214); **Railways Golf Club,** Box 40476, Nairobi (tel. Nairobi 22116); **Kiambu Club,** Box 139 (tel. Manager—Kiambu 2336).

OCEAN FISHING. The big game fishing areas of the world lie roughly between latitudes 30° north and 35° south of the equator. Of the three great oceans within this belt, the Atlantic is most heavily fished; the Pacific has yielded the records so far; and the Indian Ocean is the fisherman's hope of the unexpected in unknown waters.

The Kenya coast extends some 480 km. (298 miles) from the Somalia to the Tanzania borders. There are six principal fishing grounds and other areas which are completely virgin. Although it is possible to fish 12 months of the year, the "season" begins in September and extends through to April or May. Many large marlin have been taken in July and August, but the sea tends to be rough during this time due to the southeast monsoon.

Among the principal game fish teeming in the waters off the Kenya coast are—barracuda, caranx, cobia, dolphin (dorado) kingfish, marlin (black, Pacific blue and striped), sailfish, shark (hammerhead, mako and tiger), yellow-fin tuna and wahoo.

Fishing is good all along the coast, but six resort centers are well developed in specialist big game fishing hotels or clubs. These are, from north to south—

Lamu, where the fishing is operated from Peponi, Petley's and Ras Kitau hotels. Mainly for light tackle sport.

Malindi, where Kenya's principal fishing competitions are organized by the Malindi Fishing Club, at this developed resort in November and December. The area is noted mainly for sailfish.

Watamu. Four hotels serve this scenic area of coral cliffs, bays and lagoons, two of which are popular local fishing clubs.

Kilifi. The Mnarani Club, situated on the southern headland at the entrance to the Kilifi creek, is among the most luxurious and best equipped of the specialist hotel fishing clubs. The sport is good enough to keep the club open throughout the year.

Mombasa. Most hotels on the holiday beaches north of the island to Mtwapa creek and south to Diani beach, either operate fishing trips or cooperate with the largest Kenyan sports fishing enterprise, "K-Boats", whose rates for fully equipped and crewed trips are among the lowest in the world. The Bahari Club, north of Mombasa island at Kisauni is another large specialist fishing operation which hires out crewed boats and looks after a small fleet of craft belonging to local residents.

Shimoni. The most spectacular marlin catches are recorded here in the 500 fathom Pemba Channel. Road access to Shimoni has recently been tarred most of the way, and the Pemba Channel Fishing Club is becoming increasingly popular for the serious local and visiting fishermen.

Seasons. There is no hard and fast season in Kenya waters, but fishing begins seriously in September and lasts until March or April. Months for billfish are October through to April and July or August, although the sea can be rough at this time. Some hotels close for a month or so in the long rains around May and June, but this may vary from year to year.

RIVER FISHING. Most of the sports fishing in Kenya is exclusively for trout. These were introduced in the Gura river, high on the Aberdares range, in 1905. Today, there are several good trout streams in Kenya; off the escarpments of the great Rift Valley and the area around Mount Kenya, which is particularly well managed by the Fisheries Department. The rivers include the Sagana, Thego, Naro Moru, Burguret, Chania/Nyeri and Gura, all in Nyeri district; Thiba, Kiringa, Rupingazi and Nyamindi in Kirinyaga and Embu districts; Thiririka and Gatamaiyu in Kiambu district; Chania/Murang'a, Thika and North and South Mathioya, all in Murang'a district. Parts of North and South Mathioya are private rivers for fly fishing clubs. The Moruny river in West Pokot district lies in the Cherangani hills and has about 50 km. (31 miles) of good water for both rainbow and brown trout.

Before fishing on any private streams, the landowner's permission must be obtained. There are also strict regulations on the use of live bait, artificial flies etc. There is no closed season for trout fishing, but individual rivers may be closed for short periods at the discretion of the Fisheries Department, the Department's Trout Hatchery at Kiganjo, or by the Mountain National Parks Warden at Mweiga.

Fishing Camps. The Fisheries Department and local private associations operate a number of simple, but attractive and inexpensive, camps at the most popular trout streams in the Mount Kenya and Aberdares area. These include— Thiba, Thego, Kimakia and Koiwa. It is not normally possible to book the camps in advance. The system is first come, first served. They are often full over the weekends and public holidays, but at other times, visiting anglers are fairly sure of finding accommodations available. Visitors need to be self-contained for camping, including food, bedding, etc. Camp rates are nominal, at around the equivalent of $7.50 per person per day. The stay at any one camp is limited to 14 days.

Fishing Lodge. A specialist trout fishing lodge is operated at Ngobit on Mount Kenya. This has six doubles, each with separate bathrooms which rent for around $45 per double per day.

Fishing Hotels. Most hotels in the vicinity of trout streams anywhere in the country will either organize fishing themselves, or advise fully equipped visiting anglers on local conditions, location and regulations.

LAKE FISHING. Four lakes in Kenya are well known and important for sport fishing; these are Naivasha, Victoria, Baringo and Turkana. Apart from the famous black bass of Naivasha, and giant Nile perch at Turkana, numerous coarse fish abound in most of Kenya's lakes and in the more sluggish rivers. In all the large lakes, there is an established commercial fishing industry. The most important of the coarse fish is the tilapia, which makes delicious eating. They are now being sold in Europe as a delicacy, and are the most common of all Kenya's freshwater fish. Other lake and river coarse fish in Kenya include various species of barbus, lung fish, cat fish, elephant snout fish, and eels, which may be taken in areas such as Victoria, Turkana and Baringo, and in the lower reaches of nearly all the rivers.

 MOUNTAINEERING. The prime attraction for rock climbers and mountaineers is **Mount Kenya,** a long-extinct volcano straddling the equator and rising 5,199 meters (17,058 ft.) above sea level. Weather conditions, a wide-range of faces, thin air—all make this mountain a challenge.

The other mountain parks of Kenya lack the high standard of technical climbing afforded by Mount Kenya, but offer other attractions.

The Aberdare National Park has a well developed road system for scenic high altitude motoring, excellent trout fishing, game viewing and high altitude walking and scrambling trails in the northern sector. The Aberdares feature a number of spectacular waterfalls and two well known game lodges.

Mount Elgon offers trout fishing, game viewing, and moorland motoring and walking. It also contains caves regularly visited by herds of elephant in search of salt.

The Marsabit National Park rises like a forested island from the surrounding arid plains. It supports a healthy population of large elephants and several charmingly hidden lakes.

Other mountains include the Mathews range, the Ndotos, Kulal, Ololokwe, the Cheranganis, the Chyulus, the Taita hills and others. These are generally undeveloped for tourism, but offer interesting challenges to the more adventurous visitor.

For more details on most of these parks, see *Mountain Parks* towards the end of the book.

The Mountain Club of Kenya has over the years opened a number of areas for technical rock climbing. These crags include Lukenya, Hell's Gate, Ndeyia, Nzaui and Soitpus. Guide books are available from the club. Each of these crags offers a particular type of technical climbing and all share a unique Kenya flavor which must be experienced to be properly appreciated.

The Guidebook to Mount Kenya and Kilimanjaro, published by and available from, The Mountain Club of Kenya, P.O. Box 45741, Nairobi.

The Mountains of Kenya, by Peter Robson, is an excellent comprehensive guide book from The Mountain Club of Kenya.

Contact The Warden, Mountain National Parks, P.O. Box 22, Nyeri, or The Secretary, The Mountain Club of Kenya, P.O. Box 45741, Nairobi.

SAFARIS. Until recently, most people visiting Kenya for anything more than a business trip to Nairobi opted for the all-in package safari for which all costs are prepaid from the point of departure (from New York or London or wherever) to the return home. This is all right for the average first-time visitor who normally wants to be fully fed, cosseted and guided step by step through the Dark Continent. But in fact, it's not necessary. Anyone can discover Kenya for himself, with applied commonsense and without someone else making all the decisions. The do-it-yourself safari has the obvious advantage of permitting total flexibility in going and staying where you please for as long as you like. You avoid rushing around the countryside on rigid pre-set itineraries, with six or seven strangers jostled together in a tin-can mini-bus. Through group packaging, the tour operator can reduce per person costs of course. But it works out the same, or less, if you arrange it all from Nairobi after arrival.

What you do is book ahead for the Nairobi Hotel through the airline. You arrive, almost always early in the morning, and transfer yourself to the hotel—most comfortably in a red Kenatco Mercedes—have breakfast and check the classified ads. section of the local *Standard* newspaper to see what special deals the hotel chains or tour operators are offering. Usually there's a fair range of cut-rate special offers over most of the year, but especially in the low season from April to July. Anyway, decide what safari you want to make and how you want to do it.

The cheapest way is probably to hire a four-wheel-drive vehicle and camping gear, stock up at the Nairobi market, buy a road map and set off. Another low-cost option is to check on a notice board at the New Stanley's Thorn Tree cafe to find out who is going where and looking for people to share costs. More often than not, someone is offering a car ride to the coast, where a bed can always be found somewhere in Mombasa or the beach even in the high season. A cheaper alternative at the coast is to rent a beach cottage privately through ads. in the local papers. These lets are usually good value with everything provided—except food and drink but including house servants—from between Shs. 500/- and 800/- a day for a cottage sleeping four or more.

For safaris, the alternative to going off on your own is to buy a package tour from any one of scores of local tour operators. The Kenya Association of Tour Operators has several dozen members. Among the up-market, expensive and totally reliable ones are: **Abercrombie and Kent Ltd.,** Box 59749, Nairobi (tel. 334955); **Flamingo Tours Ltd.,** Box 44899, Nairobi (tel. 28961); **Rhino Safaris Ltd.,** Box 48023 Nairobi (tel. 28102/25419); and **United Touring Company,** Box 42196, Nairobi (tel. 331960). Others, with tie-ins to lodges are: **African Tours and Hotels Ltd.,** Box 30471, Nairobi (tel. 336858/336165/336976); **Thorn Tree Safaris Ltd.,** Box 42475, Nairobi (tel. 25941/25641/28981).

WHICH SAFARI? There is a vast variety of holiday possibilities on offer in Kenya—vast, that is, with a choice between a magnificent coast and endlessly fascinating inland territories. The main problem, when planning your trip, is to decide which you wish to concentrate on and how much you are prepared to spend on what may well be the vacation of a lifetime. The main options divide themselves fairly easily, and range from champagne cocktails under a technicolor sky to el cheapo camping. The main thing to remember, as we have already said, is that a great proportion of whatever you are prepared to spend on your trip is swallowed up by the mere act of getting to and from Kenya.

The Solid-Gold Land Rover Approach. Hunting is banned in Kenya following the wholesale slaughter of the wildlife. Most of the "white" or professional hunters went out of business with the ban, but a few kept going, switching to specialized photo or adventure safaris. They try, where possible, to keep up the old maharajah style of absolute, civilized comfort in an elegant perambulation of the African bush.

The only way to convey what you get for your money—up to $1,000 a day for the whole works—is to cite an example. We'll take a luxury camel trek into the blue and desert-browns of Kenya's Northern Frontier District.

You fly from the States (first class of course), say to London. Stopover at Claridges; collect your safari gear from wherever in Savile Row; and embark the following day on the overnight, seven-hour flight from Heathrow to Nairobi. The "hunter" (grizzled, iron-grey, handsome) meets you at Jomo Kenyatta

International Airport and transfers you—*de rigeur* by Land Rover rather than limousine—to the selected hotel. Possibly the presidential suite at the Nairobi Intercontinental, but better at one of the spacious cottages at the old Norfolk.

A day is allocated for getting your bearings and coming to grips with the height above sea level, then, the following day, a light aircraft flight 402 km. (250 miles) up-country to Wamba, just outside Samburu National Park on the southern edge of the desert. A base camp has been set up previously a few miles away, shaded by acacia and wild fig on the bank of a wide dry river. The Seyyia Lugga in this case.

For a party of four, 17 African staff and twice as many camels are engaged—together with (if you're exceptionally lucky) a drover-in-chief who, for years, was a game warden in the area. Urbane (he plays Bach in the bush on his portable tape-recorder); something of a wit and story teller—ask him about Hemingway's lost weekend at Shimoni in 1954, or about Prince Charles, happily relaxed and unshaved for five days on a camel in the same area.

The safari accommodations—moved ahead every day by camel or truck—is a room-size tent with verandah, a detached ablutions arrangement (called a "choo" tent), and a bucket-fed hot and cold shower. Breakfast is around dawn, after a wake-up cup of tea in bed. It's full English, possibly with kippers or kidneys, but certainly juice, hot coffee, fresh bread from the bush oven (an ammunition tin box buried on embers, Hawaiian style); cereals, fresh fruits and bacon and eggs.

The hunter and the game warden lead off once the camels are packed and the riders schooled in the balletic movements involved in getting on and off the beasts. Progress is then leisurely, along the sand river bed, endlessly snaking back on itself and lined with bright greenery—riverine trees and grass verges close-cropped into lawns by the goats of the local Samburu tribe. Both guides, and some of the staff as well, are encyclopaedic on the local flora and fauna. The warden, in particular, is a bird nut able to spot a rarity in the thicket a mile away.

The trek usually stops around noon; before it gets a slog in the heat. The distance has been carefully measured and there's a fly camp under shade trees just where the unseasoned traveler would be about to flake out.

Lunch is the fabled Kenya cold table and the excellent light lager of the region which has kept cool in wet straw in canvas slung round the camel's neck. Americans could order, possibly, a champagne cocktail. But no ice. The safari is elegant but no mobile Hilton, and lugging around a gas-fueled fridge is not on.

Towards evening, there will be a foot-trek after some wild beast or other, possibly a greater kudu antelope or an elephant. It's precisely the old-style hunt, complete with native trackers reading the pebbles and bent grass, but without the kill at the end of it. If you're lucky, you can get a shot at it with a Nikon and 250 mm. lens.

Dinner is pure romantic fiction. The blazing camp-fire; the varied and alarming sounds of the African night; a retinue in mess kit serving *haut-cuisine* in at least three courses. Wine, cognac with the coffee; and the hosts with their after-dinner stories which, of course, would make a book.

And so it goes on, day after day, following the lugga up towards the Jade Sea. Amazingly, it never gets boring. The scenery round the next bend is always more or less the same as it was round the previous meander. But a fascination—almost an obsession—develops. It somehow becomes necessary to see and experience the magnificent space up ahead. It ends eventually, after two or three weeks, at no particular destination with nothing monumental achieved. Except, perhaps, an increased capacity to cope with the real world back in Nairobi and beyond.

You don't have to take the camel trek, of course. This exclusive type of operation is usually carried out with Land Rovers and five-ton trucks for the loads, and tends to circuit round areas of wildlife concentration in the parks and reserves. Prices range downwards from U.S. $750 to $250 per person depending on the size of the party.

Comfort at a Price. There's one constraint with pre-arranging the luxury type of safari, apart from the cost. And that is finding out who is operating in which area of the country at any particular time. They are individual operators mostly, without the means to advertize themselves abroad to any significant extent, so they're not easy to identify and locate—although some of them are represented by up-market travel brokers, mostly in the States, who specialize in Africa. An alternative approach (in about the same price range) is to write to one of the established, top-rung tour operators in Nairobi, set out roughly the safari you want, and ask for offers.

In this case, you might buy a custom-made safari for your private party—wife, friends and maybe the children. You could have it hand-tailored to your specifications in advance through correspondence with an up-market, established tour firm in Kenya, like Ker and Downey. Or you could opt for trusting to the fertile imagination of someone who is steeped in Africa, its off-track possibilities and the safari business itself. Someone like Geoff Kent and his classy *Abercrombie & Kent* safaris. There's no Mr. Abercrombie, incidentally. He's added to promote (subliminally) the idea of quality by association with the upper-bracket U.S. sports house. Anyway, what's in a name?—it's the safari that counts and A & K offer a high-class range. The following are a couple of examples—quoted in sterling in mid 1986, but which are certainly liable to inflation: *Luxury Tented Safari*—12 nights, around 30 departure dates during the year, flights to/from London, Heathrow, third week on coast optional, £1,196. *Northern Wildlife Safari*—16 nights, £1,245, including flights. Both safaris include all park fees, services of professional guide, overnight in Nairobi and so forth.

A & K also offer all kinds of optional goodies including hot-air balloon trips. Details of this and other trips available on request.

From the States, *Percival Tours* offer a Jambo Safari with visits to Nairobi and several game reserves, 14 days for U.S. $1,899—but that does not include the transatlantic airfare. This safari can be extended to take in Egypt.

Standard Package Safaris. These are all-in city stop-overs; short excursions: beach holidays or mini-bus runs round to game parks, with accommodation in first-class lodges. The itineraries and rates tend to differ only marginally between the dozens of Kenya-based tour-operators. Most of these have overseas representation, but the big-one—with extensive worldwide connections—is U.T.C., the United Touring Company. They run the largest fleets of safari vehicles in Kenya and have a major share-holding in a number of A-class lodges and hotels. Their main competitor—the single largest hotel/lodge owner—is African Tours and Hotels Ltd. which is mostly Government-owned through the Kenya Tourist Development Corporation. Either one of them are fine for the standard tours.

The price range is extremely variable, and depends entirely on which components you want to include from the wide assortment of beach and safari possibilities available.

Budget Safaris. Nothing is stable at the lower end of the world tourist market, and that includes Kenya. Prices and offers are in a constant state of flux, so for the budget-conscious, it's a matter of ringing round the tour agencies to find the deal of the moment. For people in the States, the most reasonable package for the grand safari will be upwards of U.S. $2,500 including the return flights.

But they don't need to be that much. The cheapest option is to make the trip via London and take advantage of the many budget safaris ex England. There are all sorts of offers which will take you to either Nairobi or the coast. Once there it's possible to take an extra week or two for low cost safaris by pre-arrangement with the European package operator. There are many options, like hiring a car and camping gear out of Mombasa and going off to one of the Tsavos. But probably the best bet is to go by bus or train to Nairobi, where there are more options including the "Thorn Tree" notice board. For example, you could stay at the YMCA for $12 membership fee and about $4 a night (six sharing a room) and then take off on, say, a fixed-departure camping safari.

SAFARI HAZARDS. If you're camping, sleep *inside* a tent, not necessarily with the flaps closed but under a mosquito net. The larger wild beasts will almost without exception walk miles to avoid human contact, unless the humans happened to be parked on the only access trail to water. The camp fire will advertise your presence, although it's probably not necessary, and the net is protection against bugs and inquisitive small-fry mammals like the ratel or honey-badger. It's probably a myth, but the story is that the ratel has a predilection for gentlemen's vitals left exposed to the African night.

Snakes and other creeping-crawling things are often a terror to the novice on safari. They take some convincing that snakes are rarely seen by anyone but a determined herpetologist. People have also spent a life-time in the bush and never once found a scorpion in their boots. Snakes are in fact fairly common on the coastal strip, but the incidence of snake bite is rare.

Insects are much more a nuisance than a danger, apart from three breeds—African bees which can be savage; the mosquito which could be carrying malaria; and the tsetse in certain bush areas which could transmit sleeping sickness, or *trypanosomiasis,* if they were to bite regularly over a period of several months. A can of spray and a fly-swat are the standard defense against these pests, except for bees where the only thing to do is either get under water or get into the car and depart at speed.

Getting Around Kenya

BY PLANE. *Kenya Airways* operate daily scheduled flights to Mombasa and Malindi. Ticket prices vary depending on the time of the flights—i.e. cheaper in the early morning—from about U.S. $40 to $60 single from Nairobi to Mombasa.

About a dozen air charter firms operate out of Nairobi (Wilson Airport), Mombasa and Malindi. The charter rates are calculated, amongst everything else, on a fairly stable basic rate per mile plus a variable fuel charge.

There are also scheduled light aircraft flights. These tend to vary among the air charter operators, but destinations generally include Lamu (or elsewhere on the Coast), Kisumu and the Masai Mara.

BY TRAIN. Long, slow, overnight sleeper, Nairobi to Mombasa, takes up to 14 hours. All compartments make up into sleepers, and the restaurant on board serves the cheapest food in Kenya. The train is not, however, air-conditioned, mainly because the mile-high altitude of Nairobi is chilly and heat suffering would only take place down at the coast, when the train is rolling through cool darkness or dawn. Passengers in the up direction *always* see wild animals from the windows as the train crosses the Athi Plains—usually zebra and giraffe.

The Kenya Railways Corporation also operates one daily service either way on the Nairobi/Kisumu route. The train leaves Nairobi at 5.30 in the evening arriving at Kisumu at 8.05 the next morning. The reverse times are 6 P.M. and 7.30 A.M.

BY CAR. Driving is generally atrocious in Kenya. The problem is there are not enough police for deterrent enforcement, and that means drivers on the road who may be barely competent, unlicensed and uninsured. Vehicles may be grossly over-loaded or greatly dilapidated. Tankers, with their trailers whiplashing across the road, are a menace, and so are the public buses, all privately-owned and often racing each other to the next passenger pick up—two abreast on a narrow road. In this event, the form for an oncoming driver is merely to take to the bush.

The point of all this is that the visiting driver should keep within the strict laws and codes he's used to, regardless of the example of the lunatics charging around the Kenya roads. It's at its worst around Easter, at the time of the Safari Rally, when half of young Kenya suddenly puts its foot on the accelerator. More so than most places, you drive in Kenya with the attitude that every single driver on the road is a kamikazi out to zero in on you.

By far the most serious hazard on the safari is the state of the roads for an inexperienced or careless driver. It's not so bad inside the parks and reserves, but the access tracks can be anything from rough to "the pits," literally. Most of them are unmade and largely untended dirt, like an obstacle course of ruts and ridges, potholes and corrugations, roots and small boulders, soft boggy sand or boggier mud. Sometimes the tracks are narrow, with near vertical cambers. Or they can disappear altogether in an expanse of flat, desert bush.

However, as unlikely as it sounds, all is negotiable even for a first-time driver in Kenya providing he's got the right vehicle for the particular terrain, and providing he keeps the speed down and concentrates on the track ahead rather than the elephant off to the left. Usually it's speed and fatigue that cause the accidents—like falling asleep in the heat of the day or in attempting to do too many miles at one stretch.

Driving Licenses. Visitors over 18 years of age holding a valid driving license can drive vehicles in Kenya for a period of up to 90 days. They should, however, have their license endorsed on arrival at the nearest Police Station.

A Kenyan driving license is normally issued automatically on production of a valid driving license, two photographs and payment of a nominal fee. An International driving license is also valid.

Motor Vehicle Insurance. Third Party Insurance is compulsory for motor vehicles in Kenya.

Fuel is so far unlimited; there are no Sunday driving bans or other restrictions. But it's all imported and pricey—around Shs. 8/50 a liter—and enough of a drain on Kenya's foreign reserves to threaten future supplies. Not that anyone expects this.

Safari Vehicles and Cars. Numerous hire companies, including the multinationals, Hertz and Avis, operate all of Nairobi, Mombasa and Malindi. It's possible to shop around for deals among the smaller firms, for instance a monthly rate with unlimited mileage. The following figures are those of late 1986, and will probably be somewhere in the region of 20% higher by mid-1987.

For a Datsun 120Y or a Charade you will pay Shs. 1,680/- a week plus 3.90/- per kilometer; for a Colt Lancer Shs. 2,640/- a week, plus 4.90/- per kilometer. A Suzuki Safari runs at Shs. 1,740/- per week, 4/- a kilometer; a Safari minibus (10 seater) Shs. 3,300/- a week, 6/- a kilometer.

You will need a valid driving license (any country) and a deposit based on estimated time out and distance, plus quite a hefty amount unless a Collision Damage Waiver is taken. The driver must be over 23 and under 70 and must have held the license for more than two years.

Only American Express, Diners and Visa credit cards will be accepted.

BY TAXI. There are very few taxis with working meters, thus the price is negotiable around 20 cents a mile or a bit over. There is a long-haul taxi service—Rift Valley Province Peugeot Service—to various set destinations, mainly in the Rift Valley, with as many people packed into Peugeot station wagons as possible. Among the destinations covered from Nairobi are Naivasha, Nakuru, Eldoret, Kitale, Kisumu, and Mombasa.

BY BUS. There are public buses, mainly for the African commuter crowds and the *matatus*—jam-packed, over-loaded covered vans for the slightly better off. Neither of these forms of transport are recommended for the average tourist.

Leaving Kenya

CUSTOMS ON LEAVING KENYA. Kenya is a signa-tory to CITES (Convention on the International Trade in Endangered Species of Wild Fauna and Flora), a worldwide organization set up to protect endangered species from commercial over-exploitation, which was ratified by Kenya on March 13, 1979. Trade in ivory, rhino horn, skins and all other anatomical relics of wildlife is disallowed. It happens occasionally that some local spiv will offer a "curio" for covert sale to the tourist. But if either one is caught, it would almost certainly mean prosecution in a country ultra-sensitive about the bad name it got for a murderous free-for-all on its wildlife in the seventies. The export of live animals, birds and reptiles is also banned, except where the dealer is a professional and licensed. The same goes for diamonds, gold and gemstones like rubies found recently in Tsavo.

Departure. On leaving Kenya an Airport Tax of Shs. 140/- per person is payable in foreign currency. There's a fairly rigorous customs and currency check on the way out, together with the usual passport and security rituals. They might ask, in particular, for proof of how you changed your dollars.

At Nairobi Airport, one or two "duty free" shops are open round the clock and might provide a sting in the tail for an otherwise memorable safari.

CUSTOMS ON RETURNING HOME. If you propose to take on your holiday any *foreign-made* articles, such as cameras, binoculars, expensive watches and the like, it is wise to put with your travel documents the receipt from the retailer or some other evidence that the item was bought in your home country. If you bought the article on a previous holiday abroad and have already paid duty on it, carry with you the receipt for this. Otherwise, on returning home, you may be charged duty (for British residents, Value Added Tax as well). In other words, unless you can prove prior possession, foreign-made articles are dutiable *each time* they enter the U.S. The details below are correct as we go to press. It would be wise to check in case of change.

U.S. residents. You may bring in $400 worth of foreign merchandise as gifts or for personal use without having to pay duty, provided you have been out of the country more than 48 hours and provided you have not claimed a similar exemption within the previous 30 days. A 10% flat rate of duty is charged on the next $1,000 worth of purchases. Every member of a family is entitled to the same exemption, regardless of age, and the exemptions can be pooled. Included for travelers over the age of 21 are one liter of alcohol, 100 cigars (non-Cuban) and 200 cigarettes. Any amount in excess of those limits will be taxed at the port of entry, and may additionally be taxed in the traveler's home state. Only one bottle of perfume trademarked in the U.S. may be brought in. Unlimited amounts of goods from certain specially designated "developing" countries may also be brought in duty-free; check with U.S. Customs Service, Washington D.C. 20229. You may not bring home meats, fruits, plants, soil or other agricultural items.

Gifts valued at under $25 may be mailed to friends or relatives at home, but not more than one per day (of receipt) to any one addressee. These gifts must not include perfumes costing more than $5, tobacco or liquor.

British Customs. There are two levels of duty free allowance for people entering the U.K.; one, for goods bought outside the EEC or for goods bought in a duty free shop within the EEC; two, for goods bought in an EEC country but not in a duty free shop.

In the first category you may import duty free: 200 cigarettes or 100 cigarillos or 50 cigars or 250 grammes of tobacco (*Note* if you live outside Europe, these allowances are doubled); plus one liter of alcholic drinks over 22% vol. (38.8% proof) or two liters of alcoholic drinks not over 22% vol. or fortified, still or sparkling wine; plus two liters of still table wine; plus 50 grammes of perfume; plus nine fluid ounces of toilet water; plus other goods to the value of £28.

In the second category you may import duty free: 300 cigarettes or 150 cigarillos or 75 cigars or 400 grammes of tobacco; plus 1½ liters of alcholic drinks over 22% vol. (38.8% proof) or three liters of alcoholic drinks not over 22% vol. or fortified, still or sparkling wine; plus five liters of still table wine; plus 75 grammes of perfume; plus 13 fluid ounces of toilet water; plus other goods to the value of £207 (*Note:* though it is not classified as an alcholic drink by EEC countries for Customs' purposes and is thus considered part of the "other goods" allowance, you may not import more than 50 liters of beer).

In addition, no animals or pets of any kind may be brought into the U.K. The penalties for doing so are severe and are strictly enforced; there are *no* exceptions. Similarly, fresh meats, plants and vegetables, controlled drugs and firearms and ammunition may not be brought into the U.K. There are no restrictions on the import or export of British and foreign currencies.

MASAI MORAN

FROM ADAM UP

A Brief History of Kenya

For the most part, any attempt at a history of Kenya before the 19th century and the coming of the Europeans to East Africa must remain a patchy and speculative business. The coastal areas, where Phoenicians and Egyptians traded long before the birth of Christ and where, from 1500 to 1700, Portuguese and Arabs vied for supremacy, have a relatively well-documented past, though there are many gaps in the story. But the vast interior presents a different picture altogether. It has practically no reliably recorded or documented history, and the would-be historian has to content himself with the legends and mysterious and ancient mythologies that the tribes have passed down from generation to generation by word of mouth. Thus the history of Kenya to a large extent starts only in the 19th century.

Yet ironically, for a place with little or no known past, Kenya has almost certainly been the scene of human activity for longer than any other place in the world. For Kenya—or more specifically the great Rift Valley that stretches northeastward from the center of the country —was in all likelihood the birth place of the human race.

Around three million years ago, a short, furry creature emerged from the forests of the Rift Valley and, finding it could not see over the long grass, stood on its hind legs. It stayed that way. The first excavations in Kenya to turn up evidence of early man were in 1959 when Louis B. Leakey and his wife Mary discovered human remains, dating from 1.7 million years ago, on Rusinga Island in the Victoria-Nyanza. They announced him as the original Adam.

They were wrong, however, according to their eldest son, Richard (well-known for the television series, *The Making of Mankind*). His African assistant found part of the skull of a hominid born a million years earlier at Koobi Fora on Lake Turkana, and the young Leakey proclaimed him "1470"—an unromantic catalog number for the new father of humanity.

Further up the Rift yet another excavation by an American team in Ethiopia then turned up a girl, subsequently named Lucy, who was said to be senior to 1470 by a few millenia. Mary Leakey, still digging around Olduvai, at a place called Laetolil, has now found bones and footprints which could place the start of the human race closer to four million years ago.

Even with the added evidence of *Homo erectus* hunting hippo at Ologesaile off the road from Nairobi to Lake Magadi, all these finds are really too sparse to add up to a clear picture or provide a solid structure upon which to build the history of millennia. But no one really doubts that somewhere in the soil of Kenya many more answers lie. As recently as 1984, an American team working with Richard Leakey found another rich fossil site on Rusinga Island. This site contained bones of 18-million-year-old creatures of a species thought to be the common ancestor of apes and humans—*Proconsul africanus*.

The Tribes of the Interior

"Modern" Kenyan and East African history starts around 4,000 B.C., the date of some Stone-Age cave paintings which have been found in present-day Tanzania. The naturalist Joy Adamson claimed to have found similar paintings in a cave near Turkana in northern Kenya. Unfortunately, she carried the secret of their exact location with her to the grave. At all events, these Stone Age peoples subsequently took to the hills of western and southern Kenya where they became forest hunters. The lands they vacated were eventually taken over by the

Bantu people who migrated into Kenya either directly from the Congo basin in Central Africa or from Lake Tanganyika. They ushered the Iron Age into Kenya (at about the time of the birth of Christ) and introduced agriculture wherever the country offered more than marginal range. Some Bantu also migrated to the coast, mingling peripherally with the already well-established Arabs and Asiatics there, a mixture which produced the coast characteristic Swahili society.

Over the next thousand years or so, migrant tribes from Somalia, Ethiopia and the Upper Nile Valley continued to enter Kenya and settle there. Known as Nilo-Hamitics or Plains' Nilotes, they constituted the principal groups of the Rift Valley. Among them were the Masai, ultimately the most successful of all the new tribes though there seems good reason to believe that they are not an indigenous African people at all. Indeed, according to a radical theory advanced in 1908 by one Captain Moritz Merkur of the German Army in Tanganyika Masailand, the Masai were one of the lost tribes of Israel. Merker's theory was mostly dependent on the Masai religion which acknowledges only one God, as does that of the undisputed tribe of Falasha Jews in western Ethiopia. His supporting texts, derived from two old storytellers of the Kisonko Masai around Kilimanjaro, read like a transcultural version of the Old Testament, from the Creation to a Moses called *Moosa*.

Later warring studies—chiefly British and German—found positive Semitic, even Babylonian, traces in the Masai language and astronomy. Others dismissed it as fanciful humbug. There, in a state of chassis, as Joxer Daly said, the debate stands.

Leaping forward a further 700 or so years, by the late 17th-century the Masai had established an empire that extended from Mount Kenya in the center of the country all the way to southern Tanzania. By 1845 they were even threatening the gates of Mombasa, but more with bravado than serious intent. Apart from any other considerations, Mombasa by that point was defended by the guns of the Royal Navy.

The Land of Zinj

The history of the coast, the *Zinj* (meaning "black"), is quite separate from that of the interior. The Egyptians may have been the first to settle there, probably around 3,000 B.C. Some 2,000 years later it seems likely that the Phoenicians were familiar with the region and that they also traveled inland as far south as Zimbabwe. Ptolemy in Egypt knew something of the interior geography of East Africa in A.D. 150. He drew a map which fairly accurately showed the source of the White Nile in two East African lakes and the Blue Nile flowing out of Lake Tana in the highlands of Ethiopia.

From the time of Ptolemy onward, the Kenyan coast was an important staging post on the Trade Wind routes between Arabia and the Far East. A fascinating, albeit brief, account of the East African coast during the Roman Empire is contained in the *Periplus Maris Erythraei* (Guidebook to the Erythraean Sea) written by an anonymous merchant around the middle of the 1st century B.C. Later travelers also left their mark, among them Judorian, who logged his visits in the 6th century, and the Persians, who colonized parts of the coast until thrown out by the Omani Arabs between the 9th and 12th centuries. Further evidence of Kenya's role in the trade routes between East and West is provided by Chinese vases of the Sung and, later, Ming dynasties. At around the same time (the latter Middle Ages), petty Arab sheikdoms, war-like but intermittently prosperous, were formed at Mombasa and Malindi and on the islands of Lamu, Manda and Pate.

From Portuguese to British

Life on the coast continued under the control of these sheiks until the arrival of the Portuguese in 1498 in the person of Vasco da Gama. For the next 230 years, the Portuguese and Arabs tussled for control of the deep-water anchorage at Mombasa. The Portuguese captured it in 1528, but soon afterwards lost it to Ali Bey, the Turk, and fell back to Malindi. Here they remained, fattening the town with their largesse, until around 1590 when they recruited a passing army of Zimba tribesmen. No one knows for sure who they were, but they were impressive if bizarre warriors, much given to eating their enemies. Having recaptured Mombasa with their army of itinerant cannibals, the Portuguese determined to consolidate their hold on the town by the construction of a massive fort above the harbor, Fort Jesus. Malindi, meanwhile, they ignored, allowing it to degenerate into a sleepy and unimportant backwater, a condition it was to remain in for the next 300 years.

The Arabs then took the offensive and the Portuguese were in and out of their citadel until 1728 when they finally gave up, sailed south and settled for the inferior coast of Mozambique. They left nothing of import behind except a few plantation crops, including white maize which spread inland to become the Bantu staple.

An immigrant Arab family from Oman by the name of Mazrui now moved into Mombasa, and the coast settled into a period of civil war and general decline which was to last throughout the 18th century and into the 19th when, in 1824, the British arrived. They established the Protectorate of Mombasa, but this was almost immediately abandoned in deference to the wishes of the Sultan of Oman who, by 1837, was undisputed ruler of the new United Republic of Zinj. In this capacity he was able to continue unhindered the traditional and profitable business of slavery, which had for long been the principal attraction of the East African coast to the Arabs. Unluckily for the Sultan, however, the British very shortly afterwards returned to Mombasa in a fine state of moral zeal, determined to end the trade in human flesh. This they achieved, though their methods were scarcely less violent than the "abomination" they sought to end.

Into the Dark Continent

It was at this point that the Europeans began to venture into the wastes of the great continent. The first white men to step into the interior were two German missionaries, Rebmann and Krapf. In 1847 Rebmann went about 129 km. (80 miles) inland from Mombasa to the Taita Hills, from where he was able to see Mount Kilimanjaro. Krapf went both further north and further inland, journeying 322 km. (200 miles) from Mombasa to the Kamba country where he caught an early morning glimpse of a shining snow peak before it disappeared into its daily mantle of cloud.

Ten years later, Captain John Hanning Speke of the British Indian Army, accompanied by James Grant, was engaged on an all-consuming hunt for the source of the Nile, spurred on by Ptolemy's beguiling indications. But it was not until 1874 that Speke's at the time highly-contentious claim to have found the source of the mighty river in a great lake in western Kenya, which he had named Lake Victoria, was proved right. Speke, a tragic figure in many ways, had unfortunately killed himself some years earlier on the morning of a highly-publicized debate on the source of the Nile with his principal rival, Sir Richard Burton. It was left to the immortal Henry Morton Stanley, of Dr. Livingstone fame, to vindicate Speke.

The next stage in the exploration of the interior was carried out by two remarkable men, the Scotsman Joseph Thomson and a rich Austro-Hungarian count, Samuel Teleki von Szek. Both discovered that the natives, though picturesque, could also be decidedly restless, not to mention hostile.

Thomson had first visted Africa in 1875 on an expedition to the Central African lakes. Five years later, at the ripe age of 28, he was the only experienced Africa hand willing to undertake an expedition to the Masai country with anything less than an artillery regiment. "Take a thousand men," Stanley had advised, "or write your will." He eventually took 143, only a dozen of whom knew how to fire a rifle. His second-in-command was an illiterate Maltese sailor named James Martin. The rest he described as "the very off-scourings of the Zanzibar waterfront." Inevitably, they mutinied a few miles out on the road to Taveta, the first Arab staging post to Lake Tanganyika. The normal form was to shoot or hang the ring-leaders, but Thomson tried his Scottish brogue and the men responded. Not to what he was saying—they didn't understand a word—but to the warm inflections in his voice. The finely-tuned African antenna had picked up the fact that the youngster, the *kijana,* might be a lunatic in the head, but was all right in the heart. They were persuaded to continue, but only as far as Kibonoto, north of Kilimanjaro. Here they caught sight of an advance guard of a tribe of Masai that had routed an ill-fated German expedition led by Dr. Gustav Fischer some five years earlier.

The young Scot was fascinated by his first contact with "the savages so long the subject of my waking dreams . . . Oh, what splendid fellows!" He led a peace party of the Masai into his camp where they delivered "a mostly friendly and encouraging greeting—and with great cheerfulness, relieved us of the care of nearly ten loads of goods."

But, as the day wore on, "matters became more ominous. The warriors grew boisterous and rude . . . and we knew they were about to take revenge on our small party for their failure to annihilate Fischer." So Thomson decided to back off and return to the coast. Jogging all the way back to Mombasa, they covered the 240 miles in six days. He refitted at the port, engaged a few more men, and, saying "Something will turn up in Taveta," was able to tack on to a large Arab caravan and make a second, more confident, move on Masalland.

He separated from the Arabs at Kilimanjaro and went north, on a direct bearing to Lake Victoria towards Amboseli, and it was there his "miseries started in earnest" in an encounter with the Matapato division of the Masai—" . . . savages who indeed look down on all other tribes as inferior beings. Even with our large caravan, we had to submit with the meekness and patience of martyrs to every conceivable indignity. Though they had pulled our noses, we should have been compelled to smile sweetly upon them."

In spite of full defensive precautions, including surrounding himself with two thick thorn fences, Thomson was harassed daily by the moran (the Masai warriors) who merely strolled past the armed guards and walked into camp. "I would have to say how delighted I was to see them and give them string after string of beads in the hope of hastening their departure. But finally, only after exhibiting to their untutored gaze all the marvels of my own white person, might they be cajoled out . . . leaving behind the most unsavoury tokens of their visit!"

Like many who followed him, Thomson was in two minds about the Masai. They were monstrous, but on the other hand "a more remarkable and unique race does not exist on the continent of Africa. Indeed I might safely say in the two hemispheres. In their physique, manners, customs and religious beliefs they are quite distinct from the true negroes and the Galla and Somali . . . They are the most magnificently modeled savages I have ever seen or read of. Beautifully proportioned, they are characterized by the smooth and rounded outline of the Apollo-type."

He was not seriously threatened by the Masai until he deviated out of the Rift towards Ol-Doinya Keri, the striped mountain, the Masai name for Mount Kenya. At first he enjoyed himself, "having the satisfaction of being enveloped in a dense raw Scotch mist with the temperature at freezing point." He renamed the Sattima spur range the Aberdares, after Scottish peer, Lord Aberdare, later to become President of the Royal Geographical Society in London. But the Laikipiak moran arrived and he was under provocation as never before. Finally he fled in the night, just escaping before a full-scale attack.

He reached Lake Victoria in December, 1883, and redrew the map of Kenya, putting in a great deal more water than there was previously. He toured Elgon and found the great caves in the mountain which Sir Rider Haggard would later use as a main setting in his novel *She*.

Thomson, a genuinely modest man, was something of a hero back in England. His heady adventures among the wildest savages of Africa —he was to make several more journeys into the interior, before dying in London in 1895 when only 39—fired the Victorian imagination and started the safari business. From his day on, there were almost back-to-back tours to Kenya for the gentlemen and politicians who, within ten years, would carve up East Africa into British and German spheres of influence.

Teleki's Trip

Count Samuel Teleki von Szek, who, along with Thomson, was to make the most substantial 19th-century discoveries of the Kenyan interior, began preparations for his trip in 1886. His was to be a monumental safari, through the Kikuyu heartland and on to Lake Turkana, at that time still known only by its Masai name of Embasso Narok, the Black Lake. The expedition amounted in all to nearly 700 men, among them one Lieutenant Ludwig von Hohnel, who was to prove himself a diligent biographer, recording practically every step of the epic journey. Von Hohnel was also quartermaster for the trip and his inventory list was a volume in itself containing everything from glass beads through jointed dolls to muzzle loaders. The Count, very aristocratic, led his grand caravan of tinkers up from the coast in January, 1887.

By April, they were camped on the Ngong Hills above Nairobi, within range of the Kikuyu's poisoned arrows. Nothing happened until Teleki moved up to the forest edge, fired a couple of shots to attract attention and thereafter received a few tattered Ndorobo thrown out as trade consuls.

They were returned alive with samples of the Count's haberdashery, after which hordes of the tribal women appeared with goats, chickens and a vast array of agricultural products. Finally, the men arrived in full battledress, looking very much like the Masai—robed, red-painted and wearing their hair in long ringlets set solid in mud and animal fat. In the trade-off, the Kikuyu received mirrors, shells and cavalry swords, while Teleki got a cape of colobus monkey skins, the mark of an honorary chief.

His position was only slightly inferior to the chief of what was probably the Waiyaki clan. The old man was intelligent and well-informed, says von Hohnel. "He lent a willing ear to our assurances that we were altogether averse to war and seemed to realize the advantages which might accrue to the Kikuyu if they gave us passage through their country."

Up from Ngong through Thomson's Aberdares to Mount Kenya, the Austrian Count found it green and pleasant, if "rather chilly at night over 6,000 ft."

The empty land which later colonists would call the White Highlands was observed to "grow nearly all the cereals and crops native to East Africa and it is, in fact, the granary of a very extended district." Von Hohnel listed the main produce as millet, maize, potatoes, beans, yams, sugarcane, bananas and tobacco.

Once out of the area, the caravan split for a while with von Hohnel taking off to trade ivory and map the northern Laikipia shoulder of Mount Kenya and to follow one of the sources of the Uaso Nyiro, the Brown River, down off the mountain into Samburu country. Teleki climbed the mountain, taking his "perishing barefoot companions" up to 4,145 meters (13,600 ft.) and then going on alone up the Teleki Valley, as it was latter called, to the ice field at Point Lenana and the jagged peaks of Nelion and Mbatian, all three of them named after Masai Laibons. For a non-naturalist, his careful notes on the changing botany down the contours are impressive.

From there on the safari continued to a spur of the Marmanet range from which they saw, way below, what von Hohnel described as "the glittering expanse of Lake Baringo." Teleki's men, mostly Swahilis, rushed down the slopes to the dry heat of the lake and to what they imagined were "the full flesh pots" of the Njemps, which the Masai had written off as the untouchables of the race. They found one of the tattiest tribes in Kenya in two permanent villages, wasted at the time with famine which Teleki temporarily relieved with the assassination of 38 large animals and the provision of "positively mountains of meat."

The landscapes from there to Lake Turkana are virtually unchanged from the poetic volcanic wasteland von Hohnel saw as "recently flung from some monstrous forge." The southern edge of the lake is one last satanic obstacle course of lava debris before the ridge which opens up a view of one of the most primitive and starkly beautiful fusions of the elements on earth. Teleki named the lake "Rudolf" after the Austrian Crown Prince, sponsor of the expedition.

Other than the discoveries of two Americans, Donaldson Smith and William Chanler, who surveyed the Tana River and the featureless commiphora bush of the northeast, the main structures of the land and its peoples were known following Teleki's and Thomson's expeditions. Thus the stage was set for the next step in Kenya's history: colonization.

The Colonial Carve-Up

The beginnings of the "Scramble for Africa"—a contest played out principally between the German and British Governments—dated from 1881. Then, the Sultan of Oman, demoralized by the rapid decline of his power and Britain's success in curbing his slave trade, offered his entire estate from the coast to Lake Victoria as a Protectorate to an enterprizing Scot, Sir William Mackinnon. Sir William accepted and started building roads into the interior, paying for them out of his own pocket since the British Government, uncharacteristically perhaps, suddenly seemed to be having second thoughts about consolidating their hold on East Africa. However, by 1888, Lord Salisbury, the British Prime Minister, was persuaded to dub Mackinnon and his company of Manchester merchants the Imperial British East Africa Company, and a royal charter was issued.

A somewhat farcical period ensued when Sir Frederick Jackson, sent out to supervise the company, was diverted on his journey by an elephant hunt on Mount Elgon. While Jackson was thus engaged, a German adventurer by the name of Karl Peters was rather unsportingly making a take-over bid. He marched 300 armed "negotiators" up the Tana River, setting up Protectorates at Baringo, Mount Kenya and wherever else he could get thumb-print signatures on his "treaties of eternal friendship." At Mumias, close to the lake, he intercepted, and read, Jackson's mail and hurried on to Uganda to get in first with a deal with the King, or Kabaka, of the Buganda.

But at this point, the busy plans of both Jackson and Peters were unexpectedly made redundant by Salisbury and Bismarck, the German Chancellor. The two old gentlemen took a ruler and drew a line from the village of Vanga on the coast to the middle of the eastern shore of Lake Victoria. The line deviated only round the base of Kilimanjaro since Bismarck thought it only fair that if Britain had some snow on Mount Kenya Germany should have some too. Salisbury was given all the land north of the line including Uganda. By way of exchange, Bismarck got the North Sea island of Heligoland which he thought, wrongly as it turned out, would make a useful naval base.

By 1891, the final lines of demarcation were drawn. And in 1895, the creation of the Protectorate of British East Africa was ratified by the British Parliament. As compensation for seven years' hard labor in the service of the Crown, Mackinnon's company was paid off with a gratuity of £250,000.

Settlement

Having finally established their East African Empire, the British were then faced with the problem of what to do with the natives, none of whom had, of course, been party to the German and British division of their lands and whose attitude toward the enforced partition was less than enthusiastic. The Nandi tribe around Lake Victoria, for instance, immediately launched a guerilla offensive that was to last for ten years, tying-up increasingly large numbers of British forces and ending only when the Nandi chief was shot dead at peace talks with the ruthless but effective British negotiator, Captain Richard Meinertzhagen. The Masai were also a considerable force to be reckoned with. At the end of 1895 they massacred half a caravan of 1,100 men in the Kedong section of the Rift above Nairobi. It started with some of the caravan crew making a play for the young warriors' women and ended with what Sir Frederick Jackson described as "merciless, bloody butchery" all the way up the valley to Mount Margaret.

At the same time as crushing native resistance, the British set about settling the interior. This they did principally by building a railway from Mombasa to Lake Victoria. The "iron rhinoceros" was started in 1896 and completed at the end of 1901, (though only after 28 Indians, an unknown number of Africans and one European sleeping in his tent had been devoured by several elderly male lions) its 584 miles costing the British Exchequer the then phenomenal sum of £9,500 per mile. Arousing enormous opposition in the British Parliament and dubbed "the lunatic line to nowhere," the railway in fact proved an effective means of colonization, as the areas either side of it, especially Thomson's Scottish-looking Aberdares, were settled and farmed by the white man. Under the unofficial leadership of the colorful and eccentric Lord Delamere, the settlers by 1912 had the Protectorate paying its way on the basis of a mixed agricultural economy.

An indication of their success was provided by the popularity East Africa began to enjoy as a tourist destination, particularly among big game hunters. Among early visitors was the young Winston Churchill, and in 1909 President Theodore Roosevelt, his son Kermit and a large party of scientists visited Kenya. They shot indiscriminately for sport, as well as selectively for the Smithsonian, and also produced the first serious natural history of Kenya. The railway also got in on the act, proclaiming, "The Highlands of East Africa as a Winter Home for Aristocrats." And they produced a poster showing a wide range of game species lined up as if to attack a train, while the caption announced, "Railway Cars pass through the Greatest Natural Game reserve in the World. Sportsmen in search of Big Game make it a Hobby. Students of Natural History revel in this field of Nature's Own Making."

World War I and After

The settled, prosperous condition of Kenya was significantly jolted by World War I. But while the East African theater of the war was nothing if not irrelevant to the main course of the war, it did provide a hint of exotic and romantic color to set off against the grim slaughter of the Western Front as some two thirds of an estimated 3,000 settlers left their farms and families to ride out after the Hun in irregular cavalry units.

The war began with a series of minor but cinematic clashes, with the German commander, Paul von Lettow-Vorbeck, far and away the star performer. He first embarrassingly thrashed the British during an attempted landing at Tanga in German-held Tanganyika and subsequently led a hit-and-run campaign against the Mombasa–Lake Victoria railway. At sea, the German battle-cruiser *Koenigsberg* was similarly successful in disrupting British trade routes to India, until it was eventually forced to hole-up deep in the Rufiji River delta in Tanganyika. It was found by an elephant hunter in native disguise, after which two intrepid pilots lobbed bombs at it from their flimsy planes.

The war later took on a more dour tone when the South African Jan Smuts, sent by the British Government to sort out the troublesome von Lettow-Vorbeck, pursued the German commander round much of Central Africa, occupying a considerable force of British troops for the remainder of the war and achieving precisely what the German had intended from the start.

After the Armistice, the major political consequence of the war for Kenya was the decision by the British to offer estates in the highlands to veterans of the European campaign in what was called the Soldier Settlement Scheme. Farms were either given away to winners of a lottery or sold at nominal prices on long-term credit. By 1920, the white population had increased to around 9,000. At the same time, the country was designated the Colony of Kenya.

For many, especially the original settlers led by Lord Delamere, this tended to advance their long-held objective of a permanent White Man's Kenya; that is to say, a country run in perpetuity by and for Europeans, the Africans being relegated to ranch hands and house servants. But they were soon disillusioned when in 1923 it became clear that official Government policy was that of an Africa for the Africans. From this date a succession of Governers were obliged to apply this policy against the cantankerous and abusive opposition of Delamere and his "Kenya Cowboys."

Highlife and Hangovers

As a result of this liberal policy, the Kenya of the '20s and '30s was a vigorous combination of native Africans, adapting rapidly to the new European way of life, Asians, and the British, who, somewhat surprisingly, divided themselves into two distinct groups, the administrators and the settlers. Nowhere was this mixture more heady than in Nairobi.

Among the Africans, the Kikuyu tribe in particular streamed into Nairobi, which in 1925 was still little more than a one-street frontier town. Their arrival represented an enormous social revolution, yet the leap from traditional tribal existence to urban living was achieved remarkably successfully. But they also managed to retain their links with the tribal way of life, principally by leaving the senior wives of the tribes on their old lands to work the patches of land. These *shamba* had retained their mystic, almost religious, significance for the Africans. At the same time, the Kikuyu were active, if as yet unsuccessful, in lobbying for the return of their highland lands.

For the white man, however, this was the golden age of Kenya. Though the long term policy of the Government may not have been in their interests, they nonetheless had things very much their own way during the '20s and early '30s. Their headquarters in Nairobi, both politically and socially, was the Muthaiga Country Club, the venue for elegantly wild parties and other revels, and an extension of the even more permissive life up-country in the Wanjoki, the "Happy Valley" of the highlands. Interspersed with the cocktails and hangovers of the settlers were moments of high drama, such as the unsolved murder of the noted ladies man, Lord Joss Erroll, a close friend of the woman who was to marry Lord Delamere's son and heir. This intriguing scandal is fully documented by James Fox in his book *White Mischief.*

Another more significant casualty of the period was the first Baroness Blixen whose husband, a hunter by the name of Bror, abandoned her for another woman and left her to go broke on a suburban Nairobi coffee farm. Her memoir, *Out of Africa*, is remarkable for its stylish insight into the country and the people, as well as providing eloquent testimony on the high life of the white community.

Uhuru

The first stirrings of an African mass movement for *Uhuru*—Freedom—came with an erosion of the settler's economic power in the '30s, the result of falling commodity prices in Europe. A number of settlers moved off the land and into commerce. Some also took up as hunters, while others moved to the coast to retire or open hotels. World War II caused a further disruption of the old order with Kenya garrisoned against an Italian attack from Abyssinia. (This amounted in the end to no more than an ineffectual two-plane air raid on Malindi.) After the war, the return of the King's African Rifles, a native African regiment, aware that the white man in the highlands was not as invincible as he appeared, added further weight to the demands of the Kikuyu in negotiating their rights with the administration.

By 1946, the independence movement was given a much clearer direction by the leadership of Jomo Kenyatta, who provided the Kikuyu associations with an infinitely more sophisticated political program than hitherto and led them and a fledgling union in frequent petitions to the administration for majority African rule. But any hopes of peaceful political change were shattered by the emergence of Mau Mau, a violent and ultimately horrifying guerilla grouping launched from the forests of the central highlands. Isolated white farms were attacked and their occupants killed, often with calculated brutality. A few Asians were also slaughtered. But the brunt of the increasing violence was taken by the Kikuyu. Simultaneously, though innocent of the charge, the Kikuyu were also identified with the Mau Mau by the white administration.

In October 1952 a State of Emergency was declared and 180 Kikuyu picked up by the British Army in an indiscriminate sweep of the leadership; Kenyatta, though he had publically dissociated himself from the Mau Mau, among them. He was sentenced to seven years hard labor at Lokitaung in the Turkana desert. The Government then went after the guerillas, first cutting their supply lines by concentrating the rural Kikuyu in secured villages. They also cleared the towns of suspected Mau Mau sympathizers. A total of 30,000 Africans, mostly Kikuyu, were detained in camps across the country.

A search-and-destroy operation was then launched, with British and African troops, an expanded police force and settlers combining to eliminate the guerillas. Finally, in 1956, the almost mystically elusive

"Field Marshall" Dedan Kimathi was caught and hanged, and Mau Mau was finished.

With the elimination of the Mau Mau, the way was cleared for an orderly transfer of power from Britain to the native Africans and complete independence for Kenya. There remained some stumbling blocks, however. Despite having been elected leader of the Kenya African National Union (KANU), a new and broad-based political party, the still imprisoned Kenyatta was refused parole by the Governor, Sir Patrick Renison, and kept out of Nairobi until as late as August 1961. Similarly, the white settlers harbored many doubts about full independence, fearing for their privileged status, many being positively hostile to the notion. Finally, despite Kenyatta, there was still an undeniable lack of political sophistication among many of the black politicians.

But with the appointment of the unorthodox Malcolm MacDonald, who had served the decolonization process with distinction in the Far East, as Governor in succession to Renison, these problems were skillfully and imaginatively overcome. He set up a series of negotiations between Kenyans of all backgrounds with the Colonial Office in London before holding a model General Election in Kenya under universal franchise. KANU was the clear victor, and in June 1963 MacDonald invited Kenyatta to form a Government.

On December 12 that same year, the Union Jack was lowered for the last time and the new Kenyan national flag run up on the summit of Mount Kenya. It had as its central motif KANU's cockerel on a shield with crossed spears. The background was a horizontal tricolor of black for the people, green for the land and red for the estimated 10,000 Africans who had lost their lives in the struggle for Uhuru. Kenyatta was elected President for an initial five-year term. But he was also invested with a traditional Kikuyu title of respect; *Mzee*—the Old Man.

Modern Kenya

The handling of the early years of independence was a model of its kind. Kenyatta's over-riding objective was to make Kenya unequivocally a black man's country. But this he chose to do gradually, largely so as not to alienate the Europeans and Asians who had made the country economically strong. Rather than break the Asians' hold over commerce immediately, for example, he prised them loose with trade and licensing restrictions. Similarly, he bought out over a period of years, with soft loans from the British Government, those white settlers who had held on to their lands. The Africans were thus eased gently into business and back onto the land, particularly the highlands, by means of favorable settlement schemes, co-operatives and individual grants of lands. At the same time he declared for a multi-racial society, offering citizenship to anyone prepared to accept the new order. His chant at political rallies was *Harambee*—all pull together.

The Kenya Jomo Kenyatta built in the '60s and early '70s proved politically stable, socially tolerant and economically prosperous. Not the least of the "Old Man's" achievements was his subtle welding together of the clashing patchwork of tribes, whose traditional and in many cases deep-seated antipathy to one another might well have sounded the death knell for the modern state almost at the moment of birth.

Kenyatta died in 1978, but the transfer of power to the Vice-President, Daniel arap Moi, proved orderly and constitutional. Moi's approach has subsequently been based on a policy of *Nyayo*. Roughly translated, this means "in the Old Man's footsteps."

The '80s, however, have thus far proved a traumatic and difficult period for Kenya. The collapse of commodity prices, upon which the Kenyan economy is largely dependant, caused by an enduring world recession, has had severe economic consequences. These have in turn conspired to destabilize the country politically, a situation reminiscent of the Great Depression of the '30s. Matters came to a head in no uncertain way in August 1982 when a military coup narrowly failed to topple Moi. Since then, there have been few signs of a return to the stability and prosperity of the early years of independence. Charges of corruption in high places and of failure to control the increasing slaughter of wildlife for profit, for example, particularly of elephants, have become frequent. Meanwhile, the gap between rich and poor has, if anything, increased.

But for the visitor, Kenya still has much to offer. The Kenyans are well aware of the importance of tourism and care is given to ensuring that tourist facilities retain their high standards. But above all, the country itself—the climate, the wildlife, the dramatic and beautiful interior and the coast—remains intact, still largely as it was many thousands of years ago.

LEOPARD

ANIMALS OF KENYA

Simba, Ngiri and Ndovu

Buried deep in the human psyche, keyed to some long-forgotten gene, is an emotion that stirs to life when confronted by the sight of an animal's true nature. Visitors—anesthetized by life in the concrete jungle—are seized by this atavistic sensation when they tour the great animal parks of Kenya. These surroundings have held and humbled the imagination for centuries, and travelers still find themselves in the grip of that primal awe. A lion feeding on a wildebeest suddenly slaps a paw, claws extended, onto the fallen animal and, no matter how long the watcher has lived among skyscrapers and exhaust fumes, he cannot help responding. He knows instinctively what his distant ancestors knew, that before him is an animal power which he may outsmart, but which he dare not confront head on.

These plants are not as abundant as the grasses, but since Tommys are much smaller than zebra or wildebeest—standing only two feet at the shoulder and weighing about fifty pounds—they don't have to eat as much as a wildebeest and have more time to search for suitable food. Their tastes do not demand the young plants zebra and wildebeest feed on, so they bring up the rear in any migratory cycle.

Tommys are particularly attractive animals. Their colors are all bright—rich tan skin, strong black stripe on side, and pure white underbelly and rump. The males have strong curving horns that can reach a foot and a half in length. Female horns are short and slender. The tails are always swishing handsomely. Tommys look at visitors with keen, interested eyes.

The three together—zebra, wildebeest, and Thomson's gazelle— show how remarkably at peace with itself the savanna's ecosystem is. The sizes, tastes, and activities of the different species are all in balance with one another.

Giraffes

The great migratory mammals of Africa are most frequently associated with open grasslands. An animal more at home in parklands or thornbush country is the giraffe *(twiga),* the world's tallest living animal. These giants are so remarkable in appearance that they have often been brought long distances in order to astonish and impress people. Lorenzo the Magnificent had one in his gardens in Renaissance Florence. Julius Caesar brought some giraffes to Rome to help celebrate his victories in Africa. Caesar, an early master of public relations, generated interest in the giraffe by dubbing it a "cameleopard" and suggesting that it was a cross between a camel and a leopard. Even today the scientific name for the giraffe is *giraffa camelopardalis.*

Despite this name, the giraffe is like nothing else on our planet. An adult male can stand 18 feet high, almost twice the height of an elephant, and when he stretches he can reach as high as 19½ feet. The markings vary from race to race, but all have brownish spots on a yellow or white background. The coloring is hard to explain. Presumably it has a camouflage value, but the markings vary so much even within a given population that there is apparently little need for a specific pattern or color. The usefulness of their size is more evident. They can reach high into trees to eat leaves nothing else can touch. Many African trees are thorny, but giraffes have a long thick tongue (it can reach 20 inches) able to strip the high branches of leaves and not be bothered by the thorns.

Surprisingly, a giraffe's great size does not seem to make it easy to see. On a safari it is common to drive within a few yards of a giraffe before noticing it, and then it can turn out that what first seemed like one giraffe is actually a group of them. The others are nearby, going unnoticed perhaps because they are so huge that the mind simply dismisses them as trees.

Giraffes often seem to pay no attention to one another, but they do interact. Particularly interesting to watch is the way they fight. They use their necks like whips and knock their heads into each other's bodies or necks. These duels are often conducted in a leisurely manner with long pauses between each swing of the neck.

Occasionally groups of giraffes are found resting. They sit with their legs folded under them but seldom let their necks lie on the ground. The best time to find a sitting group is around midday. They do not seek out shade to rest in and can be found right out in the open, in the manner of mad dogs and Englishmen. They are so well adapted to the savanna life that the African sun seems to pose no special problems, and they are easily found when other creatures have fled open spaces to take a siesta. Nor do they try to cool off by having a good wallow, unlike all other giant African mammals—elephants, rhinos, and buffalos—who wallow or dust themselves frequently.

Warthogs

Some way below the giraffe's head level is the warthog *(ngiri)*. It too is associated with parklands and light woodland areas. The word most often used to describe these animals is "ugly." Their faces are elongated and flattened and they have protruding warts behind and below their eyes.

Yet, because they are so entertaining to watch, most people who see them harbor a secret affection for warthogs. They run holding their tails erect, a strangely charming way to flee. Often they are accompanied by a group of small piglets who also manage to shoot their tiny tails straight up as they run in single file beside their mother. When they eat, warthogs often kneel on their forelegs and attack the grass like determined lawnmowers. When they fight or romp they press their foreheads together and try to push each other. Travelers on safari spend a lot of time trying to get pictures that capture the spirit of their run. Since they are active only by day, they are often seen; but they usually run away from cars, and good warthog pictures are rare.

Warthogs stand about two-and-a-half feet at the shoulder. Males are much larger than females, sometimes weighing over 200 pounds. Warthog tusks curve out of both sides of the mouth and are really long and twisted canine teeth. The lower canines are used to keep the tusks sharp and, when trapped, warthogs are dangerous.

Rhinoceroses

An animal with altogether different statistics, except for the dangerous horns, is the rhinoceros *(faru)*, a massive animal of prehistoric
appearance. The skeleton is astonishing for its resemblance to some
dinosaur skeletons. After its great bulk, the rhino's most prominent
feature is the double horn on the end of its snout, which sometimes
grows to be over 50 inches long. There has long been a superstition that
powdered rhino horn can restore sexual potency. It is probably this
notion that has reduced Asian rhinos to near-extinction, and now
African rhinoceroses are seriously threatened as well, a problem com-
pounded by the fact that black rhinos are slow to re-establish themselves from poaching attacks. The horn brings twice its weight in gold
on the black market. Rhino horn, by the way, is not true horn; its
material is similar to the substance that forms animal hoof, which in
turn is related to human fingernails.

The most abundant rhino species is the black rhinoceros, which, if
you ever find a clean one, is not black but gray. Normally their color
depends on whatever they last wallowed in, for rhinos love to roll in
mud or dust. They are hairless except for the tips of their tails and ears,
and they need to wallow in order to keep cool.

The black rhino is probably best known for its unpredictably aggressive temper. It can and sometimes does charge cars. Usually it stops
short, but occasionally it dents a fender or a door. Since they commonly
weigh one or one and a half tons, they are free to charge most anything
they wish without fear of serious injury. The most exciting rhino charge
comes when two run at each other. Occasionally a male and female
dash straight for one another with heads lowered. It looks like the
prelude to a catastrophe, but then they stop and just look at each other.
Black rhinos can be aggressive toward other black rhinos, but it seldom
leads to serious injury.

An animal of a very different temper is the white rhinoceros. It too
is gray and cannot be easily distinguished from black rhinos on the
basis of color. White rhinos are even bigger than black ones, weighing
two tons or more and standing almost six feet at the shoulder. (The
black rhinoceros reaches only five feet.) They eat mainly grass and have
a wide mouth shaped for easy grazing; black rhinos eat leaves and
herbs, stripping branches to find most of their food, and their lips are
narrow and pointed, jutting forward a bit for wrapping around
branches. Although this difference in the mouth sounds too subtle for
easy spotting, it is actually an obvious feature, and it does not take
much experience to tell the two species apart.

Meru, the only place in Kenya where they can be seen, has a small number of white rhinoceroses. They are not indigenous, having been imported from South Africa. The importation has not been a great success. The terrain appears to be perfectly satisfactory, but the predator population, in the form of poachers, is too powerful. The rhinos are kept penned up at night and are herded by armed guards during the day. Even so, the poaching continues. While they last, the white rhino can be seen along the stretch of road between park headquarters and route marker number 12.

Both species of rhinoceros are dependent on water and cannot go for long periods without drinking. During droughts they concentrate more and more tightly into waterhole areas. Severe droughts take a heavy toll on rhino populations.

Rhinos are also sensitive to heat and sleep during the midday hours. During long hot spells they are usually hard to find even though they may be plentiful. It seems strange that an animal so dependent on steady water and so unhappy in great heat should be a common feature of the hottest savanna areas, but somehow they survive.

Antelopes Abounding

Most of the animals encountered on the savanna are some form of antelope. They often have a limited range, but some live throughout much of Africa. Particularly widespread is the impala, one of the easiest animals to find on any safari. The impala *(swala pala)* is a medium-sized antelope, standing three feet at the shoulder and weighing 100 to 180 pounds. Full-grown males have beautiful lyrate horns which grow to 30 or more inches. Young males have arching horns which have not yet spread into a lyre. Impala are found in woodlands, parklands, and even open grasslands. They must drink water about every other day and so they stay away from the most arid spaces.

Most of an impala's feeding takes place during the day. They are up with the dawn and quickly groom themselves a bit. Then they begin eating and continue to feed until late morning. During the midday heat they keep cool by standing in the shadows and chewing their cud. This is also the preferred time for drinking. By late afternoon they are back to feeding, and only lie down after dark. Even then they do not sleep much. Usually they are quietly chewing a cud as they rest.

The eland *(pofu)* is the largest of the antelopes, standing almost six feet at the shoulder and weighing three-quarters of a ton. Both sexes have twisted horns that extend straight back; male horns are usually a bit more than two feet long. They display agile strength when they run; they are also great jumpers and sometimes leap over each other as they go. For some reason they are extremely shy, and are one of the last species to have lost their fear of automobiles. Consequently good eland photos are rare trophies.

Another large, shy antelope is the kudu *(tandala)*. It has the most magnificent horns of all, although only the males carry them. The greater kudu's horns spiral through three graceful twists. Measured along the curve, these horns are usually about four feet long, but the record horns were almost six feet long. They stand five feet at the shoulder and weigh 600 to 700 pounds. Their faces are beautifully marked with a white chevron, and they have enormous ears. Their preferred habitat is fairly thick woodland.

There is also a lesser kudu *(tandala ndogo)* which is considerably smaller than the greater. It stands three-and-a-half feet at the shoulder and weighs about 200 pounds. It too has spiral horns, but they are set closer together and grow to only two-and-a-half or three feet. Greater kudus have a prominent throat fringe; lesser kudus have none.

Sable antelopes *(pala hala)* are to be seen in the Shimba Hills, though only rarely. Both sexes have horns, though the male's are longer and scimitar-curved. Length of horn varies with location: two-and-a-half feet is about the norm in Kenya.

Roan antelope *(korongo)* are also to be seen in the Shimba Hills. Slightly larger and heavier than its relative the sable, roans have a reddy-gray wiry coat, a black-and-white face, long ears tufted at the tips, and short stout backward-curved horns in both sexes.

Grant's gazelles *(swala granti)* are larger than Thomson's although they are similar in appearance and occupy the same general range. Like the impala, Grant's gazelles are a medium-sized antelope. Their preferred habitat, however, is open grassland, and they seem to be able to survive on the water found in the food they eat. Their horns are long, curving backwards and out. Female horns are much smaller. The horns are subject to many distortions, and Grant's gazelles have been divided into races based on horn shape; examples of the various races seem to turn up anywhere, however.

Waterbuck *(kuro)* are the most common of the large antelopes. Only the males have horns, which are heavy-set symmetrical objects that curve up and out. Horn length averages two-and-a-half feet. Their meat is generally considered to be untasty; it is greasy and smelly. It is commonly reported that lions don't like waterbuck for this reason, but investigation of this story always brings the reply, "That's in the other parks. Lions kill plenty of waterbuck here."

Hartebeest *(kongoni)* are found in most savanna areas. As a rule hartebeest are fast animals and run in herds. Their horns (found in both sexes) take many shapes, but generally they rise from a stalk at the center of the head and then bend out toward the sides.

There are varieties of hartebeest throughout Africa, but Kenya has three: Coke's, Hunter's and Jackson's, of which Coke's, with its creamy-white rump, legs and underbelly is the most common.

Among the many other varieties of antelope in Kenya are topi *(nyamera)*, a hartebeest-like antelope found only in the Masai Mara National Reserve in western Kenya and in the Dodori National Reserve inland from the coast near Lamu. Standing between 48 and 50 inches at the shoulder, the topi is a rich reddish-bay with slate-gray markings on the upper forelegs, hips and thighs, and yellow legs below the knees. Horns, present in both sexes, are heavily ridged and slightly lyrate.

Bushbuck *(pongo)* are found in thickly-wooded or forest country, and along the bushy margins of streams. They are never far from cover of some sort. They are most commonly seen in the mountain parks, particularly at Treetops in the Aberdares and the Mountain Lodge in the Mount Kenya National Park. Males are a dark reddish-brown, ranging to near black, with vertical white stripes on the body, a few white spots on the haunches, a white half-collar round the base of the neck, and with stout single-spiral pointed horns. Females are hornless, smaller and much more reddy-chestnut. The neck hair is very short in both sexes.

Reedbuck *(tohe)* come in two species in Kenya: Bohor and Chanler's, with Bohor the more commonly seen. Bohor reedbuck are sandy-red, with a bushy tail with a white undersurface. Horns are carried by males only and are hooked sharply forward. This reedbuck inhabits swampy surroundings among reeds or papyrus, or long grassland at higher altitudes. They are most frequently seen in the grasslands surrounding Lake Nakuru National Park. Chanler's, or mountain reedbuck, is similar in size to Bohor's but inhabits rough hills over 4,000 feet. It is also slightly grayer than Bohor's, and the horns are shorter although similarly hooked sharply forward.

Klipspringers *(mbuzi)* are also scattered throughout Africa, living only on rocky hills. They have a thick coat that protects them from bumps and scrapes as they bound up the rocks like mountain goats. They stand less than two feet at the shoulder and weigh about 35 pounds. Their horns are short and straight. In southern Kenya both sexes are horned.

The steinbok *(dondoro)* is about the same size as a klipspringer but looks more like a tiny gazelle. It eats grass and prefers open grassland or light bush country. Horns are present in the male only. Best chance for a photo is to wait a moment as it flees. It usually pauses after a short zigzag and looks directly at the camera.

Smaller yet is the dikdik which reaches only a little more than one foot at the shoulder. They are hardly larger than rabbits and are difficult to photograph, since they are nocturnal, shy, and prefer bush country. They are fairly easily spotted in the Samburu, Tsavo, Amboseli and other Parks.

Lions

Because the savanna is able to support so many animals, it is also home to a number of predators that feed off the grazers. No predator is more famous or more sought after by the visitor than the lion *(simba)*, and they remain the most popular animal in Africa. Observers who grow restless after watching a zebra herd romp for two minutes are often willing to sit patiently by a sleeping lion for a quarter of an hour in the vain hope that perhaps it will do something. This continuing interest is justified, for the lion is indeed a magnificent animal.

It is said that the lion is lazy, slow and only a so-so hunter who misses three times as much as it catches. Yes, the lion is lazy during the hours when visitors most commonly roam the parks, but when it has a reason to do so the lion shows a surprising ability to hustle. Its low hunting efficiency is balanced by its very great power; lions have been recorded bringing down animals that weigh over three-quarters of a ton. Naturally lions prefer to hunt prey that is a bit easier to kill, but none of the other predators can hope to hunt animals of such sizes. Occasionally a visitor will encounter such surprising sights as an exhausted lion beside a slain giraffe.

Lions are also faster than they are generally given credit for. Their top speed is about 38 miles per hour, the same as a leopard's and only slightly slower than a hyena's. A lion's stamina, however, is not very good when compared to other animals, and anybody able to run the 100 meters in five seconds can probably outdistance one. Since a lot of animals do run at such speeds, lions do not engage in lengthy pursuits. They prefer to use cooperative hunts or stealth to come within pouncing distance of their quarry.

Nobody has tried to argue that an adult lion is anything but huge. Except for the crocodile, no other predator in Africa rivals the size and strength of a lion. A lioness weighs twice as much as a male leopard, while an average male lion approaches a weight of 400 pounds. Lionesses average over eight feet in length (including tail) and males average more than nine feet. Yet they still have the grace of cats and, despite their great size, they can disappear completely in the grassy plain. Even in short grass they can crouch very low. Their coloration blends perfectly with the dry savanna, and a person on foot could easily step on one before noticing it.

Of course a lion is seldom so careless as to let a hiker come that close. Hunters report seeing fresh tracks and even hearing lions move through the grass, yet they are unable to spot the animal as it hides from danger. The lion's tendency to relax in groups also lessens the chance of surprising one, though occasionally a single lion will be encountered. Adult males are often nomadic, wandering from one pride to another. Lone females, however, are seldom nomads, and one on the move is almost certainly going somewhere specific—water, food, a pride—or else she is out hunting. The least active time of day for a pride is the heat of the noonday. From late morning to mid-afternoon lions generally sleep pretty soundly. Often during this hot time lions will not even look up when you arrive in your car.

People tend to go a little crazy when they see their first wild lion. Their often-voiced slogan is "You can't have too many lion pictures," but that theory is disproved when the film comes back from the developers. The best counsel is patience; don't take more than a couple of shots of lions sleeping with their backs to you. Most safaris of any length present numerous opportunities to photograph lions in many poses, and even if the first five do not provide interesting pictures, there will be others.

One of the reasons lions are so often found and photographed is their amazing calm in the presence of cars. Adult lions everywhere permit automobiles to approach extremely close, often so close that a telephoto lens is too strong. A common tale of people returning from the African parks is of the time they encountered a sleeping pride and saw a great black-maned head rise at their approach, give a snort as though to say, "Oh, tourists," and flop back to sleep.

A visitor's chances of seeing lions in a restless state are better during the cooler parts of the day. For several hours after dawn and in the late afternoon, they stretch, play, and pay attention to one another. Depending on when they last ate, they may prepare for a little hunting.

The hunting technique of lions depends on terrain, size of prey, and the number of other lions present. Lions prefer to come very close to an animal before making their final rush. Usually a lion must be able to grab its prey before the victim has had time to accelerate to full speed. In dry seasons, or during migrations, lions frequently plant themselves by a convenient water source and let the quarry come to them. Killing methods vary, but strangulation and neck-breaking are the most common. If lions are found feeding on an animal, you cannot assume they themselves made the kill unless the victim is larger than a wildebeest or a zebra. Lions frequently scavenge the kills made by other animals, and it is common for them to chase away the hyenas or cheetahs who did the actual work. Lion manners at mealtime are notoriously greedy.

Lions at a kill are on their most aggressive and individualistic behavior. Normally cars are able to approach very close to lions, but at a kill it is wise to keep the car back. Of course, around lions no one should ever get out of his car, open a door, or roll down windows; nevertheless observers get a little careless sometimes, poking their heads out of open-topped Land-Rovers or even making noises to try to provoke a lion into providing a more interesting pose. But no matter how blasé a person has grown toward wild lions, he had better give them their full due at a kill.

Cheetahs

One animal that often loses its kills to lions is the cheetah *(duma)*. Biologists are hard put to classify this animal. Its ancestral linkage with other big cats seems to be quite remote, though the cheetah surely looks like a cat; moreover, it purrs. Unlike other large cats, however, it cannot roar, or retract its claws, and it limits most of its activity to daylight hours. This last habit makes it much easier to find than the nocturnal leopard, but it is a shy animal and unless it is thoroughly familiar with tourists, the approach of a car is likely to send a cheetah scampering for safety. This timidity in an animal that lives by killing may seem surprising. But the cheetah is specialized for only one thing —catching and killing running animals. The cheetah is the fastest animal on earth, reaching 70 miles per hour for short periods. (Some studies have estimated that the cheetah runs at 80 miles per hour.) It seldom has to run at top speed for more than eight seconds, but during those few moments it can cover 275 yards.

The whole body of the cheetah is designed to accomplish this monumental dash. Some of its running features are obvious enough. It is built like a greyhound—long and lean with plenty of leg. The nonretractable claws work like the tread of a tire, providing plenty of traction at high speeds. Photographs have shown that the long tail is used to maintain balance while making turns at full speed. There are also a number of more subtle internal adaptations for running. Its spine is flexible, to allow maximum stretching of the legs. Heavy breathing during running is permitted by large lungs, bronchial passages and nostrils. An oversized heart permits the rapid pumping of blood during the race, and large adrenal glands can kick the whole system into a rapid start.

Kills are normally made on the run. A fleeing antelope is seized by the neck and knocked over. The violence of the fall breaks the animal's neck and suffocates it. This single event, the killing of an animal in full flight, is what evolution has shaped the cheetah for. The ferocious kind of wrestling engaged in by lions and leopards is no part of a cheetah's hunting technique. Thus, the cheetah is overmatched whenever it is challenged by one of the other large carnivores. Lions, hyenas, and leopards all help themselves to cheetah kills. Since the sound or smell

Elegant cheetahs, showing clearly the distinctive dark tear stripe.

A gazelle in Tsavo East National Park.

A young Masai warrior with his magnificent lionskin headdress.

A grouping of giraffe and zebra, demonstrating the height of a fully grown adult giraffe.

of a kill usually brings predators and scavengers running to have a look, cheetahs have developed what must be the fastest teeth in Africa. They eat their kills right away and don't waste much time about it, bolting food down in order to get as much as possible before some rival predator comes and steals a free meal.

Cheetah cubs are attractive little animals. At first they are gray with few markings; their fur is rough and seems to stand straight out, giving their round heads the look of old dandelions. The adult cheetah is one of the most beautiful animals in Africa. Their spotted fur is a gilded yellow. Their long lean bodies are seven feet long or a little more; one-third of that length is tail. Cheetahs stand about two-and-a-half feet at the shoulder and weigh a little over 100 pounds. Typically they have a tear stripe running down from the corner of each eye.

Hyenas

Less beautiful is the spotted hyena *(fisi)*, otherwise known as the "laughing hyena." There have been many recent attempts to upgrade the reputation of the hyena. Most important has been the discovery that in many if not all areas hyenas are predators rather than simple scavengers. Experiments have shown that lions are more likely to investigate the sounds of hyenas eating than hyenas to be attracted by lion noises.

Hyenas have also been denounced as cowards. Ridiculous as it is to try to impose macho values on the animal world, the hyena is not a coward. After all, they do run up to kills where hungry lions are still present and steal bits of meat. It takes a fairly brazen sort to try that stunt.

Tradition assigns hyenas a rather gruesome idiosyncrasy: tearing at a fellow hyena like a crazed shark the moment one begins to bleed. Actually, hyenas are firmly established in clans. They care attentively for their young and work together on hunts. The most common fight between hyenas is over territory. Each hyena pack establishes clear boundaries and defends them against invaders. Hyenas who, in the excitement of a chase, make a kill in some other clan's territory are frequently driven off their victim and chased back to their own territory.

Physically hyenas are splendid. They can run at 40 miles per hour for several minutes. Their jaws are exceedingly strong and they can bite through bones. Yet when all is said in praise of them, hyenas remain a public-relations man's nightmare. They are dreadfully ugly, with a sloping back and bald face. The high-pitched giggling sound they make is too weird to inspire anything except shudders. They are not large or powerful enough to kill zebras or wildebeest cleanly. Their method of hunting is to chase a herd, select a weaker runner, and start tearing at its hind legs, literally eating it alive.

Jackals and Wild Dogs

Another animal that is thought of as a scavenger but which does a lot of its own hunting is the jackal *(mbweha)*. These are small coyote-like carnivores, standing about a foot and a half at the shoulder and weighing only slightly more than 20 pounds. They hunt small birds and mammals and young gazelles, as well as helping themselves to the remains of larger animals' kills. They are often seen waiting patiently near feasting lions or cheetahs. Some remarkable instances of coopera-tive hunting between jackals and cheetahs have been observed in Nairo-bi National Park, but once the kill was made the jackals had to wait until the cheetahs were done. Jackals also eat eggs, insects, and fruits.

The African wild dog *(mbwa mwitu)*, or "hunting dog," is seldom seen. Their packs cover a large area and remain in one place only if they have small pups to care for. The legendary cunning and ferocity of wild dogs is largely based on fable. Probably the most famous myth is that they chase a herd in relays. One or two dogs are said to keep a herd running at full speed while others jog behind. As the lead dogs tire they are spelled by fresh runners until the herd gives in to exhaustion, slows down, and a victim is taken. But fields studies of wild dogs have found that chases normally last only three to five minutes, and the dogs that make the kill are the ones that begin the chase. They run at about 35 miles per hour and generally select an animal that is a bit slower than the main herd. Like the hyena, they are not powerful enough to make clean kills of large prey and they eat zebras or wildebeest alive.

They seem to occupy a niche that is similar to the hyena's; they hunt the same species, select the same weaker runners, and even need to eat similar amounts of meat. The chief difference between wild dogs and hyenas is that the dogs hunt by day, thus getting a chance to eat while the hyena rests. But in areas where hyena populations are strong, wild dogs tend to disappear.

Wild dogs look like patchwork alsatians. They stand two to two-and-a-half feet at the shoulder, making them a little smaller than hyenas. Their odor is strong and quite noticeable. At the site of a kill they give some priority to older or young dogs. Adults also regurgitate food for pups to eat; however, their infant mortality rate is still 50 percent.

Ostriches

The ostrich is the largest bird in the world. Males are over nine feet tall and weight over 300 pounds. They also produce the largest eggs in the world, measuring five or six inches in length and weighing two pounds. Eggs weighing over three pounds have been found. Breaking out of this prison is a large task, and ostrich chicks stumble forth into the world in a state near total exhaustion. At birth they are comparatively small, no larger than an adult chicken; but it only takes about six months for them to reach full size. They grow at the rate of about three inches a week.

It was once supposed that ostriches were a sort of primitive bird whose ancestors predated flight; but their ancestors could fly, and flight feathers are still present in the degenerated wings of the modern ostrich. While they are now much too large to fly, they can run extremely well, maintaining a speed of 30 miles per hour for more than 30 minutes. A most charming use is still found for their wings in the provision of shade for their young. The wings are held out like a fancy parasol and the chicks flock together for comfort.

Wings are also used in dancing displays between the sexes. The male beats his wings in front of a group of females. As they approach he chases off the yearlings and then leads the others back to his territory. The mating ceremony is also accompanied by mutual dancing and beating of wings. Any distraction during this dance brings an immediate end to it, so dancing ostriches should not be approached. During courtship the noise of a male ostrich sounds like lions roaring in the distance.

Ostriches are omnivorous, eating grasses, bushes, leaves, insects, and even small reptiles. When they drink they lower their heads and scoop up the water in the style of someone shoveling coal.

Secretary Birds and Vultures

A number of predator birds also live on the savanna. The strangest looking of all is the secretary bird, a distant relative of the hawk and falcon. Its favorite victims are snakes, which it kills with a kick. Just before assaulting the snake the secretary bird spreads its wings, perhaps as a distraction. It also eats lizards, insects, and other small animals.

The bird's name comes from the long feathers that stick out of the back of its head, rather like old-fashioned quill pens. When hunting it spreads these crown feathers into a circle. They are large birds, standing over three feet tall and enjoying a wing span of six and a half feet. They seldom fly, but they do take advantage of their wings to nest safely on top of thorn trees or bushes. Secretary birds are monogamous, and if one is seen there is usually a second nearby.

Larger and uglier is the marabou stork, a true stork that has changed from predation to scavenging. Marabou stand five feet high and have a wingspan of almost ten feet. Their shabby gray feathers and white front give them the look of a comic tramp dressed up in a worn tuxedo. Their most obvious characteristic is a long naked throat pouch, which is believed to be a sanitary resting pad for the bill. The massive wedge beak can cut open the abdominal wall of carrion. Marabou young hatch out at the end of the rainy season, since drought inevitably leads to an increase in food for scavengers.

Also on hand to fight over the last remains of any kill are a number of vultures. For hygienic reasons these birds and the marabou have naked heads and necks, which does nothing to make them more attractive to the visitor. Often they can all be seen along with the marabou at a kill. How so many species can feed off the same carcass is a mystery. According to the theory of evolution, they should not be in competition with each other, but they certainly look as though they are.

Animals of the Wetlands

The contrasts of African geography have astounded travelers for centuries. Great mountains leap without warning from perfectly flat plains and, following this unexpected pattern, water habitats are often set in the middle of some other ecological system—enriching rather than overwhelming it. The fauna and flora of another habitat are commonly found along the banks of a river.

Most important in determining the particular role of a wetland area is the condition of the water itself. Is it swift-moving or still? Deep or shallow? River or lake? Most bodies of water begin as swift-moving streams. If these are small and shallow, they may not be enough to provide a very extensive wetland habitat, and the wildlife along their shores will consist almost entirely of forest or savanna animals that have come for a drink. But as the river grows, it takes on enough of its own character to support the wetland creatures that use water for more than quenching thirst. These rivers then provide a double habitat. There are both wetland animals and the wildlife from the surrounding area. Naturally enough, such animal-rich areas have been attractive sites on which to establish reserves.

Water habitats get a chance to assert themselves more fully when the river flows into a lake, particularly if the lake is essentially a dead end. Many rivers feed water into hollow depressions where it cannot escape. The result is either a swamp or a bitter-water lake. In some cases, swamps occur even if eventually the water does find an exit and starts to flow again.

Another form of badwater wetland is found in Africa's many bitter lakes. Often quite shallow, these lakes are drainage dead ends associated with rifts or surrounding mountains. Water trickles or rushes down to them but can go no further. It might seem reasonable to expect such lakes to keep growing until they could spill over into something; but this is prevented by evaporation, which is very great in the tropics. As the water evaporates, the impurities stay behind, and the mineral content in the remaining water steadily increases.

During the wet season fresh water floods the lakes, greatly expanding the shoreline and overwhelming the lake's mineral content. At this time the lakes are far less bitter, much more like ordinary bodies of fresh water. Then, as the dry season begins to take hold, the lakes shrink and much of the floating minerals are stranded on dry land. Exposed to the sun, the salts harden and form a permanent crust around the lake's edge. This crust keeps many land animals away from the shore but provides an optimal habitat for large birds that can safely assemble in large numbers.

The crust also poses difficulties for human observers. It can make reaching the lake shore as difficult as trying to travel across the trembling land of a swamp. As a result, a number of Africa's bitter lakes now have permanent blinds nearby. From them observers with binoculars or telephoto lenses can watch the lake. This solution is generally better than trying to move all around the lake. Not only is it easier, it is also less disturbing to the wildlife. It is hard to sneak up on animals when you have to cross a wide, flat, barren land. Bitter lakes require patience and perseverance if they are to be seriously explored.

Easier to approach are the freshwater lakes. These too are found in abundance in Africa, though wildlife is not always so heavily concentrated around them. As a rule these lakes are larger and deeper than the dead-end lakes. They are home to many fish, and their shores tend to be settled by fishing communities.

Hippopotamuses

An animal that enjoys many different sorts of wetland is the hippopotamus *(kiboko)*. Hippos thrive in rivers, swamps, bitter lakes, and even on dry land. They can travel far overland, and during the wet season any large pool on a flood plain is liable to contain a few. They are a real benefit to the water itself. In swamps and shallows hippos churn up the mud and help keep the water from becoming even more stagnant and oxygen-starved. They also eat a lot of floating sedge and thus help prevent flowing water from becoming clogged with vegetation. River regions in which hippos have been cleared out sometimes turn into semi-marsh areas with astonishing speed. Hippopotamuses also eat a lot of grass on the shore; but in only a few places do they spend many daylight hours on dry land. Usually they pass the days snoozing in the water. The water helps support their enormous bulk and keeps them cool. It also hides most of their bodies. Typical hippopotamus photographs show nostrils, eyes and ears poking above the ripples.

This standard view of the head is a good illustration of how specialized for floating the hippo has become. Its vital sense organs all protrude above the animal's huge snout, and the nostrils even close when the hippo dives under water. This view also shows the thinking behind the animal's name, which is Greek for "water-horse." They are related to pigs, not horses, but the submerged hippo head does look something like a horse's head. As another result of spending so much time floating in the water, hippopotamus often have easily observed bathtub rings running lengthwise around the middle of their bodies; frequently, the ring has a gilt quality to it that sparkles in the sun.

Hippos are bigger than the absurd proportions of their stubby legs and almost invisible necks can suggest. For many travelers the first time the enormous size of a hippopotamus hits home is when one opens its jaws. A grown man could sit down in a hippo's mouth. Hippopotamuses stand from four-and-a-half to five feet at the shoulder and usually weigh about a ton-and-a-half, although some giants have approached three tons. They are about 12 feet long. The lower jaw contains two ivory tusks which usually measure two or two-and-a-half feet long on the front curve. Hippo ivory is soft and pliable and far less valuable than elephant ivory; for that very reason, however, it is the most popular ivory for the manufacture of tourist souvenirs.

Hippo tusks are dangerous. Most adult males have been in several fights, and to see what a tusk can do just look at their scarred sides. These scars almost never reflect a narrow escape from a lion. They come from other hippos.

For all their stubby appearance, hippos move quickly and easily on the ground. Fortunately their tempers are usually calm and they do not seem to be territorial. It is quite unusual for one to attack a boat, although they can be unintentionally dangerous if they suddenly emerge in front of a small craft. On land they are dangerous primarily if encountered on one of their pathways. The most convenient trail through wetland vegetation is often a path made by hippopotamuses. People on foot commonly follow these routes, which lead straight to danger, especially at night. Frightened and startled, the hippo charges, and it moves fast. When afraid its tendency is to run for water, and if a person is between it and safety a hippopotamus can become ferocious.

The routines that hippos set themselves—complete with regularly used trails and places to defecate—make a hunter's task an easy one. There are a number of places where it can be predicted that a hippopotamus is likely to appear within the next 24 hours. Hippos have been regularly hunted for food, ivory and hides. Dried hippo skin can be made into a dreadful whip, which was used in the early days of colonial rule for judicial punishment. In Swahili the word *kiboko* can mean either "hippopotamus" or "whip."

Because of the animal's nocturnal habits, most people on safari encounter hippos floating in the water. It soon becomes obvious to anyone watching that they are fine swimmers and divers. A hippopotamus can stay under water for five or six minutes, although the average dive is probably closer to two minutes. They like to walk on the bottom of rivers or lake beds. When they surface, they reopen their nostrils and blow out the used air, creating a spray like a whale's spout.

Buffalo

Less formidable in appearance than the hippopotamuses but more ferocious are the African buffalo *(nyati)*. They prefer to graze along the edges of rivers and lakes because they must drink water every day. In theory they could spread out over a dry plain so long as they were within a few hours' walk of a waterhole. In practice, however, they stick close to the wetlands. Buffalo are the largest herding animals that do not migrate to grassy plains during a rainy season. Their best habitat is along the bank of a river that is bordered by patches of savanna or forest. When they can have their druthers, they graze by a lagoon where the water is still but not stagnant. In the real world, of course, things are seldom so perfect. Buffalo end up spending most of their time near water in either forest or savanna, and they shape their lives accordingly. (They do not walk well in really boggy areas.)

The ferocity of buffalo is legendary, and many people are surprised to see that usually they look as gentle and harmless as a herd of dairy cows. (In fact, buffalo are related to domestic cattle.) Their reputation is based on their short tempers and fighting strength. Buffalo do not take kindly to predators. If they see a lion pride resting nearby, the buffalo are likely to charge and send the lions fleeing into trees. They are seldom so bold with humans unless they have been wounded, but if they do charge they are almost impossible to stop. Artful dodging is also difficult since they run with the head up. Their speed of about 35 miles per hour is not much in the animal world but will do nicely against humans.

Buffalo are primarily nocturnal animals, so travelers usually find them chewing their cud, lingering in one place and generally asking no more than to keep cool. Daylight is their laziest time. Their one active pastime is a good mud wallow. Wallowing cools them off, and they roll about in a stiff-legged display of sensuality that is in marked contrast to their normal puritan disdain for comfort. A few minutes in the mud renders the animals thoroughly filthy but in a most photogenic way. A buffalo's head, encrusted in dried mud, looks like the very soul of the African bush country.

A good sign to help locate buffalo when they are hidden behind a stand of grass or papyrus is the presence of cattle egrets. These large white birds are common in wetland habitats and like to eat the bugs that cling to animal hides or which are kicked up when buffalo walk. The egrets can be seen flying above the grassy areas where buffalo are hidden. When at last they are located, the buffalo are usually peering straight at you. They stare intently because their sight is not very good. Their hearing is also poor, but they have an excellent sense of smell.

Sitatunga

Another grazer that is marvelously adapted to wetlands is the sitatunga, also known as the marsh antelope. Its most remarkable feature is undoubtedly its hooves, which are long and splayed, allowing it to walk across soggy swampland. Sitatunga footprints appear in the shape of a long V. The hooves bend on almost a 90-degree angle and extend forward in the manner of the human foot. When frightened, sitatunga are said to leap into the water and submerge almost completely, exposing only the tips of their nostrils for breathing. They are expert swimmers as well, an unusual quality in an antelope.

Sitatunga are shy and nocturnal, so sighting one is rare and worth a special effort. During the heat of the day they are generally hidden among the papyrus. They are more interesting than attractive. Their coat is a shaggy grayish brown and looks a little motheaten, though it is perfect for the aquatic life of the animal. The horns, found only in the males, are long (up to three feet) and twisted, but would be more graceful if they were wider or more lyrate. Sitatunga are medium-sized antelopes, reaching four feet at the shoulder, and weighing 200 or more pounds.

The physical adaptation of the sitatunga is specifically suited for swamp life, but its habits are those of the typical forest antelope. It does not move about in herds. Usually only one or two sitatunga are in one place, and they flee at the first hint of danger. Little detail is known about their life or activities. Although they are not the easiest of beasts to see while on safari, they are sometimes spotted in the Saiwa Swamp National Park near Kitale.

Crocodiles

Strictly swamp creatures like the sitatunga are not much bothered by forest or savanna predators. Cats in particular are not fond of water and usually avoid marshy areas, but wetlands have produced the most dangerous of all predators, the crocodile. They kill more people than any other carnivore, probably because they are less intelligent than mammals. Crocodiles act far more mechanically than do cats or hyenas. Their lives are controlled by instincts more than by learning, and the discriminatory capacity that makes leopards and lions wary of humans may be beyond the ordinary understanding of a crocodile.

Crocodiles are marvelously suited for their wetland environment, and fossils show that they have retained the same basic anatomy for the past 60 million years. Like the hippopotamus, their eyes and nostrils protrude above the snout so that these vital spots can be above the water when the rest of their bodies are fully submerged. The crocodile is also able to seal its nostrils shut when under water. One additional capacity found in the crocodile that is absent in the hippo is the ability to pull its eyes into its head and streamline its body even further. Such streamlining is important to the crocodile because, as a predator, it has to be able to move as quickly as possible through the water. Several other special adaptations are designed to maximize its ability to swim and hunt at the same time. For example, the crocodile can seal off the back of its mouth so that it can open its jaws while swimming forward and still not flood its lungs.

The crocodile's common mode of attacking a large land animal is by swimming rapidly under water, accelerating enormously at the end of the swim, and bursting out of the water with its jaws about to slam shut. If everything has gone properly, the prey will be at the water's edge, bending forward to drink. The crocodile seizes the victim's head and pulls it under the water. The jaws crush the skull and lock tight while the water drowns the prey. It is simple and brutally effective.

The most frightening, and most visible, feature of the crocodile is its extraordinary teeth. When a crocodile lies still on land, its jaws are wide open and the rows of sharply pointed fangs are readily apparent. The teeth are not designed for chewing but for tearing large chunks of meat out of a body. The chunks are then bolted down. The stomach and intestines can swell several times their normal size to hold and slowly digest the large bites of food.

The general impression crocodiles give casual observers is that of lazy giants who pass most of their lives basking in the sun, and they do bask in the sun for much of the day. Like all reptiles, crocodiles are cold-blooded, which is to say they must keep their blood temperature up by external means. Basking raises the blood temperature and conserves energy (energy consumption drops blood temperature), so when the crocodile does begin to hunt it will have the energy reserves necessary for the final burst of strength used in attacking the quarry. Thus, a crocodile's hunting ability depends as much on the weather as it does on the availability of prey. When the temperature drops, a crocodile does not hunt.

Flamingos

In the water itself is the most spectacular of all of Africa's bird sights: the enormous flocks of flamingos that assemble in groups of several hundred thousand or even a million. African flamingos are not as brilliantly red as those of the Gulf of Mexico area. Their coloring is more a pastel shade. Flamingo coloration is due to the massive doses of carotene (vitamin A) in their diet. (This same phenomenon explains the red-orange color of lobsters and many other water creatures.) Captive flamingos used to fade in color, but zoos have found that the pink brightens up when carrot juice is added to the birds' diet. In the wild, they make for stunning color photographs.

Two species of flamingo live in Africa; however, the lesser flamingo comprises about 98 percent of the population. The other species, the greater flamingo, is taller by over a foot and lighter in color. Greater flamingos are commonly present in flocks of several thousand and therefore ought to be easy to identify, but 2,000 greater flamingos tend to disappear when they are in the midst of 100,000 lesser flamingos.

The easiest way to distinguish between the two species is to keep in mind that the greater flamingos are generally closer to the shore. They feed on small creatures found in the mud of a lake, and have to stay in areas shallow enough for them to reach down to the bottom. Lesser flamingos, on the other hand, are specifically adapted for feeding on minute bits of life floating in the water. Both species have bills that are curved so that they work most efficiently when placed upside down in the water, as happens when the birds bend over to feed. The bill of the greater flamingo is flesh pink, and that of the lesser flamingo is maroon.

During the day flamingos stay where they are. If a huge flock is reported in a distant lake at dawn, it will probably be there all day, and a traveler can set out confident that the flock will not have departed when he arrives. But flamingos do migrate at night, sometimes as far as 400 miles. The reasons for these movements are not understood. The lakes do not run out of algae, so it cannot be a migration in search of food. Perhaps it has something to do with the changing quality of the water. A million birds feeding and defecating in a narrow lake must have a considerable impact on the water's mineral content.

Crowned Cranes and Sacred Ibises

Patroling the grasslands along the water's edge there is often a crowned crane, also known as the crested crane. One look at its head is enough to identify it. A tuft of golden bristles stands on top of a white and red face. Crowned cranes are over three feet tall and are one of the most eye-catching birds in the world.

The sacred ibis, which frequents the same areas enjoyed by the crowned crane, is dull by comparison. Shorter (two and a half feet tall) and with a face that is entirely black, it might go unnoticed except for the long, thin, arching bill that characterizes it. It was the Egyptians who proclaimed the bird sacred. The ibis can be seen to great advantage in the area around Kisumu.

Egyptian Geese

It is in the wetlands that people who had previously scoffed at the idea of birdwatching start to find it not so strange an occupation after all. Naturally enough, Africa's waters have ducks and geese. The most commonly observed is probably the Egyptian goose. This medium-sized waterfowl frequents inland water sources, and during the rainy season it ventures well out onto the open plains where it can be found happily splashing about in mud puddles. Its generally brown coloration contrasts vigorously with its white shoulders. It has been semidomesticated for centuries and appears in many of the frescos of ancient Egypt. It is an alert animal, and has sometimes been used as a watchdog. The call of the Egyptian goose is a heavy-breathing sound like an old-fashioned steam locomotive. It is generally found in pairs or flocks and is one of the many attractions of such areas as the lake behind the Aruba Dam in Tsavo East, among many other places.

African Fish Eagles, Spoonbills and Herons

Perched on a branch above the water is often an African fish eagle. The white heads and tails of these large birds make them easy to spot and identify. As their name implies, they feed mostly on fish, but they will also rob nests of their young and even kill or scavenge water birds. They are also piratical, swooping down and snatching fish from the beak of another bird, including fellow fish eagles.

Young fish eagles have a streaky breast that grows progressively clearer until it eventually becomes fully white. Their first flight comes at the age of about six and a half months. They reach full maturity at about five years old. Fish eagles live as breeding pairs, and the bond between the couple is strong enough to permit them to share their food. They have a long life span, from 20 to 28 years.

Scattered among these large and easily noticed water birds there are usually a few examples of other wading-bird species, such as the African spoonbill and the goliath heron. The spoonbill is three feet tall, shorter than the lesser flamingo, and it has a white body. Its most prominent characteristic is the way its bill spreads out like a spatula at the end. The goliath heron is much larger, growing to five feet. Its height and reddish neck make it easy to spot.

Animals of the Forest

In the equatorial jungles, trees of every size are tangled with bushes, shrubs, vines and grasses. Only a thoroughly trained botanist can make sense of the scene; to everyone else it is a riot of living things piled on top of one another. The ferocity of the competition for space, light and water can be startling, even a little frightening to an observer who is used to thinking of plant life as passive. The trees and shrubs of the African forest assert themselves.

In some parts of the forest the competition for light is so intense that three distinct layers of plant life have appeared. On the ground, growing to a height of from six to ten feet, are the grasses, shrubs and ferns. Just above them are the short trees and palms that range from 20 to 40 feet in height. They are often wrapped, or choked, in woody vines called lianas. Towering above this middle layer, rising to as high as 150 feet, is the forest canopy. With such intense growth it would seem that the soil must be rich. Large projects for clearing and developing forest areas have been attempted, but consistently it turns out that the land's fertility was only an illusion. The African forest is not so much rich as it is a precariously balanced whole that depends very much on its trivial parts. Strange as it sounds, the land can support a lush forest but not much else.

Africa's forests are far less dominated by one species of tree than the climactic forests of the north. Most African forests of any size contain several hundred species of trees, bushes and vines. Not surprisingly, this complex pattern of vegetation is able to support a much more varied animal population than northern forests.

The conditions can be pretty demanding for wildlife. If the overhead canopies are too dense, low-lying shrubbery cannot get enough light to survive. The forest undergrowth disappears, and with it go the animals that feed on it. Even in areas capable of supporting browsers, forest wildlife is difficult to locate. The habitat has no vast expanses capable of revealing distant herds, and visitors should not expect to see the great numbers of animals that can be photographed in savanna parks.

Elephants

Since forest creatures cannot see through trees any more than we can, the likelihood of their being surprised by a predator is unusually great. The same trees that make viewing difficult for travelers pose special problems for the animals who live there, and two basic responses have been developed. The first and more cautious is to run away at any hint of danger; however, elephants *(ndovu)* rely on a second possibility. They live in large societies where there are many eyes and ears. Instead of having to flee all the time, the elephant finds security in the herd. It is rare to encounter a truly solitary elephant.

Usually forest creatures are the hardest to find, but almost everyone returning from a safari has stories about elephant-watching. The best places to spot them seem to be in the edges of forests and at water holes, though they can turn up anywhere. The forest is their favorite habitat, but they do not limit themselves.

Since elephants generally regard the approach of a tourist or tourist car as at least mildly threatening, the first thing a visitor is likely to see is an alarm display. Only elephants that are completely used to tourists pay no attention at all. An alarmed elephant puts out its ears and holds up its trunk, trying to get as many clues as possible to what is happening. Elephants' eyesight is poor and they rely mainly on sound and smell. If they make a show of strength and then charge, chances are good that it is a bluff. If, without display or hesitation, they just come on the run, they may actually attack. Hunters have found that elephants charge sounds more than they do objects, and it was often sufficient for hunters just to step out of the line of charge. Cars, however, are noisy, and an elephant has no trouble keeping track of a fleeing automobile. Even so, it is safer to be in a car than anywhere else when one or more elephants are in a rage.

A real charge is rare, fortunately, and even a bluff charge is less common than a group display. A seriously alarmed elephant seeks the security of the group. The elephants run together, form a solid phalanx of tusks and trunks, and raise their ears at the intruder. This instinct for herd unity is one of the strongest features of elephant society and is easily noted by an observer. Elephants appear to know one another as individuals and they seem to like one another. They touch one another with their trunks. Older sisters are attentive to young calves. Cows are alert to the whole group and serve as leaders, choosing the time and direction of march. Some of these individual relationships within the herd can be detected after only a few minutes.

Of course, the thing an elephant-watcher first notices is quite different. Elephants fairly spin the imagination with their size. All the figures are gargantuan. Average bulls weigh about six tons, stand ten feet at the shoulder, and carry tusks with a combined weight of 110 pounds. Record bulls have been known to carry tusks of well over 100 pounds on a side, and some bulls have been reported to stand 12 feet at the shoulder. Cows are smaller, but can be called "little" only when compared to bulls. They are about a foot and a half shorter and perhaps two tons lighter. Their tusks are considerably smaller, commonly weighing only about 15 pounds apiece.

Elephant size is particularly impressive from a distance, where there is a sense of perspective. Observers on cliff tops, for example, are often struck by how clearly elephants can be seen when other species are no more than vague dots. From a distance it is also impressive to see how rapidly elephants move. Close up they seem to be running, but from further away one begins to see that their gait is really quite deliberate, and their speed is a result of their great strides.

And yet they are skittish creatures. Because elephants are so big, people are often surprised that they behave so cautiously. Lions hunt only young calves, but elephants do know about one other formidable enemy—us. For thousands of years people have managed to slaughter adult elephants. In some areas elephants were once so extensively hunted that they have become nocturnal animals who venture away from the cover of deep forest only after the sun has set.

Elephant caution has made them alert to new forms of danger and new ways to avoid old risks. The creation of national parks has definitely affected their behavior. Ideally, elephants should migrate over large territories, but these days they tend to confine themselves more and more to the relative safety of parks. There they eat, eat and eat some more. Apparently they can eat almost anything vegetable. Bark, woody stems and twigs go into their mouths along with leaves, flowers, fruit and grass. They can also stand on their hind legs, lean against a tree, and reach high into the foliage with their trunks. If they want even higher leaves, some elephants are skilled at knocking over trees. The process turns forests into woodlands, woodlands into grassy expanses, and grasslands into desert. A herd of elephants can be established in a thicket and, without going anywhere, eventually find itself living in open bush country. Such a change is disastrous for other forest animals, but there is something of eternity in the African elephant and, like people, it adapts rapidly to the world of its own making.

Leopards

Stealth is the secret of a forest hunter's success. Forest predators move alone and, like all the other solitary figures of the forest, they flee at the approach of people. They are the hardest to find and the least studied of the hunters. The largest is the leopard *(chui),* the predator most subject to legend and superstition. Its ferocity is its most feared characteristic. Africans consistently maintain that they would rather encounter a lion than a leopard, though in fact man-eating leopards are just about as rare as man-eating lions.

But they are bold enough to enter villages at night, and are especially tempted by chicken coops, though they are also fond of dog flesh. The missionary's watchdog is a tempting attraction in any village. They may get more blame than they deserve, however, for any domestic animal found slain in the night is said to have been taken by a leopard. The thought that it might have fallen to some smaller, less majestic predator is dismissed out of hand.

Since leopards are wary of people, especially during the day, their signs are seen more often than the animals themselves. The most impressive indication of the leopard's presence is the discovery of an antelope carcass high in a tree. Most predators eat only what they can gorge at the time of a kill, but the leopard will drag the kill into a thicket and then haul it up into a tree. This is a tremendous feat of strength, well beyond the capacities of most predators. The carcass may weigh as much as the leopard, yet it is often hung as high as 15 feet. When a carcass is found in a tree, it is a good idea either to wait or return periodically to the site, since the leopard is almost certain to return to its cache. In fact, food secured in trees is fairly safe from theft. Hyenas and jackals have no way of climbing after it. Scavenger birds generally, but not always, ignore a kill in a tree. Lions sometimes climb after a carcass, but more commonly they seem confused. The leopard has developed one of the safest ways of storing its kill.

When sighted at last, the leopard makes no secret of its power. It has the lean muscular look of a killer. It weighs about the same as a cheetah, 75 to 120 pounds, but has a much stockier build. The head in particular is impressive, being square and muscular. The leopard's skin is commonly regarded as the most beautiful of the spotted furs. Each spot is composed of four black dots in a field of tan. The fur between the spots is a yellowish white. The reason behind this beautiful coloration is obscure. Certainly it has camouflage value in the forest, but as in the case of the zebra there would seem to be simpler ways of achieving the same end.

Leopards are extremely solitary, even for cats. They roam through a large territory and do not like to share it with other leopards. Males associate with females only for brief courtships. Females are not quite so lonesome since they often have a litter to care for. Cubs are placed in some secure and isolated spot, such as between large rocks or in the hollow of a tree. It is not until the cubs are well developed that they begin to emerge regularly from the thickest parts of the forest. At about a year-and-a-half the cubs and mother part, although they seem to share the same territory for several more months. Apparently young leopards do not need much persuading to go their own way.

Since leopards are so fiercely independent and territorial, they have been forced to expand into many sorts of habitat, including desert fringes. Their preference seems to be for open forest or savanna woodland. They are excellent tree climbers and can successfully pursue fleeing monkeys. They do not seem to be much faster than lions, although some people claim that they have greater hunting success. If true, the leopards' advantage probably comes from their forest habitat. It is easier for them to approach unseen, and it is difficult for most grazers to accelerate fully in woodlands. The leopard's method of killing is the one common to most cats. It grabs its victim by the nape of the neck and then bites. Like the lion, it is able to kill its prey cleanly and quickly. In fact, it likes its meat to age a little before eating.

The leopard is generally silent. Its solitary habits do not demand much communication. Its cough is always described as sounding like the sawing of wood; however, this sound is described far more frequently than it is heard. Because it is hard to locate and thrilling to see, it is worth making a special effort to find one on any safari.

Servals and Genets

Another attractive and hard-to-locate forest cat is the serval (mondo). It is most easily recognized by its long and slender legs. The serval stands about two feet at the shoulder, weighs about 35 pounds, and is spotted. Its erect ears are another easily noted characteristic. Since it lives in the forest, it is commonly thought of as a small leopard, but it is more like a forest cheetah. It, too, is swift and built for running. Its long legs and slender body are similar to the cheetah's, though its body is not so long. It also has nonretractible claws like a cheetah; however, it is nocturnal in its habits. Its largest prey are the forest duikers (see below) though it catches rodents and snakes as well. It is a good climber and has been seen chasing small animals through the trees. Not much is known about its activities, except that they are solitary.

Not all forest predators are cats. The genet (kanu) is often called a cat but is actually related to civets and mongooses. This nocturnal creature is seldom seen except in chicken coops. It is about 20 inches long, but the tail doubles that figure. Its short legs and slender body permits it to wriggle through quite small spaces. It can give off a strong musky scent from glands at the anus. Its spotted body and ring tail give it the appearance of an unattractive forest cat, but this coloration developed completely independently of the cat's spots and argues forcefully that spotted fur is a real advantage for nighttime hunting in the forest.

Wild Pigs

As well as the warthog, there are two other species of wild pig in Kenya, both of which live in the high mountain forests: the giant forest hog *(nguruwe wa mwitu)* and the bush pig *(nguruwe)*. Giant forest hogs are huge, black, heavily-built and hairy, carry tusks similar to the warthogs', and have large semicircular warty growths on their cheeks. All in all, in other words, they do their best to live up to their name. Bush pigs are slightly smaller than the giant forest hog, and have a wiry, reddish-brown coat with a white ridge along the back and a grayish white face. Their tusks are short and knife-like.

Bongos and Duikers

One animal that shows no sign of being able to adapt to conditions outside the forest is the bongo, largest of the forest antelopes. Antelopes on the plains tend to form herds of loosely united individuals, but the bongo does not often move in large groups. It has perfected the other form of forest defense, extreme wariness. At the first hint of danger it flees. Its reputation for speed of disappearance has given the bongo an almost mystical place in the lore of forest wildlife. A sighting must always be considered a piece of extraordinary luck.

Bongos are specifically adapted for fleeing through a forest. Since they are not large enough to bludgeon their way through the woods like an elephant, they have developed an unusual style of running that permits them to race through a thicket without becoming entangled in the undergrowth. Their gait has an odd, downward sort of motion that avoids low-lying branches. At the same time they hold their heads up and lay their horns flat against their backs so that they are not snared from above. Older animals often have bare patches on their backs where the tips of the horns have been regularly pressed. The horns themselves often show the effects of this habit, for the fronts tend to be badly scuffed.

Bongo horns are quite attractive—long and spiraled with one full twist, similar to eland horns. The average length of the horn measured along the front curve is about 33 inches, the record being 39 inches. The female's horns are generally smaller than those of the male.

Bongos are rather large for forest animals. The males can stand as high as four-and-a-half feet at the shoulders, and adults weigh about 485 pounds. Cows are smaller, perhaps 100 pounds lighter. Their bright reddish coloring is darker in males, eventually reaching a mahogany brown. They have about a dozen thin white vertical stripes on their bodies, a near-perfect forest camouflage. Undoubtedly this protective coloration has persuaded many an observer that he saw nothing when he was looking squarely at a bongo.

The many types of forest duiker *(nsya)*—an animal of the genus *cephalophus*—are almost as elusive as the bongo. Duikers are all small antelopes that feed on the forest undergrowth. Their size and habitat makes them difficult to spot. The males and, in some species, the females have short straight horns a few inches long. Duikers are found in almost all the thick forests of Africa; however, the range of any one species is usually limited. Abbott's duiker, for example, is found only in the forests of Mount Kilimanjaro and nearby mountains. But it is typical of the species, standing about 26 inches at the shoulder and weighing approximately 120 pounds. Its color is chestnut brown. It uses the whole forest as its range and climbs as far as the timberline. Like the bongo, forest duikers do not have much in the way of social defense. They run at the first suspicion of danger. Sightings are unusual, and good photographs trophies to be proud of.

Baboons

The easiest ape to find is the baboon *(nyani)*. When first encountered, a baboon troop does not seem to be much different from or more complicated than a plains herd. Troops average about 50 members, although groups of several hundred are far from uncommon, and upon the arrival of a car they all beat a short, hasty retreat. Physically too the ordinary members of a baboon troop seem no more individualized than a herd of antelope. All have dog faces, a protruding naked muzzle and sharp canine teeth. The only hint that something special can be found here comes from the large, showy manes of the dominant males.

Ordinarily, the most arresting baboons are these dominant males. Adult females are only half their size and have none of the spectacular hair that seems to endow the males with so much authority. Among the olive baboons of East Africa, dominant males average about 65 pounds and have a head and body length of 30 inches (excluding tail).

Although the dominant males are the first to attract the observer's attention, the real life and variety of the troop is to be found among the ordinary baboons. Soon after making their short retreat, they return to their business, for they are not terribly afraid of people. Many things interest them, and relationships among troop members are intricate.

Baboons are omniverous. Usually they eat vegetation, but will kill and eat an animal if they stumble upon it. Their inquisitiveness and willingness to eat almost anything has enabled them to spread all over sub-Saharan Africa, including even desert areas, though they are still primarily associated with forest and woodlands. They sleep in trees and are agile climbers and jumpers.

It is impossible to say how much of a concept of "self" baboons have, but they do look out for number one. Squabbles, greeds, envies and lusts unknown to herd societies continually plague baboon troops. The other side of the coin is the display of generosity, personal concern and affection within baboon troops. The dominant males see to it that none of these individualistic forces threatens the troop's ability to act as a group. They have all the vices of petty bureaucrats enamoured of their badges, and they also have the same purpose. Without them the status quo would soon dissolve.

Guenons and Colobus Monkeys

The most widespread monkey family in Africa is that of the guenons *(tumbili).* They are great tree climbers, able to go into the deepest parts of a forest which are ordinarily closed to ground browsers because of a lack of undergrowth. The most commonly encountered guenon is the vervet, which lives on forest or woodland edges and sometimes ventures as far as a quarter of a mile into the savanna itself. They are average-size guenons, weighing about 10 pounds, and are about two feet long (excluding tail). The tail is held out behind them when they walk. The young often use the tail to hang on firmly to their mothers. Despite the human way they look at something, they have few facial expressions. Lip-smacking is rare and grinning seems to be unknown. They communicate through a variety of shrill chirps. Like many other monkeys, they have an irritating method of defending their territory against intruders. They hurl branches, and defecate and urinate on the invader. The accuracy of their aim is reputed to be appallingly good.

Despite the great size of the family—21 species, 67 subspecies—they have much in common. Like the apes, their hands have opposable thumbs (i.e., they can be placed against one or more of the remaining digits on their hands) and their eyes are close together, giving them a very human gaze. Their fur is thick and colorful, the main colors being green, reddish, black and yellow. Typically, the males have a bright blue scrotum which is often quite noticeable. They are all gregarious, living in bands of about 50 members.

The great monkey of the highest parts of the forest is the colobus *(mbega).* They live in the topmost part of the forest canopy, swinging 100 or more feet above the ground, and hardly ever come down. They are seen in parts of the forest where few or no other animals are encountered. Favoring as they do such tall trees, they are generally free from predators, except humans. The colobus monkey has beautiful skin and was long a prized trophy. The black-and-white colobus can be seen

in the Jadini Forest or the Aberdares, or in the Mount Elgon and Lake
Nakuru National Parks. The red colobus, an endangered species, is
now well-protected, living in the Tana River Primate Game Reserve.

Not much is known about their habits. About all a person is likely
to see of a colobus is how well it can leap through the trees. They can
jump quite far from branch to branch, breaking falls by grabbing leaves
as they fly by. They can also slow their leaps by using the tail as an air
brake. Apparently, they move in small bands of four or five members,
and are territorial. It is most unusual to get a close view of one in the
wilds, but their physical characteristics are distinctive. Like humans,
their hind legs are much longer than the forelegs, but they lack thumbs.
A male may be as much as 27 inches long with a tail 34 inches long.

Francolins and Turacos

Forests make poor flying areas and are not a good habitat for most
birds. It is not surprising that one bird that favors the woods is a ground
bird, the francolin. This is a chicken-sized game bird with a feathery
neck. The throat is usually white, the underbelly is speckled and the
wings tend toward a chestnut brown. The francolins' range varies with
the species; some prefer open woodland while others move far into
mountain forests. They travel in small flocks and always flee an observer, but they seem to be a little sloppy about it, for it is not unusual to
come around a corner and see them scampering away.

The most colorful of the forest birds are the turacos, also known as
plantain-eaters. They are found throughout the forests of Africa. Most
turacos have crimson flight feathers. The variety most commonly seen
in the Great Rift Valley is called Hartlaub's. It has a bluish-black crest
and round white patch above and in front of the eye.

Honey-Guides

Remarkably, there is a forest and woodland bird which actively seeks
out people. When the honey-guide makes a rapid one-note call, it is
signalling that it knows where honey is to be found. If a person on foot
begins to approach, the bird will lead him to a beehive. The honey is
usually within a quarter of a mile, so there is no need to worry about
being led deep into the unknown on the word of a bird. After smoking
out the bees, the person returns the bird's favor by putting aside a
chunk of honeycomb for it to feed on. Honey-guides also eat beeswax
and bee larvae.

The honey-guide is recognizable by its pink bill and fairly large size;
it is about eight inches tall. The male has a black throat.

ZEBRA

NAIROBI

Nairobi is a young city, growing fast. For a new arrival, its size is unexpected, and for the regular visitor there is a perceptible difference every year in the skyline and international ambience of the holiday and business center of Africa. Now, with a main U.N. agency established in the striking Kenyatta Conference Center, the image of Nairobi is changing yet again: "The City in the Sun" . . . "The City of Flowering Trees" . . . is becoming "the conservation capital of the world."

80 years ago, there was no more than a cold river *(Enkare Nyarobe)* in an empty wilderness. An early European arrival said it was "a bleak, swampy stretch of soppy landscape, devoid of human habitation of any sort." But his view may have been obscured by the colonial pith helmet, because the Masai knew the place as *Nakusontelon*—"the beginning of all beauty."

In 1897 a British sapper, Sergeant George Ellis, hammered in Mile Peg 327 of the Mombasa–Lake Victoria Railway and set up a depot before attempting the steep gradient of the Kikuyu Escarpment and a precipitous drop into the Great Rift Valley beyond. Four years later, when 916 km. (572 miles) of "the most expensive scrap iron in history" terminated at Kisumu, the tented encampment at the Nyarobe depot had been replaced with wooden shacks, and Indian coolies had started a bazaar. The fledgling town was ill-conceived, however, and lacked any decent sanitation. This led to an outbreak of bubonic plague and as a result the town was deliberately burnt down. But despite this setback, the continuing health hazards of the nearby swamp, and the ever-present danger from wild animals, Nairobi's foundations were permanently laid in the black-cotton swamp.

The Growing Capital

In the years that followed the fire the town was rebuilt and quickly took on an air of permanence, to be confirmed in 1907 when it replaced Mombasa as the administrative center of the British East African Protectorate. The European population of Nairobi had by this time grown to several hundred as a result of British Government incentives to settlers to farm large tracts of the highland region. It thus became the commercial and social center for a fast growing white farming community, but at the same time was attracting world attention as a frontier town. The reason was the rich game, and Nairobi soon became the center of big-game safaris for the rich and the famous. Perhaps the greatest of these was the safari of Theodore Roosevelt which needed 500 porters to carry supplies and returned with 500 trophies—even by the standards of those days a shocking tally.

In the next few decades, European administration of the "White Highlands" continued and, by the time Baroness Blixen's coffee farm was sold in 1931 for housing and a golf course, Nairobi had 50,000 residents and was the seat of the colonial administration. The city now has a fast-growing population of around a million.

A National Assembly was built for the white settlers who enjoyed their reputation as the most pedigreed and argumentative parliament in British Africa. Indians multiplied and took control of commerce and light industry and thousands of Africans moved in from their home-lands, initially as the new urban working class.

During World War II, Nairobi became a garrison town against the threat of an Italian invasion from Abyssinia and one consequence was the slaughter of local wildlife to feed the troops. Thus in 1947, the first of Kenya's National Parks and Reserves was set up to prevent further indiscriminate plunder, this time by the world's sporting aristocracy. Nairobi National Park was situated 12 km (eight miles) from the main Post Office, fenced off from the suburbs but left open to the seasonal game migration from the Athi Plains beyond. In the same year, a master plan for Nairobi's development was announced. Thereafter, recreation parks and broad avenues, lined with exotic trees and shrubs, were laid out so that the town should proceed from its tangled bazaar center with more "order and charm." In 1950, Nairobi was created a city by Royal Charter.

After *Uhuru* in 1963, the infant independent Republic of Kenya flourished. A mature political tolerance by President Kenyatta's young government attracted vast investment and also greatly reduced tribal and racial separatism which might have retarded the country's self-help prosperity.

20 years later, visitor arrivals had increased from 10,000 to 400,000 and somehow Nairobi has kept pace with an always urgent demand for quality accommodations and sophisticated business and safari services. Today there are more than 8,000 hotel beds in the city, ranging from economy to top international standard.

Transport services are highly developed. There are two airports which handle international and scheduled internal flights as well as a whole range of air safaris and private charters. The safari industry is flourishing even more than in those early days with numerous public companies offering all-inclusive tours of various durations or self-drive safaris. The major car hire firms are all represented in addition to many local businesses. Traveling by local bus has not generally been recommended for tourists in the past, but new tourist services now operate from the capital to the coast and many other main places of interest. Rail travel is limited and slow but the overnight sleeper to Mombasa is a popular trip.

Nairobi is well situated at the center of the country's good network of highways, from which most destinations described in this book can be comfortably reached. But it is not just a starting point for the many safaris, it is a popular holiday destination in its own right. The climate couldn't be more perfect, being springlike for most of the year, for although only 140 km. (87 miles) from the equator the altitude of 1,676 meters (5,500 ft.) tempers the sun so that temperatures rarely rise above 27°C (80° F) during the day. Nighttime temperatures rarely fall below 10° C (50° F).

Discovering Nairobi

The layout of the City Center is based upon the grid pattern set out in the 50s and the architecture is an interesting mixture of old colonial buildings and new developments. It is always colorful and there is always some part of the city's abundant flora in full dress any month of the year, but October is most impressive, when Nairobi is curtained —and carpeted—with lilac jacaranda.

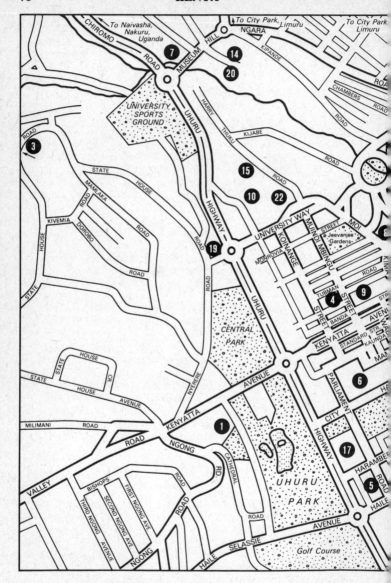

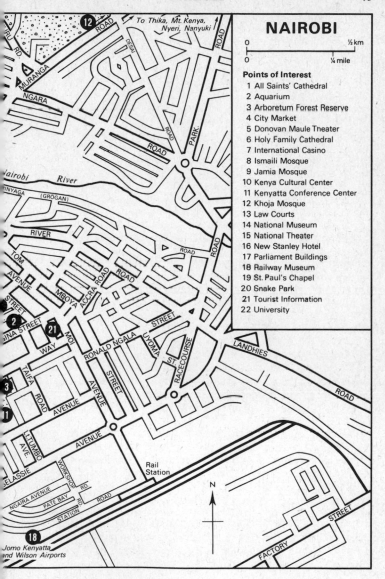

NAIROBI

0   ½ km

0   ¼ mile

Points of Interest

1 All Saints' Cathedral
2 Aquarium
3 Arboretum Forest Reserve
4 City Market
5 Donovan Maule Theater
6 Holy Family Cathedral
7 International Casino
8 Ismaili Mosque
9 Jamia Mosque
10 Kenya Cultural Center
11 Kenyatta Conference Center
12 Khoja Mosque
13 Law Courts
14 National Museum
15 National Theater
16 New Stanley Hotel
17 Parliament Buildings
18 Railway Museum
19 St. Paul's Chapel
20 Snake Park
21 Tourist Information
22 University

To Thika, Mt. Kenya, Nyeri, Nanyuki

MURANGA

NGARA

Nairobi River

(GROGAN)

TINYAGA

RIVER

TOM

AVENUE

MBOYA   ACCRA   ROAD

GINA STREET

WAY

TAIFA

ROAD

AVENUE

KITUMBO AVE.

GELASSIE

NGAIRA AVENUE

PATE BAY

STATION

DESAI   ROAD

ROAD

PARK

ROAD

ROAD

ROAD

MOI

RONALD NGALA   STREET

UYOMA

ST.

RACECOURSE

STREET

AVENUE

WORKSHOP   RD

ROAD

LANDHIES

ROAD

Rail Station

N

FACTORY   STREET

Jomo Kenyatta and Wilson Airports

The harlequin crowd in the streets provides yet more animated color. People wear *kitenge* prints, or saris, or formal suits, turbans or Maasai togas, or often the traditional Sanders-of-the-river safari gear. On the whole they are a friendly people, not so surprising in Nairobi with its sunshine and permanent holiday mood.

Another friendly aspect of the city is that many of its sights are within walking distance of the hotel district and this really is the best way to see it. Shopping, for example, is a leisurely stroll since it can be confined to a compact area around Kenyatta Avenue. Best buys are carvings and cultural artefacts, silks, semi-precious stones, and tropical fruits and flowers from the City Market. If you want to enjoy the passing scene, one of the best places is the traditional Thorn Tree café, outside the New Stanley Hotel—new, that is, around 70 years ago—where everyone who is anyone eventually comes to rest.

The fact is that Nairobi is essentially an outdoor city. It has ten golf courses, a park-like race track, and most other sports from the nationally popular athletics and soccer to an exclusive pink-coated hunt straight out of Shropshire. An annual fever at Easter is the world's toughest Safari motor rally.

Nightlife does not compare with any of the wilder cities of the western world, but there are smart casinos and grill rooms, dance-bars, several cinemas and two theaters, occasional star concerts, and the boundless hospitality of the residents.

Among the civic buildings that should be visited is the Conference Center, Kenya's pride and joy; entirely financed locally and housing the world's second-largest conference hall. It stands in the spreading complex alongside Uhuru Park, together with the Parliament Buildings and the Law Courts. There's a touch of "anything you can build I can build higher" about the area as each succeeding building overtops the one before. But the 1972 Conference Center takes quite a lot of topping at 28 storys. Needless to say it has a revolving restaurant, the Restaurant La Tour.

The Parliament buildings can be visited by calling the Serjeant-at-Arms (tel. 21291, ext. 256). Tours can be arranged at any time that Parliament is not in session (except Saturday afternoons, Sundays, and public holidays), though you can also get Gallery Cards to allow you to listen to a debate in either Chamber. The tour of the buildings is very interesting, not only for a glimpse at African democracy at work, but because there is a good sprinkling of local crafts around, wood carving, tapestries and so forth. The Parliament Buildings also contain the tomb of the "Father of the Nation," Jomo Kenyatta, guarded with solemn pomp. There's a fine view obtainable from the top of the high clock tower.

The National Theater (opened by Sir Ralph Richardson in 1952) is close to the Kenya Cultural Center, at the edge of the University's attractively cultivated grounds, best approached from Harry Thuku Road and the famous old Norfolk Hotel. The Theater has followed the lead of All Saints' Cathedral in having a magical bit of Britain embodied in it—in this case a piece of stone from the Shakespeare Birthplace in Stratford. The capital's other theater is the Donovan Maule on Parliament Road, with a repertory company presenting a series of plays throughout the year.

Churches and Mosques

Nairobi has a fine crop of religious buildings, Christian and Moslem. All Saints' Cathedral, situated along Kenyatta beyond Uhuru Park, is a prime example of the Church of England abroad, with bits from three of the most notable Christian sites in Britain—St. Paul's, Canterbury and Lindisfarne—buried in the walls, all the accoutrements of C. of E., choir stalls carved and brass plaques ashine, proclaiming Christ Colonial. For a modern version of church architecture, you should visit St. Paul's Catholic Chapel, at the other end of Nyerere Road from All Saints', along the side of Central Park. Worth seeing, too, is the Holy Family Cathedral, along City Hall Way, not far from the Inter-Continental Hotel. This cathedral is, again, fairly new—consecrated in 1963 —with a simple interior and a high, free-standing, bell tower.

If you turn left off Kenyatta Avenue onto Wabera Street you will come to the Jamia Mosque. It is a feature of the Nairobi skyline, with its silver domes and tall minarets. Inside, it is an archetypal mosque, slightly garish but full of quiet calm. Visitors are permitted, but you will have to take off your shoes. The Jamia Mosque is of the Sunni persuasion. The other main mosque in town is the Khoja, on Moi Avenue, nearly across from the Jeevanjee Gardens. This mosque, too, is worth dropping in to; both are strikingly illuminated during religious festivals and other times of celebration. The Ismaili mosque is situated at Ngara roundabout, north of the city center.

Museums

The National Museum is situated on Museum Hill close to Uhuru Highway. It is within walking distance of the center of the city (two km.) or can be reached by No. 18 bus from the rear of the Kenya Commercial Bank, Tom Mboya Street.

Exhibits include collections of Joy Adamson's paintings of wild flowers and the peoples of Kenya; a marine section on fish and molluscs; an African butterfly collection (said to be the world's largest), sections on birds and mammals of East Africa and a minerology section.

The section on pre-history is of particular interest with new exhibits and information on the recent important finds to the east of Lake Turkana (Rudolf) and the geology of Kenya. Another section is on African artefacts including musical instruments, gourds, masks; personal ornaments, weapons and pottery.

There is a museum shop with a selection of local crafts, books, postcards and general ethnic goodies.

Across the way is a fairly small bird collection—the Nairobi Aviary —where you can see some of the country's native birds in captivity and, next door, if you want to see snakes alive alive-o, there is the Snake Park. This reptilian haven contains around 200 species of snakes and also needle-nosed and common Nile crocodiles, tortoises (including the giant model) and turtles. The venomous snakes are milked on Wednesdays between 4 and 6 in the afternoon to obtain raw material for anti-venom serum.

Back in town is the excellently kept and interesting Railway Museum, only 800 meters from the main Railway Station but tucked away and difficult to find. The route for walkers is off Haile Selassie Avenue into Workshop Road, right into Pate Bay Road and left into Ngaira Avenue. Where Ngaira Avenue turns into Station Road a murram track directly ahead leads to the museum in 100 meters.

The museum contains historical photographs of the building of the "Lunatic Line" Railway with many relics from the early trains and lake steamers. Outside are four old locomotives in spotless condition and among the old carriages is the one from which Police Superintendent Charles Ryall was taken by a lion in 1900.

Outside town once more are the Bomas of Kenya—not really a museum, but rather a living introduction to the ethnic ceremonies and the way of life of the region. This Kenyan cultural center is situated just beyond the main entrance to Nairobi National Park on the Langata Road. It can be reached by No. 24 bus from Development House, Moi Avenue, near the Railway Station.

The Bomas offer traditional dancing displays; model African dwellings and a night club (daily from 9 P.M.). Dance performances are at 2.30 P.M. Mondays to Fridays: 3.30 P.M. Saturdays, Sundays and Public Holidays.

Parks

The main visit during your stay should be to the Nairobi National Park, which we cover under our section on Parks and Nature Reserves. There is nothing like it anywhere—a genuine primeval plains' sector of a city. This is the essential contradiction in the personality of Nairobi which can be seen from the summit of the Ngong Hills flanking the Park. In one direction the view is of the prehistoric age of the mammals; in the other, a 20th-century city of a million inhabitants—and, for the moment, the two extremes rest easily side by side. But there are some other more traditional parks to see either actually in—or very close to—town.

The Uhuru Park is slap in the middle of the city. It is extremely well manicured—almost as if in protest at the normal unkempt look of most African vegetation—with lawns, flowers and a small boating lake, where you can hire various sizes of boats from early morning till evening. You can get a good view of several of the city's main buildings from the park; directly opposite are the Parliament buildings. Across Kenyatta Avenue is the Central Park, with the bulk of the Nairobi Serena Hotel to one side.

The extensive City Park is three km. (two miles) from the city center. (No. 11 or 12 bus from the rear of the Kenya Commercial Bank, Tom Mboya Street.) It contains a maze, sunken gardens and lily pools alive with fish and frogs. There are swings and slides near the attractive Valley Gardens, and the Boscowen Memorial Collections of rare and exotic plants. The park is open to the public mornings and afternoons Monday, Wednesday and Friday and afternoons Saturday and Sunday.

Nairobi Arboretum Forest Reserve is two km. from the city center. (No. 28 bus to State House Road.) It is spacious, green and shady, and contains more than 270 species of trees, all labeled. Broad paths, with benches, wind amongst the trees. The Arboretum is open from sunrise until half an hour after sunset. No charge for admission. For anyone who loves trees, this is an especially rewarding experience.

Since we have had collections of birds and snakes, it is the turn of the fish. Back in town, on Mama Ngina Street, not far from the Hilton, is the Marine Aquarium. It houses a representative gathering of typical sea-life from Kenya's coastal waters.

Five Short Excursions from Nairobi

1 Lake Magadi and Olorgesailie Prehistoric Site. Of all the Rift Valley lakes only Lake Turkana (Rudolf) is lower than Lake Magadi whose altitude of 580 meters (1,900 ft.) produces a climate radically different from Nairobi's. Striking scenery, abundant waterbirds. Masai herdsmen and the Olorgesailie Prehistoric Site combine to make the 110 km. (68 miles) drive from Nairobi more than worthwhile. As the road is in good condition it is an easy journey for any car.

Exit from the city is via Langata Road past Wilson Airport and Nairobi National Park. One km. after the Park entrance, Magadi Road is sign-posted to the left. In five km. (three miles) the tarmac finishes and there is a bumpy section for 11 km. (seven miles) to Kiserian village where the new road begins and provides smooth traveling.

After Kiserian the route climbs over the southern end of the Ngong Hills for fine views of the spacious ranching landscape. Volcanic hills rise out of the plain as the road drops into hot, dry country where the Masai graze their herds. At the village of Olepolos the track off to the right leads to the Ngong circular tour.

65 km. (40 miles) from Nairobi, the Olorgesailie Prehistoric Site is well signed two km. to the left of the road. This site is a tiny National Park and is well set out for visitors. A small museum together with exhibits of hand axes and animal bones *in situ* give a clear impression of the stone age culture which existed there about 200,000 years ago. Discovered in 1919 by the geologist J.W. Gregory, the site was excavated by Dr. and Mrs. Leakey in the 1940s and made a National Park in 1947. It is now administered by the National Museum. There are unfurnished bandas for those who wish to stay the night, but visitors must bring all implements and bedding.

The route to Magadi continues for another 45 km. (27 miles) past Olorgesailie. Flanked by hills the road follows the valley of the Olkeju Ngiro river where Masai water their cattle in an impressive gorge close to the road. The country drops steadily towards the lake with views of the Nguruman Escarpment framing the pink waters of the lake.

The trona—natural crystalline soda—is exploited by the Magadi Soda Company. But the factory and drying pans only intrude in the bizarre lake landscape at the central section, where the company's causeway gives access to the western side. Even close to the factory, water-birds are plentiful. African spoonbills, wood and sacred ibis and pelicans are all common but the lesser flamingos are most prolific.

A road south along the east side of the Lake goes past the company's houses, golf course and air-strip to a fine view point overlooking the southern end of the lake. There are usually large numbers of flamingos here and always hot springs.

By crossing the causeway, it is possible to reach the Nguruman Escarpment and eventually Narok; this route is across remote and difficult country, for four-wheel drive self-contained parties only. But it is full of game and a wildly beautiful setting.

2 Lake Naivasha, Mount Longonot and Hell's Gate. Roughly circular and 15 km. (nine miles) in diameter, Lake Naivasha is a magnificent fresh-water lake offering many facilities to visitors and being particularly rich in bird life. Mount Longonot (2,770 meters, 10,880 ft.) overlooks the Lake and makes an interesting climb. Longonot is an old volcano with fumaroles still active in the crater area. Close to Lake Naivasha is Hell's Gate Gorge which has hot springs and geysers.

Exit from Nairobi on the A104 via Kabete, which after 39 km. (24 miles) reaches the main Limuru intersection; bear left (signposted to Narok) along the old B3 Naivasha road. This passes through forest and then descends the rift valley escarpment in a series of zig-zags stretching eight km. (five miles). Part way down the escarpment on the left is the forest picnic site which gives superb views of the rift valley, across to Mount Suswa and north to Mount Longonot, with the Narok road streaking between them across the valley floor into the distant haze. Below also is the satellite tracking station of Mount Margaret.

Continuing down the escarpment further viewing points by the roadside are shared with vendors of local handicrafts and sheepskins. After passing a small Italian Chapel on the right, the road reaches the valley floor. Shortly off to the left is the road to Narok and Masai Mara, but straight on after a further 13 km. (eight miles) the road crosses the railway line at the village of Longonot. Just before this, the level-crossing, a track leads off left towards Mount Longonot. From the head of this track it is easy to walk up the mountain and around the crater rim. It is wise to leave a guard with the car, or leave it at the railway station and walk the extra five km. (three miles) each way.

Soon after Longonot railway station, the road breasts a rise and Lake Naivasha appears in the distance. Plains' game, especially Thomson's gazelle, is almost always seen just off the road as it drops towards the lake. A lake circuit road turns left two km. before Naivasha town, and there are a number of hotels and campsites along the shore which offer accommodations and boating facilities.

The Naivasha Marina Club offers day membership to visitors. There is a restaurant and bar overlooking the lake. Small boats with outboards give access to the Crescent Island Wildlife Sanctuary—location for many wildlife films including the *Born Free* TV series. Thomson's gazelle and waterbuck are common on the island, but perhaps the most noteworthy feature is its birdlife; over 450 species have been recorded.

The road continues past Fisherman's Camp (17 km., ten miles, from the turnoff) and eventually circles the lake. The best views are from just beyond Fisherman's Camp. After this the road descends and passes through dry country to rejoin the A104 six km. (four miles) west of Naivasha town. Refreshments are available at the Bell Inn.

Close to the lake is Hell's Gate Gorge (Njorowe), open to visitors via the track off left just past the Safariland hedge. The gorge is an impressive place, with towering cliffs 200 meters (655 ft.) high where a pair of lammergeyers nest regularly. Fischer's Tower, in the center of the gorge, has a resident family of rock hyrax.

The track continues for several kilometers. From the end of the gorge, a footpath continues down the stream to hot springs and geysers which can be reached in two hours.

3 Mayer's Ranch. A visit to Mayer's Ranch, on the escarpment overlooking the Rift Valley, makes a very pleasant afternoon outing from Nairobi. Here you can enjoy Masai culture and customs and watch their ceremonial dancing and chanting, followed by a country-style tea in Mrs. Mayer's farmhouse, with its delightful old English-style garden and spectacular views.

To get to Mayer's Ranch, leave Nairobi on A104 via Kabete, bearing left at the Limuru intersection on the old B3 road to Lake Naivasha and Narok. Partway down the escarpment after the left turn to the forest picnic site, take a sharp left down the farm road. After a short way, you arrive at the ranch, about 40 km. (25 miles) from Nairobi. For the return journey you could take the Limuru road, passing through the numerous tea estates of this beautiful countryside and re-entering Nairobi at the Muthaiga traffic circle.

4 The Ngong Hills. Famed by Karen Blixen's poetic description in *Out of Africa,* the Ngong Hills stand sentinel 25 km. (15 miles) southeast of Nairobi, on the very edge of the Great Rift Valley. Rising to 2,460 meters (8,070 ft.) they form a scenic backdrop to Nairobi National Park and create a natural divide between small-scale farming developments on the Nairobi side of the hills and the unchanged African plains where Masai graze their herds.

A fine ridge walk along the grassy crest of the hills gives spacious views of both the city, to the east, and sometimes Mount Kenya beyond, and the hot dry country, studded with distant volcanic hills, to the west; and a drive round the Ngong Circular Road encompasses a contrast of 20th-century city with timeless Masai pastoralist, spacious views and rugged scenery in less than 100 km. (62 miles). The hills are six km. (four miles) from Karen in the western city suburbs.

The summit is accessible to saloon cars along a rough, steep track from Ngong village, and it is easy walking along the ridge. Buffalo are sometime seen.

The Ngong circular tour can be joined from the south from the Magadi road at Olepelos. Alternatively it can be started from the village of Ngong, easily reached from Nairobi by the main Ngong road which passes the race-course then through the Ngong Forest before climbing through Shambas. The circuit is signposted right from the main street and winds across the northern shoulder of the hills, bearing left at the junction, to the dry thornbush and acacia country of the rift valley floor. The track skirts the foot of the hills which climb 1,000

Nairobi City Square, showing its traditional and modern architecture. *Above*, the Kenyatta Conference Center; *below*, the Law Courts, with Jomo Kenyatta's statue.

The Outspan Hotel—built around the former home of Lord Baden-Powell, founder of the Boy Scouts. Two safari vehicles, one with zebra-style paintwork.

Two portraits of animal strength—a buffalo with its mud-caked hide, and the huge ears of an alerted elephant.

Kikuyu warriors, painted and dressed for a tribal dance.

meters (3,280 ft.) to the left before gradually rising to meet the main Magadi road at Olepelos, 26 km. (16 miles) from Ngong. Here local Masai sell their bead ornaments and wear traditional dress. A left at the village leads back to Nairobi via the Langata road, past Nairobi National Park and Wilson Airport, a distance of 40 km. (24 miles).

5 Ol Doinyo Sabuk National Park. This small national park is a forested mountain rising to 1,240 meters (4,067 ft.). Bush-buck, impala and buffalo live on the mountain (the Swahili name *Kilima Mbogo* means Buffalo Mountain). The animals are shy, however.

There is a stony track you can drive up to the summit with extensive views over the surrounding countryside. In clear weather Mount Kenya is prominent to the north and the Aberdares to the west. The graves of Sir Northrup and Lady McMillan and their servant Louise Decker are just off the track about halfway up the mountain.

Exit from Nairobi is on the A2 for Thika. After 44 km. (27 miles) on good motorway there is a flyover for Thika town. The name will no doubt be familiar from the book by Elspeth Huxley, *The Flame Trees of Thika,* or from the excellent TV series made from it. But a great deal has changed since the days of which she wrote. From Thika the route is the A3 (signposted Garissa). After 23 km. (14 miles) follow the signpost to Ol Doinyo Sabuk. After one km. the route turns left at a T-junction and two km. further on crosses the Athi river.

Just below the bridges, the Athi goes over the Fourteen Falls—a horseshoe shaped net of waterfalls which is spectacular in the rainy season. There is a parking area, from which a vantage point can be reached on foot, down a turning to the left, just before the bridges. Immediately after the bridges is a small market and a right turn, signposted to the National Park. The park entrance is four km. (two miles) from the market—85 km. (52 miles) from Nairobi. At present there is no charge for admission.

PRACTICAL INFORMATION FOR NAIROBI

ARRIVING AT NAIROBI. Transportation from Nairobi's Jomo Kenyatta International Airport is easy. The Kenatco Company operates a limo service; there are taxis (yellow-striped); and mini- and regular buses. The trip is around 20 km. (12 miles) on new motorway all the way.

The airport itself, no more than a few years old, has restaurants, information desks, hotel and tour booking offices and car-hire firms.

Hotels

Expensive

Hilton, Box 30624 (tel. 334000). Corner of Mama Ngina St. and Kimathi St. Wide range of facilities, all well up to Hilton standards. Pool on roof terrace, and a number of good restaurants, including a bargain coffee shop.

Inter-Continental, Box 30353 (tel. 335550). Just off Uhuru Highway. Centrally-located and highly recommended. Cabaret restaurant—one among a number of better-than-average eating spots—with great views; pool.

New Stanley, Box 30680 (tel. 333233). Corner of Kenyatta Ave. and Kimathi St. Lots of character, and, though it can be noisy, worth it for the experience.

Norfolk, Box 40064 (tel. 335422). Faces the University on Harry Thuku Rd. For old Kenya atmosphere; boasts a long and distinguished history. Excellent management by the best-known hotel group in Kenya, Block Hotels Ltd.

Serena, Box 46302 (tel. 337978/337614). On Nyerere Rd. and Kenyatta Ave. beside Central Park. Well-run and imaginatively designed, plants aplenty.

Moderate

Ambassadeur, Box 30399 (tel. 336803). On the corner of Moi Ave. and City Hall Way. Central and busy spot; good value.

Excelsior, Box 49584 (tel. 26481). On the corner of Kenyatta Ave. and Koinange St. Central; quite good value.

Pan Afric, Box 30486 (tel. 720822). On Valley Rd., just beyond the Anglican Cathedral. Up-market hotel with smart atmosphere, grounds and pool.

Safari Park Hotel, Box 45038 (tel. 802311/802611). On the Thika Rd. at Ruaraka eight km. (five miles) from the city center. Good food, lovely garden and large swimming pool. Next to the Casino de Paradise.

Sixeighty Hotel, Muindi Mbingu St., Box 43436 (tel. 332680). City center just off Kenyatta Ave., near the post office. Large modern hotel. Conference Room, shops, hairdressing, commercial rates. Convenient to main shops.

Inexpensive

Boulevard, Box 42831 (tel. 27567/9). Attractively-sited just off Uhuru Highway beside the river. On the simple side. Close to the National Museum.

County, Box 41924 (tel. 26190/337621). Centrally-located on Haile Selassie Ave. near the Parliament Buildings.

Fairview, Box 40842 (tel. 723210/1/2/3). On Bishop's Rd., a couple of kilometers from the city center. Family hotel with five acres of beautiful grounds. No pool.

Grosvenor, Box 41038 (tel. 21034/5). At top of Valley Rd., beyond the Pan Afric hotel, outside town. Oldtime Kenya design, with good garden; pool.

Heron Court, Box 41063 (tel. 720740/3). On Milimani Rd., west of the city center. Apartment hotel.

Jacaranda, Box 14287 (tel. 742272/6). At Westlands. Many recreation facilities, and good Italian restaurant.

New Mayfair, Box 43817 (tel. 742731). Five km. (three miles) out of town. Friendly atmosphere; pool, sauna and extensive grounds.

Milimani Hotel, Box 30715 (tel. 29461). New hotel on Milimani Rd., west of the city center. Pool.

Silver Springs, Box 61632 (tel. 720545). On Valley Rd., past the Pan Afric.

Utalii, Box 31067 (tel. 802540/802088). On Thika Rd., a fair way from town (18 km., 11 miles), but part of the country's hotel-training school, so service is extremely attentive.

 RESTAURANTS. Nairobi restaurants are good, sometimes exceptionally so. Prices are generally low—certainly by American and European standards—and ingredients of very high quality. The Asian restaurants, again very reasonably priced, can be excellent, but most visitors will nonetheless probably incline toward the many International spots. Note that all the larger hotels have one or more restaurants, those at the Inter-Continental and Norfolk being especially good. The Muthaiga Country Club and Nairobi Club are both good, but you must find a member to take you to either.

African Heritage, Box 41730, Banda St. (tel. 333157).Traditional African dishes served buffet-style. Ethiopian buffet served in the evening.

Alan Bobbe's Bistro, Box 44991, Caltex House, Koinange St. (tel. 21152). Good, if a little expensive, French food in small chic restaurant. Run by a local character, Alan Bobbe. Must book.

Carnivore, Box 56685, Langata Rd. (tel. 501775/501709/501779). Out of town towards Nairobi National Park. As much as you can eat of the best of Kenya's protein, including *mbuzi* (goat) and *swara* (venison).

Casino de Paradise, Safari Park Hotel, Thika Rd. (tel. 802673). Casino at the Safari Park Hotel some way out of town at Ruaraka. A Korean restaurant goes with the Korean casino. Reasonable food at reasonable prices.

Corner Bar, Nginda St., Murang's Rd. (tel. 200911/27172). Indian food; good for red-hot chicken curry.

French Cultural Center, Box 49415, Monrovia St. (tel. 336263). A shade on the expensive side, but authentically French.

El Patio, Reinsurance Plaza, Taifa Rd. (tel. 340114). A reasonably priced restaurant favoring Spanish cuisine. Lunchtime salad bar.

International Casino, Box 45827, Museum Hill (tel. 742600). Restaurant on the ground floor below the casino. Good Italian food in plush setting, with cabaret. Prices are reasonable, if not budget.

Kentmere Club, Banana Hill, Limuru (tel. 865253). Olde worlde English restaurant with thatched roof; on the outskirts of town. Expensive and not always reliable food, but mostly good.

Mandarin, Box 44834, Tom Mboya St. (tel. 206001). Excellent Cantonese food; one of the best Chinese restaurants in Nairobi.

Marino's, Box 72549, International House, Mama Ngina St. (tel. 27150/337230). On mezzanine floor; mainly Italian food.

Minar, Box 41869, Banda St. (tel. 81382/29999). Some international dishes, but mainly Indian food. Watch out for the *cayenne!*

Pagoda, Box 49806, Shanker Dass House, Moi Ave. (tel. 27036).

Red Bull, Box 49230, Mama Ngina St. (tel. 335717/28045). Fairly expensive but very popular spot offering mainly Swiss-German food.

Tamarind, Box 74493, National Bank House, Harambee Ave. (tel. 338959/20473). Chic, expensive and very, very good. Seafood specialties, notably spiny lobster (with butter and white wine) and crab *chinoise.*

 TOURIST INFORMATION. Visit the Nairobi Tourist Information Bureau in front of the Hilton Hotel. In addition, the magazine *What's On,* published monthly, and the two main daily papers—*The Nation* and *The Standard*—give details of many upcoming events.

Embassies and High Commissions. *United Kingdom High Commission,* Bruce House, Standard St., Box 30465 (tel. 335944). *United States Embassy,* Embassy Building, Haile Selassie and Moi Aves., Box 30137 (tel. 334141/334150).

 SHOPPING. For gemstones, try *Elton's Kenya Ltd.,* on Standard St.; *International Gems,* Standard St.; *Gemstones of Africa,* Kaunda St.; or *Al Safa Gemstones* in the New Stanley Hotel. *Rowland Ward* on Standard St. has big-game hand-engraved glass among many other upmarket items. For Makonde and Wakamba sculptures and carvings, indigenous contemporary and traditional African art, batiks, masks, drums, etc., try the *African Cultural Gallery,* Esso House, Mama Ngina St.; *Batiks & Jewellery Ltd.,* in the lobby of the Inter-Continental Hotel; *Gallery Watatu,* First Floor, Consolidated House, Standard St.; *The Art Gallery,* Corner House, opposite the Hilton Hotel; or *Craft Sales,* University Way, near the Norfolk Hotel. Look into *Pwani Arts* behind the New Stanley Hotel, Standard St., for artifacts and furniture from Mombasa and Lamu; and *African Heritage* on Kenyatta Ave. for intriguing crafts.

 TOURS AND TRANSPORT. There are a wide variety of tours around Nairobi. Check the magazine *What's On* or ask your hotel porter. Alternatively, try the Nairobi Tourist Information Bureau. The Automobile Association (AA) is also good for road and safari information. It's located in the Westlands suburb, a short taxi ride from the city center.

Taxis are readily available from in front of the main hotels, either the regular kind or the more raffish and cheaper *matatu* variety. The train station and main bus depots are all within easy walking distance of the city center. You would be wise not to do too much walking around alone.

HIPPOPOTAMUS

MOUNT KENYA SAFARI
CIRCUIT

This circuit is described in a clockwise direction out of Nairobi, although it works equally well the other way round. The main tourist route, including an excursion safari to Lake Nakuru and the Mountain National Parks, extends as far north as Nanyuki before turning back for Nairobi via Nyeri. The circuit as described is by road, but the main centers of interest are all accessible by light aircraft as well. The railway also covers part of the route, from Nairobi to Nanyuki.

With a generous allowance for game runs and other excursions, the main circuit involves about 700 km. (430 miles), all on good roads, and can be done comfortably in five days.

Out of Nairobi

Leaving Nairobi for Naivasha, the most direct route is to take the broad Uhuru Highway which bisects the city in a northerly direction from the center of town, signposted to Naivasha and the A104. Passing the International Casino and exit for the Museum on the right, the highway then goes through the Westlands suburbs as the Waiyaki Way. This is one of the oldest stretches of road in the country, since it was built on a track to Lake Victoria and cut in 1896 by British Army engineers led by Captain Sclater, after whom the road was once named.

At Kabete a junction left brings in the alternative route from West Nairobi and the Karen district, via Dagoretti Corner. All this time the road has been steadily climbing and to the left there are distant views over to the Ngong Hills.

From Kabete the road continues to climb, no longer through smart suburbs but past steep hillsides heavily farmed by the Kikuyu for crops of maize, banana and the white flowers of Pyrethum—used in the manufacture of insecticides. Passing Kikuyu town and Mugaga the road then reaches the major Limuru junction after 39 km. (24 miles), and is now over 2,134 meters (7,000 ft.) high.

Limuru township is a colorful market for the agricultural produce of the former Kikuyu Reserve—parts of which were excised in the colonial period as "White Highlands." Limuru is the site of Kenya's main shoe factory (visitors welcome). Not far away, on the old Banana Hill Road, is a cottage-style gourmet restaurant, the Kentmere Club Hotel. There is also an attractive Farm Hotel in the Limuru area which provides good country-style meals. For sport, Limuru offers horse racing, golf on a scenic nine-hole course, and racquet sports at a non-exclusive country club.

Reverting to the junction, signposted off left is the old Naivasha road, the B3, which winds down the face of the escarpment at one of its steepest points. This road should be taken by those traveling to Narok, or visiting the Rift Valley view, Mayers Farm or Mount Longonot. (It is described in the section on excursions from Nairobi.)

Straight ahead at the junction is the newly constructed A104 highway, probably the best in Kenya, which now forms the main route from Nairobi to the centers of Naivasha and Nakuru in the Rift Valley. It travels first along the edge of the Rift escarpment from which there are two spurs, 14½ km. (nine miles) and 34 km. (21 miles) from the junction, where visitors can take in the magnificent view. The broad floor of the Great Rift Valley stretches across to the mist-blue western wall of the Mau Range, punctured by volcanic cones and rising steam jets. From the second spur it is just possible to see into the crater of

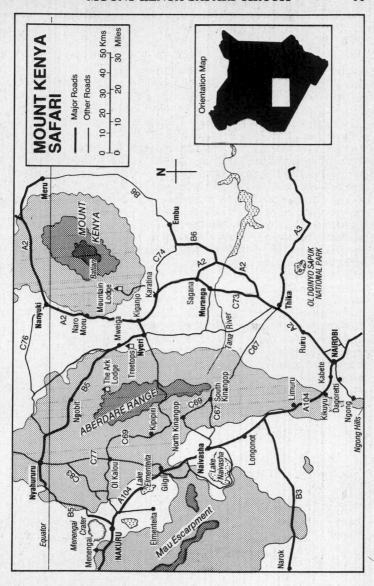

Mount Longonot from where ancient lava flows spill across the valley
floor. Beyond lie the sparkling waters of Lake Naivasha.

The road now descends gently across the slope of the escarpment to
the valley floor, giving good views ahead to Lake Naivasha. At the
bottom of the decline, signposted right is the turnoff to N. Kinangop
and the Aberdare National Park, 92 km. (57 miles) from Nairobi.
Shortly afterwards is the junction left to Naivasha.

Lake Naivasha

Lake Naivasha is a favorite weekend spot for Nairobi residents.
About 72 sq. km. (28 sq. miles) in area, the lake has no apparent outlet,
but remains fresh and changes noticeably in size according to rainfall
on the basin slopes of the Mau and Aberdare ranges.

There are accommodations to suit all tastes on the lake shore, including camping. There are two full-service hotels—Lake Naivasha Hotel
(Reservations, Box 40075 Nairobi, tel. 22860), with wide grounds beside the lake and with excellent fish from the lake in the restaurant; and
the Safariland Club (Box 72, tel. 29), with all the fun of messing about
in boats, plus a wide range of prices for hotel rooms, deluxe cottages
and tents. Local attractions include sailing, water skiing, fishing for
black bass and tilapia, and bird watching. Ornithologist John Williams
has described Lake Naivasha as "a bewilderment of birds," and there
are estimated to be more than 400 species on the lake and papyrus
fringe, including the magnificent fish eagle.

Crescent Island is a private but accessible bird sanctuary which also
provides visitors with the opportunity to photograph various her-
bivores, including hippo, at close range. Access is gained from the
Marina Club, a right turn just past the Lake Hotel.

Visitors should take local advice about boating on the Lake—clog-
ging weed, hippo and sudden squalls are occasionally dangerous.

The Lake Ring Road

A rough road circles the lake, beginning a couple of miles south of
Naivasha town on the old road and rejoining this road north of the
Lake, just past Morendat station: it provides access for hotels, holiday
villas, farms and fishing clubs. Also on the lakeside, off this road, are
the homes of the late Joy Adamson *(Born Free)* and Mirella Ricciardi
(Vanishing Africa), and an incongruous but impressive Moorish villa—
"Oserian", or the Djin (Gin) Palace, a locally notorious weekend party
house for English aristocrats in the playful thirties. There is also a
variety of wildlife in the lake hinterland (including the big predators)

which may soon be given protective reserve status in an initiative of the World Wildlife Fund.

The road continues along the far shore of the lake at the foot of the Eburru mountain, a slumbering volcano where local farmers once capped steam jets with condensers to obtain water and used the natural heat to dry their pyrethrum crops. Close by is one of Kenya's rare china clay pits, which supplies the potteries in Nairobi. A sign-posted murram road at a fork leads directly to Gilgil and affords a magnificent view towards and including Lake Elmenteita. Otherwise straight on to rejoin the main road.

Hell's Gate is another scenic detour reached by a track which forks left from the lake ring road about 15 km. (nine miles) from the Naivasha road turn off south of the town. This is a huge gorge (Njorowe), once the outlet of an enlarged lake system which filled the Rift Valley floor after the last Ice Age. It is an Arizona-style valley landscape flanked by sheer cliffs, the isolated "Fischer's Tower" pinnacle, standing at the entrance to the gorge. At the end of the gorge (eight km., five miles) a footpath leads down to the hot springs, where steam jets are a main feature of the lower section. The cliffs are also a popular excursion for ornithologists in search of the rare lammergeier and Verreaux's eagles which nest on the basalt cliffs.

Naivasha Town

The Masai's "En-aiposha" (the Lake) is a bustling trade center which began as a single food store for the railway workers at the turn of the century. It grew as the headquarters of what was then the Eastern Province of Uganda and is now the commercial center of an expansion of the Kikuyu. It is also a popular watering place for travelers (at the Bell Inn) before continuing north to Nakuru, or detouring right off the paved road to the Kinangop and the Aberdares.

The Aberdares

This area lies due east of Lake Naivasha and is well signposted from the center of town and from the A104 highway. After 14½ km. (nine miles) the tarmac runs out and the road forks left—signposted Aberdare National Park—across the Kinangop plateau. Lying at an altitude of 1,980–2,130 meters (6,500–7,000 ft.) this plateau was a favorite farming area for European settlers, its rolling grasslands and rich woodlands being reminiscent of the English countryside. On *Uhuru* (Independence) it was the first area to be purchased by the government for distribution as smallholdings amongst African farmers.

After 24 km. (15 miles) of rough track, some murram and some broken paved road, the base of the escarpment is reached from where a steep climb leads to the west gate of the National Park through hairpin bends. Before getting this far visitors intending to cross the Aberdares should first check road conditions with the A.A. in Nairobi or at the Bell Inn at Naivasha.

Alternative routes heading north, forking left along the way, lead to Gilgil and Nakuru along the farm-belt arteries and past the Kipipiri mountain. Heading south is the settlement of South Kinangop, near the Sasumua Dam which is one of the main sources of Nairobi's water supply and an excellent spot for trout fishing. A track from here leads over the southern saddle of the range eventually to reach Thika.

Lake Elmenteita

Back on the main route, the road runs through dryish ranch land from Naivasha to Gilgil, a garrison town and the junction for a tarred road, by-passing Nakuru to Nyahururu (Thomson's Falls). Gilgil has a pleasant country club, a nine-hole golf course and the active Kinyatta Polo Club. Just after the town is Lake Elmenteita, a seldom-visited soda lake with a large flamingo population (greater and lesser), which can be seen on the left from a meandering escarpment off which there is a viewing point. Kariandusi, soon after, is a small L.S.B. Leakey excavation site for relics of Stone-Age man. Nearby there is a modern high-quality diatomite mine.

The track to Elmenteita—left off the main highway to Nakuru—is the road to *King Solomon's Mines*. At least the author, H. Rider Haggard, and knowledgeable locals believed it to be part of an ancient hunting trail to elephant country—and therefore ivory—also passing through the Mau range.

Lake Nakuru

Back on the main route the highway shortly reaches Nakuru, 156 km. (97 miles) from Nairobi. In 1902 it was just a small railhead but is now the third largest town in Kenya with a population of over 100,000. It is the Pyrethrum capital of the country and a major agricultural center, with many institutions having their headquarters there.

Nakuru is attractively laid out between the Lake and the slopes of the 11 km. (seven miles) wide Menengai Crater, where there is a camping site and further on a fine 18-hole golf course. The town has two modern hotels and two lodges within Lake Nakuru National Park —Lake Nakuru Lodge, converted from an original farmhouse, and Lion Hill Camp with deluxe tented accommodations. For stopover entertainment Nakuru offers cinemas, a theater and Kenya's principal motor racing track.

Lake Nakuru National Park is on the south side of the town and is well signposted. It covers the entire lake and bordering grass plains and acacia woodlands, and is popularly described as "the greatest bird spectacle on earth" for its concentration of flamingo and up to 350 other bird species.

Menengai

A worthwhile deviation off the main route is a ten km. (six mile) drive north of Nakuru town up to the 2,278 meter (7,475 ft.) rim of the Menengai Crater. The view from there is spectacular over the lake and surrounding patchwork of farms. The crater—or more correctly caldera—itself is 89 sq. km. (34 sq. miles) in area, one of the largest and deepest in the world with its floor 500 meters (1,640 ft.) or more below the rim. It was here at Il Menenga (The Dead) that the Laikipia Masai were said to have been driven to a precipitous death by the Naivasha Masai; and the belief persists that at dusk the low moaning of ghosts can be heard.

Another visitor attraction in the Nakuru area, signposted from the town, is the Hyrax Hill prehistoric site, which contains evidence of early settlements on what was then the lakeshore of both Neolithic and Iron Age vintage. The Gambles Cave and Njoro River sites, also near Nakuru, can only be visited by arrangement with the National Museum in Nairobi.

Nyahururu–Thomson's Falls

Beyond Nakuru, a left turn off the main road leads west to Londiani and Kericho, the principal tea-growing area of Kenya, passing through fertile wheatlands and the edge of the western Mau Forest. The main tourist circuit branches right off the main road at Nakuru for Nyahururu.

There are two principal access routes to Nyahururu—the slower murram road out of Nakuru being the more picturesque. It passes alongside the fertile Solai sisal estates, and then up a steep escarpment.

The other route, all asphalt, starts out from Gilgil (a right turn opposite the Gilgil Club) and by-passes Nakuru. This runs through the major settlement schemes and is joined at Ol Kalou by dirt roads from Nakuru (left) and the Kinangop (right). Off to the right of the road above Ol Kalou is the swampy Lake Ol Bolossat, a favorite haunt of gentlemen duck shooters.

Until recently, Nyahururu was known as Thomson's Falls after Joseph Thomson who discovered the falls on his *Journey Through Masailand.* The falls plunge more than 70 meters (230 ft.) into a steeply eroded gorge at the foot of the lawns of an attractive and old, though now somewhat dilapidated, hotel. The town itself is small, serving the needs of the farming community around it. From here a road due north leads to Maralal and the eastern shores of Lake Turkana. But for the purpose of this Mount Kenya safari circuit, the route is east.

A new paved road runs from the town southeastwards to Nyeri, 97 km. (60 miles) of good road across the lower northern slopes of the Aberdares. From there the A2 highway heading northward can be joined and it is another 64 km. (40 miles) to Nanyuki. A direct route to Nanyuki leads off left from the paved road just outside the town to travel directly eastward across the Laikipia plains, through large cattle ranches. Although only 97 km. (60 miles) against the 161 km. (100 mile) detour it is extremely rocky in some sections, which could wreck the tyres on an ordinary saloon. For visitors valuing their nerves and their vehicle the roundabout route through Nyeri is strongly recommended.

Nanyuki

This is a clean country town, lying on the equator and arranged along a broad avenue lined with flowering trees and shrubs. There is a rail terminus for the surrounding ranches, and the town is the base for several safari companies specializing in the Northern Frontier District and Mount Kenya expeditions. Nanyuki is also sports-oriented, particularly equestrian, with show jumping at the old-style country club as well as polo. The Sportsman's Arms at the edge of town is an old-established, family-run hotel with a friendly atmosphere and good home cooking.

Facing Mount Kenya, about eight km. (five miles) from the town center, are the sculptured lawns and gardens of the Mount Kenya Safari Club. A group of Americans, including the late film star William Holden, developed the old Mawingo Hotel first as a private residence and then for top-drawer paying guests. It is a magnificent rest up at the ultimate point of this main northern circuit—with well-appointed suites and family cottages, superb cuisine, and a full range of leisure diversions including Chuka dancers, swimming, disco, sauna and riding. Attached to the club is a private game ranch and wild animal orphanage, a fully-equipped film studio and a nine-hole golf course.

Nanyuki is the departure point for the northern game areas, for the Samburu-Isiolo-Shaba Reserves, Marsabit National Reserve and Meru National Park. In addition a full circular tour of Mount Kenya through

Meru and Embu is 257 km. (160 miles). But for the purposes of this particular circuit the route returns south back down the A2 highway in the direction of Nairobi, all the while being overlooked by the towering peaks of Batian and Nelion, their snows glistening in the equatorial sunshine.

Naro Moru

Just outside Nyeri on the A2 highway to Naro Moru is the Silverbeck hotel, noted for the pleasurable fact that you can have a drink in the bar with one foot in each hemisphere, north and south of the equator. It is also said that the bath water runs out in different directions at each end of the hotel. Trout fishing and pony treks on Mount Kenya can be organized at the Silverbeck.

Naro Moru itself is a riverside hamlet, where, close by, much of *Born Free*—the story of Elsa the lioness—was filmed. The Naro Moru River Lodge is the most popular base camp for climbing expeditions and is the main access to Mount Kenya National Park (see page 216). After Naro Moru, the paved road runs past the huge Solio Ranch, maintained as a private game park which, unfortunately, is closed to visitors.

Mount Kenya Forest

Below Naro Moru and just before the Police College township of Kiganjo, there is an excursion on murram roads off to the left and looping back towards Mount Kenya National Park. On this route is the Thego Fishing Camp and Sagana State Lodge, Kenya's wedding present to Princess Elizabeth, who learned of her accession to the British throne here in 1952. Past the magnificent grounds of Sagana, replete with trees donated from all parts of Kenya, is Mountain Lodge, a first-class treetop hotel overlooking a salt lick and water hole. A long verandah and an underground chamber provide close up views of Mount Kenya's forest wildlife including occasional leopard. An alternative route to this lodge (which must be booked in advance in Nairobi) is via Karatina, but this road is not advisable in wet weather.

Nyeri and Treetops

A right turn from the A2 at Kiganjo leads to Nyeri, the administrative headquarters of Central Province and the principal town of the Kikuyu. It lies at the base of the Aberdare's eastern slopes and is the center for this farmland plateau. The main hostelry here is the distinguished Outspan Hotel which is found on the edge of the town, opposite the golf course and en route to the National Park. It was here that

Lord Baden Powell, founder of the boy-scout movement, retired and his cottage, Pax Tu (Just Peace), still stands in the hotel's beautifully landscaped grounds. He is buried along with his wife in the town's cemetery.

The Outspan owns and manages the world-famous Treetops Hotel. Visitors arrive in time for lunch at the Outspan and then continue in hotel transport to Treetops, 16 km. (ten miles) out of town in the Abedares National park. Heavy baggage is left at the Outspan for collection the following morning. Just beyond the Park boundary, the transport stops at a clearing in the forest and an armed professional hunter escorts visitors on foot to the famous hotel built high in Cape chestnut trees. Floodlighting illuminates an impressive nightly parade of forest wildlife at a natural waterhole—elephant, rhino, buffalo, giant forest hog and numerous antelope.

The Ark

Close to the mountain parks headquarters at Mweiga, back tracking a few kilometers on the Nyeri–Nyahururu road, is the Aberdare Country Club, another first-class hotel which, like the Outspan, processes visitors to The Ark—a luxury game-viewing lodge deep in the Aberdares Park. Built in cedar and brown olive, the lodge is a representation of the biblical ark and has a high overview of the wildlife and a ground-level pillbox close to the waterhole. The lodge is noted for regular visits by the rare and shy Bongo antelope.

Kikuyu Country

From Nyeri, back to Nairobi, there is a choice of two roads, both eventually converging above Thika. The better and faster road is straight ahead and well signposted. For the alternative and perhaps the more interesting route turn right at Sagana through the densely cultivated ridges of the Kikuyu heartland to Muranga—formerly the British district headquarters of Fort Hall. The township is only of marginal interest to tourists, although the murals by the Chagga artist Elimo Njau in the St. James and All Martyrs' Church, which depict an African Christ in a local setting, are worth seeing. An excursion is also possible to the historical site of the Makurwe Wa Gathana where, according to legend, Gikuyu and Mumbi, the mother and father of all Kikuyu, raised their nine daughters from whom the Kikuyu tribes are descended.

Thika

From then on, the road winds down the ridges to Thika, a fast-developing light industrial satellite of Nairobi, set amid sisal, pineapple and coffee plantations. It was pioneered by—among others—the authoress Elspeth Huxley who wrote *The Flame Trees of Thika*. The Blue Posts Hotel at the northern entrance to the town is a pleasant refreshment stop and a view-point for the broad Chania Falls.

A short excursion from Thika takes one out along the Garissa road to the Athi River's 30 meter (98 ft.) Fourteen Falls and Ol Doinyo Sabuk National Park. The Park is mainly a viewpoint and picnic spot, but there are buffalo to enliven the trek. A track to the summit at 2,150 meters (7,050 ft.) is accessible by car when dry.

From Thika a two-lane highway leads past the township of Ruiru, Kenyatta University College (the country's main graduate teacher training facility) and the Kahawa Barracks and thence back into Nairobi at Muthaiga.

BUFFALO

EXCURSION SAFARI

The Samburu–Isiolo–Shaba Game Reserves and Meru National Park

This safari is an excursion from the Mount Kenya circuit, starting from and returning to Nanyuki, though most tour operators' trips to both the Samburu Game Reserve and Meru National Park are part of their northern circuit out of Nairobi. The total distance of the excursion, excluding game drives in the Reserve and Park, is about 450 km. (280 miles), all on good all-weather roads. A minimum of five days should be allowed. Alternative routes returning to Nairobi from Meru National Park are also given.

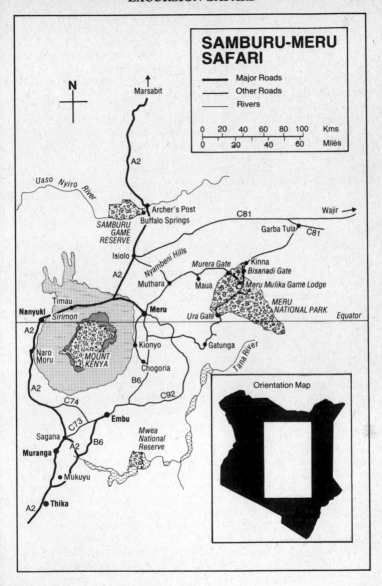

SAMBURU-MERU SAFARI

——— Major Roads
——— Other Roads
——— Rivers

0 20 40 60 80 100 Kms
0 20 40 60 Miles

N

Marsabit

A2

Uaso Nyiro River

Archer's Post
Buffalo Springs

SAMBURU
GAME
RESERVE

C81
Wajir

Garba Tula
C81

Isiolo

A2

Nyambeni Hills

Murera Gate
Kinna
Bisanadi Gate

Muthara

Maua
Meru Mulika Game Lodge

Timau

Nanyuki

Sirimon

Meru

Ura Gate

MERU
NATIONAL PARK

Equator

A2

Naro
Moru

MOUNT
KENYA

Kionyo

Gatunga

Tana River

Chogoria

B6

C92

Orientation Map

C74

C73

Embu

Sagana

Mwea
National
Reserve

Muranga

A2

B6

Mukuyu

A2

Thika

Out of Nanyuki

Fifteen km. (nine miles) on the new Great North Road towards Ethiopia, the Sirimon Track turns back to Mount Kenya. This is a good route for those who want to drive up to see the mountain moorland, but less satisfactory than the Naro Moru access for climbers with limited time.

Soon after the ranch lands of Timau, the road reaches the edge of an impressive escarpment, with wonderful views to the horizon over the semi-desert of Kenya's northern province. There are isolated craggy peaks pushing up into the heat haze, while below the tin roofs of Isiolo reflect the near perpetual sun of the district.

The road then descends steeply from the northern shoulder of Mount Kenya; signposts warning of an accident blackspot should be heeded. At the junction, 53 km. (33 miles) from Nanyuki, one road continues straight on to Meru, the other turns left to Isiolo, a further 24 km. (15 miles) of straight, gentle descent away from the mountain.

Isiolo is an African version of a Wild West frontier town. Although nothing much to look at, it is an interesting melting pot of tribes, cultures and customs, and represents a crossroads between the traditional pastoral life of the Samburu and Turkana people to the north and the modern, settled agricultural ways of the south.

Samburu–Isiolo–Shaba

The paved road stops at Isiolo, and there is a police post for travelers heading north on the wide, but often rough, all-weather roads to Marsabit and Wajir, and then to El Wak on the Somali border. But most visitors passing through Isiolo are heading only a further 40 km. (25 miles) north to the Samburu–Isiolo–Shaba Game Reserves which straddle the Uaso Nyiro River. (See the *National Parks* section.) These are among the wildest dry-bush gamelands in Kenya, and one of its premier wildlife attractions.

From the Game Reserves, the long excursion to Lake Turkana continues north through the township of Archer's Post, but for the present safari the route backtracks to Isiolo, where there is a choice of two access roads to Meru National Park. One, the shortest route, is via a murram road, turning left at the Caltex gas station in Isiolo, skirting the airstrip and crossing 40 km. (25 miles) of bush country to join up with the main Meru–Nanyuki tarred road. This route should not be attempted in wet weather.

The alternative route is to return south from Isiolo on the main tarred road for approximately 30 km. (19 miles) before branching left at the signposted intersection to Meru. This is in fact the main Meru–Nanyuki road, which continues all the way to Maua in the Nyambeni Hills. For Meru National Park, turn left at the signpost before Maua. A further 24 km. (15 miles) on murram brings you to the Murera Gate entrance to the park.

Meru itself is the "county" town of the Meru tribe. Closely related to the Kikuyu on the opposite side of the mountain, they are equally industrious farmers, making full use of the well-watered slopes to grow crops of pyrethrum, coffee, tea, bananas and miraa, a mild stimulant habitually chewed by the peoples of the north. They are also energetic drummers.

The town has a colorfully dilapidated hotel, The Pig and Whistle, and nearby there are a number of places of interest: lakes sacred to the Wameru, waterfalls, caves and forest glades. Lake Nkunga is easily accessible just south of the main road to Embu, ten km. (six miles) after leaving town. Instructions and/or guides for reaching the other sites can be obtained at the hotel.

The countryside here is lush and green, and heavily populated. Along the road, you'll see Meru farmers—usually women—carrying heavy loads of bananas and miraa. Further south, are the Embu, known for their unique stilt dance.

Meru National Park

The Park is fully described in our *National Parks* section. It is one of the more recently developed tourist destinations, as well as being one of the most scenically diverse of Kenya's wildlife sanctuaries. For the purpose of this circuit, the entrance is at the northern Murera Gate, the exit at the southern Ura Gate, the latter leading to a newly-developed circuit road through Watharaka agricultural country and the villages of Marimante and Gatunga to the main Meru–Embu road.

Deviations

By backtracking to Meru, an alternative route to Embu is possible through forested ridges high up on the shoulder of Mount Kenya. The scenery is of lush and undulating greenery relieved by sparkling streams and grass-thatched villages. This is not an area for the visitor in a hurry, or for travel in the wet season, when to the hazards already imposed by the tortuous bends and hills is added the problem of an ice-like muddy road.

From this road at Chogoria, a track leads up through the forest to Mount Kenya. Though less used than the Naro Moru and Sirimon tracks, as well as being considerably longer, it is perhaps the most beautiful trail up the mountain and leads to the self-help Meru Mount Kenya Lodge.

A third exit from Meru National Park northward through the Bisanadi Gate is at present seldom used. A rough dry-weather-only road runs through Kinna to Garba Tulla, before dipping southeast toward a new game reserve at Kora, where George Adamson is rehabilitating lions into the wild. A new bridge over the Tana river connecting Meru National Park and Kora Game Reserve is at present under construction. Until this bridge is finished Kora Game Reserve is inaccessible from Meru National Park.

This is the beginning of the development of the Tana River excursion safari, which will take in the new riverine reserves centered at Buru-Wenje (the Tans Primate Reserve) and Pandanguo close to Lamu.

At Garba Tulla, another main, though difficult, road runs northeast through the Ogaden Desert to Wajir, and eventually to Ethiopia through Moyale. Wajir is a Beau Geste-style desert outpost, complete with fort, palm oasis and camels. The Royal Wajir Yacht Club is the wry British name for a shanty bar here, in the shape of a ship, which was most recently used by the local Somali camel "corps." Although both the Tana River and Wajir routes are possible, they are really only suitable for self-contained explorer visitors using a sturdy four-wheel drive vehicle and prepared to camp out.

Embu

Back on the main circuit road from the Ura Gate of Meru Park, the route passes through Embu, main town of the tribe of the same name and an agricultural center. There is the Izaak Walton, a pleasantly run-down inn which specializes in trout fishing trips in the area. From Embu, a tarred road leads back to the main Mount Kenya circuit road at Sagana, thence right on to the A2 back to Nanyuki. In the opposite direction it is less than a two-hour drive through Muranga to Nairobi.

Tana River

Alternatively, for visitors returning to Nairobi from Embu, there is a paved road through the Mwea-Tebere rice scheme, where the Tana River is used to irrigate an extensive area of paddy fields. This is a marvelous place for seeing water birds in large numbers, especially early in the morning and in the evening. The paved section of the road ends at the Tana, and a murram road links up with Thika via Mukuyu.

ELEPHANT

WESTERN KENYA

Western Kenya contains a remarkable range and wealth of land-scapes, making it one of the most appealing and fascinating areas of the entire country. A north–south line drawn through the area cuts through semi-desert, alkaline lakes alive with flamingoes and other birdlife, fertile farming-lands, montane forest and grassland savannah teeming with game. And all these vastly different terrains are less than 200 km. (125 miles) apart. But in addition, the area also contains one of the best wildlife reserves in Africa, the continent's largest lake, a 4,300-meter (14,110 ft.) peak, and the only tropical rain forest in East Africa.

Although the circuit we describe in this chapter is not yet fully developed, there are nonetheless moderate to good accommodations. Similarly, the complex network of minor roads is complemented by good, fast trunk roads, allowing an infinite variety of routes. At the same time, a number of new full-service hotels and lodges are planned, while improvements are already under way to many roads.

The main roads from Nairobi to Kisumu and Kitale make it easy to reach western Kenya in a half-day's drive. So visitors with limited time could select one of the excursions below and complete it in two or three days. All the excursions listed here can of course also be tackled in reverse.

Suswa and Narok

The exit from Nairobi is on the paved A104 road to Naivasha and Nakuru. From the capital, the road climbs steadily through small-scale Kikuyu farming country until, after 40 km. (24 miles), it reaches the Limuru intersection. Here, the left exit should be taken to Narok, which leads down the face of the escarpment in a series of hairpin bends. There's a chapel at the foot of the escarpment. Five km. (three miles) on from the chapel, our circuit route turns left on to the B3 to Narok. This is a good paved road which passes close to the Mount Margaret satellite station and between the two volcanoes of Suswa and Longonot.

The distinctive Mount Suswa volcano (2,500 meters; 7,200 ft.) is accessible in a four-wheel-drive vehicle or a strong saloon car up to the northern rim of the crater where the track forks. The right hand branch leads across the crater floor, where the Masai graze their cattle, past lava flows and steam jets to a sheer moat between 200 and 500 meters (656 and 1,640 ft.) deep. It guards a huge table of lava covered with cedar forest. The left fork leads to a part of the mountain riddled with a complex system of caves or lava tubes. These are up to two km. in length and should only be explored with proper equipment.

Past Suswa, the road runs through dryish country and then, like a roller-coaster, dips and rises over the southern end of the Mau Escarpment to Narok, 140 km. (90 miles) from Nairobi. Narok is the center of the northwestern Masailand and is usually crowded with colorful Masai—the young men, the *moran,* in their striking red-ocher shuka togas, often carrying spears and the traditional short sword, or simi.

The paved section of the road runs out at Narok, but the B3 continues as an all-weather murram road. Just past the hamlet of Ewaso Ngero 18 km. (11 miles) from Narok, the road forks. Our circuit turns left on to the C12, another all-weather dirt road, which leads across gentle savannah hills dotted with manyattas and usually thick with game before eventually reaching the Masai Mara Game Reserve on the Tanzania border. The right fork of the B3 continues on to Sotik and Kericho. However, it also provides good access to the northern game areas of the Masai Mara and a number of lodges.

Good game watching is almost guaranteed in the Masai Mara Reserve. It is particularly noted for its lions, which thrive on the large

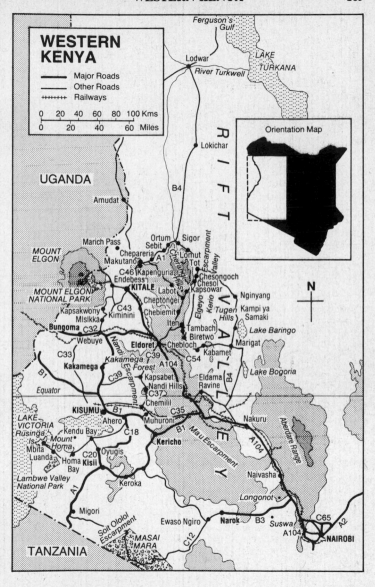

WESTERN KENYA

— Major Roads
— Other Roads
+++++++ Railways

0 20 40 60 80 100 Kms
0   20   40   60 Miles

Orientation Map

N

Ferguson's Gulf
Lodwar
River Turkwell
LAKE TURKANA

UGANDA

Amudat

Lokichar

B4

MOUNT ELGON

Marich Pass
Ortum   Sigor
Sebit
Chepareria   Lomut
Makutano   A1   Tot
Endebess   C46 Kapenguria
MOUNT ELGON   Chesongoch
NATIONAL PARK   Labot   Cheso   Kapsowar
KITALE   Cheptongei
Kapsakwony   Chebiemit   Iten   Nginyang
MIslkka   C43   Kampi ya Samaki
Kiminini   Tugen Hills
Bungoma   C32   Tambach
Webuye   Biretwo   Lake Baringo
C33   Eldoret   Chebloch   Marigat
Kakamega   Kakamega   C39   Kabamet
Forest   A104   C54
C39   Eldama   Lake Bogoria
B1   Kapsabet   Ravine
Equator   Nandi Hills
C37
KISUMU   B1   Chemilil
Ahero   C35   Nakuru
LAKE   Muhuroni
VICTORIA   Kendu Bay   B1   A104
Rusinga   C18
Is.   Mount   Kericho   Mau Escarpment   Aberdare Range
Mbita   Homa
Luanda   Oyugis
Homa   Kisii   Naivasha
Lambwe Valley   Bay
National Park   Keroka   Longonot
A1
Migori   C65
Ewaso Ngiro   Narok   B3   Suswa   A2
TANZANIA   Soit Ololol   C12   A104   NAIROBI
Escarpment   MASAI MARA

RIFT

VALLEY

Cheran Hills
Elgeyo Escarpment
Kerio Valley
Kerio
Nandi Escarpment

concentrations of plains' game. Elephant and buffalo are also common and (counting bats and rodents) about 100 mammal species have been recorded. (See the *National Parks* section.)

Take the Mara River Gate exit at the northwest corner, from where a left turn, on to the C13, climbs up the Soit Ololol escarpment. The C13 continues for a further 65 km. (40 miles) to Migori—gasoline available—where it meets the A1 paved road. Take the A1 north to the little town of Kisii—which has a reasonable hotel—a pleasant drive through well-kept farms.

Kisii and Kericho

Kisii is well-known for its soapstone carvings, produced in large numbers for sale all over Kenya and beyond. But Kisii is otherwise essentially a market-town for the hard working Kisii farms that surround it and is of only marginal interest to tourists, other than as a base for excursions to the Lambwe Valley National Park, Homa Bay, Rusinga Island, Kendu Bay and the pelicanry at Oyugis—all on the eastern shore of Lake Victoria.

From Kisii, a twisting paved road, the B3, leads through Sotik to Kericho, a total of 100 km. (62 miles) through farming country which, after Sotik, gradually gives way to tea estates.

Kericho lies at an altitude of 2,000 meters (6,560 ft.), giving the town a pleasantly cool climate. There is an airstrip 6 km. (4 miles) outside the town. The Tea Hotel, in the town itself (Reservations, Box 75 Kericho, tel. 40), offers comfortable accommodations in the old style. The hotel organizes tours of the tea estates and factories; these are model operations and well worth seeing. Kericho is also a center for the Kipsigis people and a visit to a Kipsigis home can also be arranged through the hotel. The excursion safaris out of Kisumu (see below) could all be tackled from Kericho; the extra 80 km. (50 miles) each way would be compensated for by the cool nights.

Towards Lake Victoria

From Kericho, our circuit continues west along the paved B1. Then, after 20 km. (12 miles) through tea estates and farms, the road drops steeply down to the Kano plains. The distant gleam of Lake Victoria can often be seen during the descent of the 800-meter (2,625 ft.) escarpment. As you descend, so the more humid climate of the lake region becomes more noticeable.

The remaining 50 km. (31 miles) to Kisumu, on the northeast corner of the lake, are absolutely flat. To the north of the road are the largest sugarcane estates in Kenya, while at Ahero there is a complex rice irrigation scheme. This area is the homeland of the Luo people, the largest tribe in the country after the Kikuyu. There are many traditional-style homes close to the road.

The Luo are the principal Nilotic people in Kenya. They number well over one million and are predominantly cattle herders. In the early days they came into conflict with both the Kalenjin and Masai, though neither of these groups was really interested in the low-lying and hot country near the lake. The Luo suffer from a kind of sickle-cell anaemia which renders them more or less immune to malaria, so eventually they were left alone to occupy the lake hinterland. Many of the Luo are fishermen and still use sailing canoes similar to those which Stanley described when he visited Lake Victoria. The tribe has never practised circumcision, but they do have an important series of initiation ceremonies in which some young men submit to the removal of two teeth from the lower jaw in order to prove their bravery.

Kisumu is the principal port of Lake Victoria and the third largest town in Kenya (after Nairobi and Mombasa). At an altitude of only 1,200 meters (3,935 ft.) the climate is much stickier than in Kericho, but Kisumu is a well-laid-out town, superior to many African capitals. It is also the principal town of the Nyanza province and center of the Luo. Accommodations are available principally at the Sunset Hotel, a modern block on the lakeshore. (Reservations Box 215 Kisumu, tel. 41100). There is an airport with services to Nairobi, a railway station, and extensive motor boat services on the lake.

Although this part of Kenya is more generally and heavily settled than elsewhere, there are a number of interesting excursion safaris which can be made in the Kisumu and Kericho area.

EXCURSIONS FROM KISUMU

Lake Victoria, Africa's largest lake and legendary source of the Nile, is, at 63,000 sq. km. (24,300 sq. miles), the second-largest body of fresh water in the world, Lake Superior in Canada being the largest.

One of the most interesting ways to explore it is on board the *Victoria,* a well-equipped vessel that leaves Kisumu once a week for a five-day cruise to Musoma, Mwanza, Bukoba and Port Bell. Several other smaller vessels also sail to Kendu Bay, Homa Bay and other settlements around the lake.

Another way to see something of the lake is to drive along the southern side of the Kavirondo Gulf from Kisumu to South Nyanza. The route takes you along the paved road to Ahero, where you turn south towards Kisii. You might like to stop first at the fishing village of Dunga, however, just east of Kisumu and home port for around 100 sailing canoes. They leave the village at first light, returning with the lake breeze around midday. The fishermen are friendly and as many speak good English it is easy to arrange for them to take you out on one of their long narrow canoes. The canoes are not built for comfort, but the fishermen are good sailors and know the waters of the gulf well. With their large inverted triangular sails and upturned prows, these canoes, reflected in the limpid waters of the lake, make a striking sight.

Ten km. (six miles) on from Ahero, turn right on to the all-weather C19 to Kendu Bay. This route also provides access to many typical Luo fishing villages, where the sailing canoes can be seen returning with their catch.

From Kendu Bay, it is easy to reach Lake Sindi by a left turn down the D219 towards Pala at the junction four km. south of Kendu Bay. Three km. (two miles) down the Pala road, there is a signed turn to the left for the remaining two km. to the lake. The lake, steep-sided and framed by wooded hills, is cradled in a volcanic crater caused by gas eruptions. It is around four sq. km. in area, and has lately become the venue for many thousands of lesser flamingoes. Since it is very rich in the blue-green algae on which the flamingoes feed, it is possible they will become a permanent feature.

Returning to the main road, it is a further 27 km. (17 miles) to Homa Bay. The route skirts the foot of Homa mountain, and affords lovely views of the bay with the Ruri Hills in the background. The town is the administrative center for the district and has regular motor-boat sailings to Kisumu. There is an airstrip nearby and a small hotel. From Homa Bay, the coastal road continues to Luana and Mbita where there is a chain ferry for cars to Rusinga Island.

An expedition in 1984, led by Alan Walker and Richard Leakey, discovered one of the richest fossil sites uncovered for many years. Thousands of fossilized bones of *Proconsul africanus,* thought to have a central role in the course of human evolution, were found. Already famous for earlier digs, Rusinga is now something of a shrine for the local Luo people, being the site of the grave of Tom Mboya, a leading minister of independent Kenya.

Just south of Rusinga Island there is the tiny uninhabited Mbasa Island, where there are plans to build a lodge. This area is rich in birdlife, especially sunbirds, unusually prolific here as a result of the abundance of aloes on which they feed.

Bird Sanctuaries Around Kisumu

Heronry. Three breeding colonies can be visited near Kisumu. The most interesting of these is the "great heronry near Kisumu"—to quote Sir Frederick Jackson who visited it in 1901. Hundreds of nesting pairs of many species gather here and create an extraordinary spectacle, one of the most rewarding sights in Kenya for the ornithologist.

African spoonbills, sacred ibis, yellow-billed storks, cormorants and open-billed storks may all be seen nesting side by side in the same tree. Black-headed heron, great white egret, cattle egret and yellow-billed egret are also normally present, though the number of birds and proportion of species vary from year to year. The nesting period coincides with the long rains, beginning in March or April, and continuing until July. Outside this period, however, there are no birds.

The heronry is off the road 11 km. (seven miles) from Kisumu on the Kericho–Kisii road, but it is rather hard to find. The best bet is to ask for directions when you see the road sign: KSI 119-KER 78.

Ibisery. There is also an ibisery, close to Ahero, where hundreds of sacred ibis breed during the rainy season. Five km. (three miles) west of Ahero—16 km. (10 miles) from Kisumu—a good murram road turns south. A further five km. on, it turns right at a market. Continue on for about two kilometers and the nesting birds can be seen on the left-hand side of the road. The birds are used to people and, with as many as 30 nests in one tree, photography is rewarding. 100 meters beyond the ibisery there is an irrigation canal which contains the irrigation waters for the extensive rice scheme here. Indeed, much of the area around Ahero is irrigated, giving rise to the large numbers of water-birds to be seen, including lesser flamingoes, as well as some non-water birds such as crowned cranes.

Pelicanry. The pelicanry near Oyugis, 70 km. from Ahero down the Al to Kisii and about 20 km. (12 miles) from Lake Victoria, has a completely different season, running from August to March. The best time to visit is between October and January. Here the pink-backed pelicans nest in large fig trees, and there is a continuous coming and going as adult birds bring food from the lake for their young.

Kakamega Forest and the Nandi Hills

This is the only forest in Kenya which is West African in character—a tropical rain forest, in other words—and its flora and fauna are of immense interest to scientists. It lies a little to the east of the Al between Kisumu and Kakamega, north of Kisumu. Driving from Kisumu, there are good views of Lake Victoria as you climb the western end of the Nyando Escarpment. 40 km. (25 miles) from Kisumu—ten km. (six miles) south of Kakamega—turn east along a murram road—the C39 —which soon reaches the forest. Accommodations at the neat but unfurnished Forest Rest House can be booked in advance at the forestry department in Kakamega.

Colobus, blue and red-tailed monkeys can all be seen with ease, and since there are no dangerous animals it is extremely pleasant to wander through the trees on the network of paths. The forest is also of great ornithological interest and although many of the unusual species need an expert eye, the great blue turaco, African grey parrot, joyful green-bul, and blue-headed bee-eater are fairly conspicuous. Butterflies are abundant and a delight as they flit among the great trees.

Having explored the forest, you can either return directly to Kisumu or take a more roundabout route back by continuing on the road through the forest and on to Kapsabet. The latter choice offers good views of the Nandi Escarpment, while from Kapsabet there is a paved road—the C37—through tea and coffee estates to the little township of Nandi Hills. From here the road sweeps down the spectacular and beautiful Nyando Escarpment, giving splendid views of the valley be-low. It then passes through the sugar estates around Chemilil, the most important in the country.

A right turn at the intersection just after the Chemilil Sugar Factory leads to the C34 and an easy drive along the excellent paved road back to Kisumu. The C34 skirts the foot of the Nandi Hills and passes close under the impressive peak from where, according to legend, wrong-doers were hurled to their deaths.

Alternatively, it is equally easy to return to Kericho from the Sugar Factory if you turn left to Muhuroni. Then, two km. past the Muhuroni Sugar Factory, there is a right turn on to a good murram road which in turn joins the B1 heading for Kericho.

Luhya Country and Kitale

The next leg of our circuit is north from Kisumu and Lake Victoria through Kakamega to Kitale, in all 160 km. (100 miles) from Kisumu. Again, take the A1 north up the western edge of the Nyando Escarp-ment. The equator is crossed soon afterwards. From there, you enter the undulating lands of the Luhya, strewn with granite boulders. Luhya is in fact a generic term for the 18 tribes, or more, of Bantu people, totaling in all more than one million, who live northeast of Lake Victoria. Many families can trace their genealogy back more than 500 years (over 20 generations). Luhya legend has it that they migrated into their present territories from Egypt and the Sudan about 250 years ago; earlier, that is, than the Luo, who eventually settled further south. Like the Luo, however, they have a complex series of initiation ceremonies, which remain important events in the lives of many Luhya. Most of the sub-tribes practise circumcision, but some also remove two teeth from the lower jaw, again like the Luo.

Kakamega, 50 km. (30 miles) north of Kisumu is soon reached. Today a thriving center, it started life 50 or more years ago as a gold rush town, and indeed small-scale prospecting continues in the nearby hills.

Continuing north to Webuye (formerly Broderick Falls), there are good views of the Nandi Escarpment. Webuye, 20 km. (12 miles) east of Bungoma, lies on the main Nairobi–Kampala road. In addition to being the site of a paper mill, it boasts a tourist hotel. From Webuye, a good all-weather murram road leads through Lugulu and Misikhu, with Mount Elgon increasingly prominent on the left, to Kitale.

Kitale, at an altitude of 1,900 meters (6,230 ft.), lies in the heart of the magnificent farming country of the Trans-Nzoia district. The town has an airstrip, the most northerly railway station in Kenya, an interesting and rapidly developing museum, the Kitale Hotel (Reservations, Box 41 Kitale, tel. 41 116), and the Country Club (daily membership for Shs. 20/-). The town is an excellent base from which to make excursion safaris into the astonishingly beautiful country of northwest Kenya, an area well off the normal tourist routes.

EXCURSIONS FROM KITALE

These journeys are through remote semi-desert country. In dry weather the tracks are perfectly all right for a strong saloon car, but there are few service and filling stations. As usual, wet weather makes these routes hazardous and it is probably best to travel in convoy.

The west Turkana safari we describe below can be done in one hard day's drive from Kitale direct to the full-service lodge at Ferguson's Gulf. For the two-day safari to the Cherangani Hills and the return from western Kenya via Lake Baringo, it is necessary to have camping equipment.

The Cheranganis

Our first two excursion safaris are to the Cherangani Hills, 80 km. (50 miles) long and 30 km. (18 miles) wide, and lying to the east of Kitale. They rise in places to more than 3,300 meters (10,825 ft.), and are the only range of "fold" mountains in Kenya. Their rugged and spectacular scenery makes them among the most scenic of Kenya's mountain regions, yet they remain little-visited.

Perhaps the most startling of the Cherangani landscapes is found on the range's eastern side, at the Elgeyo Escarpment which drops from 3,000 meters (9,840 ft.) to 1,000 meters (3,280 ft.) in little more than six km. The upper slopes of the main range are clothed with bamboo, magnificent montane forest and the strange ten-meter (32-ft.) high plants of the equatorial moorlands.

The hills are also home to many animals and a profusion of birds. Indeed the whole area, with its widely differing habitats, supports a large number of species.

The colorful Pokot people provide a further attraction. In spite of their similarity to the Nilo-Hamitic Turkana, the Pokot are in fact a Kalenjin tribe with a different language and important differences in customs. Like other Kalenjins, they practise circumcision as part of an important series of initiation ceremonies.

Many of the Pokot are cattle herders, but those who live on the Cherangani hills and on the Sekerr range grow crops on carefully-terraced hillsides. These hills are obviously more fertile than the semi-desert plains, an advantage that is further consolidated by an effective irrigation system. These irrigation channels are something of a mystery, for they seem to have already existed when the first Pokot moved in.

Perhaps because of close contact with their neighbors, the Pokot style of dress is similar to the Turkana. There are differences, however; in addition to the coiffure of matted and dyed hair, for which they also use a neck stool, many Pokot men wear elaborate and colorful bead necklaces similar to those worn by Masai women. Many of the men carry bows and arrows instead of spears and they also carry the wrist and finger knives of the Turkana. Pokot women wear their hair longer than their Turkana neighbors, and wear more colorful necklaces. In the past they have often been called the Suk, but this is really the name of a region and the people themselves should be called Pokot. They are friendly and more forthcoming on first contact than the more dour and taciturn Turkana.

First Cherangani Safari. Our route into the Cheranganis from Kitale is along the all-weather C46 to Makutano, 40 km. (30 miles) from Kitale. Five km. (three miles) after Makutano, there is a left fork for Ortum and Sigor. From this junction, the road twists and turns as it descends 500 meters (1,640 ft.) to Chepareria, leaving the farming country behind and entering an attractive stretch of forest which continues 25 km. (15 miles) to Sebit.

After Sebit, the road travels alongside the Muruny River with the Cheranganis rising abruptly on the right, sending down spurs and ridges into the valley for all the world like the Cumberland hills in the north of England. At Ortum there is a Catholic mission with hospital, school and pretty stone-built church.

North of Ortum, the Muruny River carves its valley deeper and the narrow road crosses several fords where streams run off the hills to swell the river's flow. To the north, the Sekerr Range becomes more prominent as river and road turn east to dart through the narrow defile of the Marich Pass. This is an attractive place, with the cool, clear waters of the river splashing over pools and boulders between the steep slopes of the surrounding hills.

Emerging from the pass, the road reaches the suspension bridge over the river which gives access to Lokichar and Lodwar (for the west side of Lake Turkana). Leaving the suspension bridge on the left, the route turns south to the village of Sigor—a Pokot market center. From the market there is a good view of the summit of Sekerr to the north. This is a sacred mountain and the dead are buried facing its summit.

Two km. south of Sigor the road crosses the Weiwei River, where there is an attractive campsite on the north bank under large fig trees. The river water is clean—although it is wise to boil it before drinking it—and deep enough to swim in. The entrance to the campsite is about 300 meters north of the ford across the river. A night or two here is recommended. The visitor may then explore the surrounding country-side which presents interesting contrast between the dry arid bush of the wide and spacious valley floor and the steep and verdant flanks of the hills.

From Sigor the road continues to skirt the foot of the Cherangani Hills through the tiny villages of Lomut, Chesogon, and Cheblil to Tot. From Tot there is a road over the Kito Pass to Nginyang and Lake Baringo, which is an alternative way of returning to Nairobi via Naku-ru. However, our chosen route continues south to Chesongoch with the towering Elgeyo Escarpment forming a dramatic backdrop.

From Chesongoch, there is a steep and rocky road up the escarpment to Chesol, perhaps the most spectacular road in Kenya. The climb was used for a dramatic sequence in the film *Living Free*. The road can be negotiated in a saloon car and provides views across the Kerio valley to the Tugen hills. From the top at Chesoi the road becomes much easier and continues through natural forest with magnificent trees up to 30 meters (98 ft.) high. South of Chesoi are the villages of Kapsowar and Cheptongei.

From here the quickest way to Kitale is to turn northwest and go via Labot and Kapcherog, but you may prefer to go to Chebiemit through more fine forest and then on south and west through increasingly rich farming country to the town of Eldoret.

A further alternative, which avoids the very steep climb from Che-songoch to Chesoi, is to continue south along the Kerio valley for another 65 km. (40 miles) and then climb the escarpment through Biretwo to Tambach. This ascent also gives magnificent views, but is easier on the car, and nerves. The Torok waterfall cascades down the cliffs on the escarpment and the blue waters of little Lake Kamnarok can be seen gleaming on the valley floor with the Tugen Hills beyond.

Second Cherangani Safari. This exploration of the Cherangani Hills follows the same route out of Kitale as our first safari until the little village of Makutano, 40 km. (30 miles) from Kitale. From Makutano, turn right towards Kabichbich and Labot at the intersection five km. (three miles) outside the village.

The route then zigzags steeply to Chepkono and continues along the ridge of the hills—the summits bare and rocky, the valleys to either side full of dense vegetation. To the northeast, range after range of hills emphasize the length of the Cheranganis.

The road passes close to the summit of Kipsait (3,000 meters, 9,840 ft.) and drops towards Labot where there are patches of cultivation.

From Labot, a track leads northeast. In dry weather this can be negotiated by four-wheel drive vehicles and gives access to the peak of Kalelaigelat (3,340 meters, 10,960 ft.) and the northern end of the range. This is a good way into the heart of the hills for those who wish to do some mountain walking or visit the beautiful forests. It is possible to return direct to Kitale from Labot via Kapcherop and the village of Cherangani, a roundtrip of 180 km. (110 miles). It is longer, but more rewarding, to return via Tambach and Eldoret.

Tambach is perched on the rim of the Elgeyo escarpment and provides magnificent views across the Kerio valley to the Tugen Hills in the distance. It is 70 km. (43 miles) from Labot to Tambach via the villages of Cheptongei, Chebiemit, Singore and Iten.

Tambach is located part of the way down the escarpment from Iten. Having enjoyed the view across the valley it is necessary to back-track to Iten before driving across country which becomes increasingly rich farming land as the road nears Eldoret.

Eldoret is a thriving center, reflecting the prosperous farming country which surrounds it. The hotel here is the Sirikwa (tel. Eldoret 31655). From here, it is a fast 56-km. (34-mile) run to Kitale on a good paved road across undulating open country. The rare Rothschild's giraffe can sometimes be seen on the way. This longer alternative is about 260 km. (160 miles) round trip. There is an hotel in Eldoret—the Sirikwa—for those who wish to break the journey.

West Turkana

A journey to Lake Turkana, the biggest alkaline lake in the world, has become fashionable for those who wish to try an adventurous safari through hot, dry country inhabited by nomadic people whose lives are much as they were 100 years ago. The road from Kitale to Lake Turkana—the A1/B4—is now paved right to the Lake Turkana Fishing Lodge at Ferguson's Gulf. The Lodge itself is at the end of a long spit; if you are not expected, signal with your headlights or a mirror

A lion at rest in Amboseli National Park.

The view of Tsavo East National Park from Voi Safari Lodge.

A reflective marabou stork in the Salt Lick Nature
Reserve.

One of Kenya's main vacation attractions is its glorious coastline—seen here along the beach south of Mombasa.

and a boat will be sent out. You can also fly there, though this naturally rules out the interest of the overland trip. In addition to its considerable comforts, the Lodge can arrange boat excursions, such as the four-day trip to Central Island, the Koobi Fora excavations at Sibiloi National Park, and Alia Bay.

The initial stages of this excursion, via Makutano and Orten to Marich Pass, are described in the two Cherangani safaris (see above). At Marich Pass, the route turns left over the suspension bridge and heads north through hot, dry country with the Sekerr range of hills rising to the left. It is 110 km. (70 miles) to the town of Lokichar and a further 80 km. (50 miles) to Lodwar, deep into the lands of the Turkana, a tough nomad tribe.

An alternative route to the one above forks left at Makutano and travels the 300 km. (190 miles) to Lodwar via Kongelai, Amudat and Lokintangala. However, Amudat and 55 km. (34 miles) of the road lie across the border in Uganda and so visitors are advised not to attempt passage unless accompanied by someone with local knowledge and the relevant permissions; from the Kenyan and Ugandan authorities as well as the owner of the vehicle.

Lodwar is a desert outpost on the banks of the normally dry Turkwell River. Most essentials are available, including gasoline. From Lodwar to the Lake Turkana Fishing Lodge at Ferguson's Gulf it is a further 70 km. (43 miles) northeast on the paved road.

The birdlife at Ferguson's Gulf is very rich and varied, with flamingos normally present in large numbers. Another attraction close to the lakeshore is a Turkana fishing cooperative. Here the local fishermen sell their dried fish, most of which is sent to Nairobi and Kisumu. It is to serve this new local industry that the road to Ferguson's Gulf was reconstructed. Some Turkana still use the old method of catching fish with inverted baskets in the shallow waters of the gulf; and the tall naked fishermen silhouetted on the shimmering lake are impressive and photogenic.

However, the fishermen, with their new life-style, are being increasingly detached from the tribe in the hinterland to the west of the lake, whose lives are strictly traditional, and have changed very little from those of their ancestors four centuries ago. These Turkana are of Nilo-Hamitic descent and are nomadic herdsmen. Their livestock is a mixture of cattle, sheep and goats with large numbers of camels in the drier areas. Their main food is milk from the animals. A camel will give two or three times as much as a cow in good weather and will continue to give milk in dry weather when a cow has dried up completely.

Their tribal traditions stress the importance of marriage and individual independence, so that it is the aim of all young men to marry and move away from their father's home—much more so than with the other nomads of northern Kenya. The Turkana do not practise circumcision but, like the Luo and Luhya, have a series of initiation ceremonies in which two teeth are removed from the lower jaw as a test of bravery.

Their traditional ornaments and decorations are distinctive; the men wear an elaborate coiffure of hair matted with clay and dung, usually dyed blue. The style of this coiffure is often elegant, a decoration of feathers and a curved reed adding the final flamboyance. To protect this at night they use a neck-stool as a pillow. This is habitually carried along with their spears and other symbols of manhood.

Wrist and finger knives are also standard equipment for the young warriors. Both men and women wear earrings and lip plugs, to which the women add necklaces made of ostrich eggshells carefully worked into small discs. The traditional leather aprons of the women and girls are still worn, along with decorations of cowrie shells traded from the coast more than 1,000 km. (620 miles) away.

When moving their huts of poles and skins, the Turkana load everything onto donkeys. Often, however, the men move around with the animals while the women remain behind at a semi-permanent manyatta. This will be near a good waterhole, usually dug in a river bed and sometimes more than 10 meters (32 ft.) deep at the end of the dry season. The women grow a few crops near these semi-permanent manyattas when they can, but this is of marginal importance to their survival in comparison to their dependence on their livestock.

Across the Rift Valley

The return trip from Lake Turkana is a straight reversal of our previously described route as far as Marich Pass. From there, an alternative route back to Nairobi is possible. Although the roads on this alternative route are mostly roughish murram, they can be tackled in any reliable saloon car in dry weather and make a much more interesting journey than that on the paved road back to the capital via Kitale and Eldoret. This route can also make a convenient end to several excursion safaris, including the Cherangani Hills and the west Turkana excursion: at Marich Pass turn left and head south through Sigor, Tot and Chepkam. Each of these could lead to the foot of the Elgeyo Escarpment just below Tambach—southeast of Kitale—and so our route description begins at that point.

From the foot of the escarpment below Tambach, a road leads across the Kerio Valley through attractive dry country relieved by groves of acacia. The landscape is also dramatized by enormous termite mounds, many with ventilation chimneys as high as five meters (16 ft.). They are among the tallest in the country. Here and there in the acacias there are hollowed out tree trunks placed in the trees to attract a nest of bees. If the trick succeeds, the bees are later smoked out for their honey.

In the middle of the valley the road crosses the spectacular Chebloch Gorge. Here the river glides between sheer walls of rock no more than five meters (16 ft.) apart and perhaps 20 meters (65 ft.) high. Downstream from the gorge the river widens out over sand and gravel banks where, curiously, the local people still prefer to wade the river than use the bridge.

Soon after crossing the bridge, the road zigzags up to the Tugen Hills with fine views back across the valley to the Elgeyo Escarpment and the Cherangani Hills. On the summit of the Tugens is the little town of Kabarnet which has a hospital, a secondary school and where essentials, including gasoline, may be purchased. From Kabarnet a scenic road runs along the crest of the Tugens affording wonderful views to east and west.

The Tugen people are of the Kalenjin group. They speak the same language as the Nandis and Kipsigis and share many of the same traditions. They are all Nilo-Hamitics and basically pastoralist, although the Kalenjin are now diversifying into millet and maize. In the past they were fierce warriors and were one of the few peoples to have been consistently successful in fights against the Masai.

The Nandi also opposed the invasion of the British more vigorously than any other group at the beginning of the century. When the railway was nearing Kisumu, the work was considerably delayed by the Nandi who stole the rails to make spear heads and the copper telegraph wires for ornaments. Many of their old customs are still practised, including the long series of initiation ceremonies. These last several months and include circumcision along with much instruction in the traditions and customs of the tribe.

Beer parties are an important part of their social lives; beer made from millet is drunk from a central pot through tubes between two and three meters long (six to ten ft.) and made from the rogaret creeper. A public beer party, or *kokwet*, is a popular occasion but drunkeness is frowned upon. At these parties there is a strict code of behavior; people are expected to speak one at a time and the host acts as chairman.

The old pride in success at war is now replaced by an even wider success in sport, for many of Kenya's world-famous Olympic athletes come from these rough highland peoples.

Lake Baringo

Out of Kabarnet, it is possible to continue south along the Tugen Hills to Eldama Ravine and then along the C55 to Nakuru. This is a very scenic route, but it misses lakes Baringo and Bogoria (Hannington) which can be reached by continuing east from Kabarnet.

On this route, a rather rough road descends the rugged Tugens to reach the village of Marigat, which is in the center of an area which has suffered from overgrazing, mainly by goats. Yet its bleak and barren nature gives it a rugged beauty.

A left turn at Marigat makes a gentle, 20 km. (12 miles) descent to the lake, brown with silt but nonetheless scenic with its pattern of islands and extensive reed beds backed by the eastern wall of the Rift Valley.

There are several alternatives for accommodations. Lake Baringo Club (Reservations, Box 47557 Nairobi, tel. 331635), a well-run Block hotel, offers full service and has more elegance than might be expected so far off the beaten track. Visitors not staying the night are required to pay for day membership. At Kampi ya Samaki (Camp of the Fish) there are self-service cottages and an organized campsite. Jonathan Leakey, son of L. S. B. Leakey (the well-known anthropologist), has a snake farm at the camp. The snakes are milked for their venom, which is used in the manufacture of serums and other medicines. Visits to the snake farm, where baby crocodiles are also kept, can be arranged.

From here, a boat named the *Islander* takes visitors to Ol Kokwa Island in the middle of the lake, site of the luxurious tented Island Camp (Reservations, Box 42475 Nairobi, tel. 25641). The island is about two km. across, and is in fact an extinct volcano with hot springs and sulphur deposits. It rises to a height of about 50 meters (165 ft.). At the other end of the accommodations scale (for completely self-contained parties), there is a lovely place to camp three km. north of Kampi ya Samaki.

Hippo and crocodile are to be found in the lake but seem not to detract from the activities of either the local fishermen or waterskiing visitors. The birdlife in the area is tremendous, with over 400 species recorded. Among the waterbirds are a large nesting colony of Goliath herons, while nesting on the basalt cliffs just behind Kampi ya Samaki there is a pair of Verreaux's eagles. Kingfishers and Madagascar bee-eaters flit along the shores of the lake watched over by the majestic fish eagles; shrikes, weaver birds and the magnificent Red bishop are found in the nearby acacia woodland. Some of the islands have natural gardens of desert roses—*Adenum Obesum*—spectacularly beautiful in bloom.

Lake Bogoria

A compulsory excursion from Lake Baringo is to the magnificent Lake Bogoria (formerly Lake Hannington) National Reserve, 40 km. (25 miles) to the south. It is, for some, the most beautiful of Kenya's Rift Valley lakes. From Lake Baringo, take the B4 to Nakuru, turning left at the signpost for the Reserve just beyond the Marigat turning, from where it is a further 19 km. (12 miles) to the lake's northern shore.

The craggy Laikipia Escarpment rises abruptly for 1,000 meters (3,280 ft.) from the eastern shore of the lake, making a dramatic backdrop for the thousands of flamingos, pelicans and many other species of migrant water birds. At Maji Moto, midway along the 17-km. (ten mile) western shore, natural hot springs spout fountains of boiling water up to four meters (13 ft.), and campers can have unlimited supplies of hot water—and boiled eggs cooked free! Early in the morning, thick clouds of steam form above the springs, beautiful in the dawn light as the sun rises over the escarpment.

Zebra, klipspringer, Grant's gazelle and Chanler's mountain reedbuck can all be seen around the lake and this is also one of the very few places in Kenya where there is a good chance of seeing greater kudu, one of the most magnificent of all the antelopes.

There are no permanent accommodations yet at Bogoria, you can camp at designated lakeside sites.

To Nakuru and Mount Elgon

The B4 from Lake Baringo to Nakuru runs past sisal estates which gradually give way to ranching and farming country. This excellent road is paved all the way and gives extensive views of Lake Nakuru with its pink rim of flamingos. Nakuru is 120 km. (75 miles) from Lake Baringo, and no more than two-and-a-half hours from Nairobi on the paved northern circuit highway.

Mount Elgon

Our final Kitale-based safari is to Mount Elgon on the Ugandan border, though the trip can also be made from the Mount Elgon Lodge in Mount Elgon National Park. (See the *National Parks* section for details.)

Mount Elgon is volcanic in origin, detached from the other mountains of the region. The diameter of its base is enormous—far greater than that of Kilimanjaro—indicating that in its youth it must have been extremely high. Today, after centuries of erosion, it is a still-impressive

4,300 meters (14,110 ft.) and provides some magnificent mountain walking country. There are plenty of crags in the crater area where serious rock climbers can find much to interest them, but the mountain is principally a high-level walk, offering glorious views and a luxuriant growth of the strange plants unique to equatorial mountains. Giant heathers, groundsels and lobelias, everlasting helichrysums and other flowers all flourish here in greater profusion than on the better known Mounts Kenya and Kilimanjaro.

There are several ways of reaching the summit, but the most convenient at present is through Kapsakwony on the southeast side of the mountain. From Kitale, take the C43 through Kiminini towards Webuye. After 42 km. (26 miles)—well before reaching Webuye—there is a right turn to Kamakoiwa on the C42 which leads to Kimilili. After another six km. (before reaching Kimilili) a right turn leads to Kapsakwony.

From here an earth road continues up the mountain through extensive plantations, natural forest and bamboo. With luck, Sykes or even colobus monkeys might show themselves. In a sturdy car, or with four-wheel drive, it is possible to reach the tiny settlement of Labot which is well into the moorland zone, an area rich in giant heathers, heaths and myriads of wild flowers. After a further eight km. is a mountain hut. This can be reached with a four-wheel drive vehicle, but most visitors leave their car lower down and walk up.

The hut, a clean wooden building, contains a locked chest with basic cooking and lighting equipment. Bookings are made with a local warden who lives about one km. downstream and will normally appear to unlock both hut and chest for bona fide visitors.

The hut is at 3,650 meters (11,975 ft.), so the climb to the rim of the crater (4,300 meters, 14,110 ft.) is not particularly arduous, though it is very rewarding. A track up the moorlands above the hut passes through fields of flowers and forests of giant senecio groundsels. Higher up, the track winds through towering cliffs and past a mountain lake (not shown on the map) before climbing abruptly to the summit of Lower Elgon.

The true summit is on the Ugandan side, six km. (four miles) round the rim of the crater. Energetic walkers could reach it in a day and return to the hut, but it is a mere 20 meters (65 ft.) higher and most visitors are content to reach Lower Elgon and enjoy the magnificent views and strange mountain plants.

The crater is over ten km. (six miles) across, and is a natural plantation of giant groundsels set amongst tussocks of montane grasses sometimes two meters (six ft.) tall. The streams in the crater drain out through the Suam Gorge, a spectacular breach in the volcano wall. Hot springs at the mouth of the gorge testify to the volcanic origin of the mountain. From the summit of Lower Elgon it is usually possible to see Kadam (3,080 meters, 10,105 ft.) to the north and the Cherangani Hills (3,100 meters, 10,170 ft.) to the northeast. On a good day Lake Victoria can be seen to the south with Mount Homa and the Ruri Hills on the south side of the Kavirondo gulf 170 km. (105 miles) away.

Another way to ascend Mount Elgon from Kitale is via Suam to the peak of Koitoboss (4,250 meters, 13,945 ft.). The route is along the C45 to Endebess 15 km. (nine miles) away. A murram road leads off right and after another ten km. (six miles) turns left, running up the mountain past the Suam sawmills. The car is left at the top of the track and a footpath leads to the crater rim to the north of Koitoboss. There is no hut on this route, but a good bivouac cave is just off the right of the path as it reaches the rim of the crater.

To reach the craggy and impressive summit of Koitoboss, traverse along its foot inside the crater before climbing to the peak from the southern side.

Visitors should be prepared for cold weather on Mount Elgon. Although there is no permanent snow, there are frequent frosts, and, during the rains, snow showers can be expected around the summit. Anyone with a bronchial infection should not attempt Mount Elgon because of the hazard of pulmonary oedema and it should be remembered that although there are no mountaineering difficulties, the peaks of Mount Elgon are nonetheless remote and lonely.

RETICULATED GIRAFFE

EAST TURKANA SAFARI

North to Sibiloi, East to Marsabit

This is still an explorer's safari, not much developed in terms of visitor facilities, human settlement and landscape since the march of the Hungarian Count Samuel Teleki von Szek and his Austrian chronicler, Ludwig von Hohnel, in 1887. They reached the northernmost lake of the Kenyan Rift after great hardship, changing its name from Embasso Narok to Lake Rudolf, in honor of the patron of the expedition, Crown Prince Rudolf of Austria. Today, of course, the lake is known as Lake Turkana. A smaller lake to the northeast, on the present Ethiopian border, was also renamed by the explorers, who changed its name from Embasso Ebor to Lake Stephanie, after Rudolf's consort.

Since then, a road has been consolidated along the old camel tracks of the Samburu and Rendille nomads. Unless there has been rain, a sturdy saloon car can undertake this route, provided you are equipped to deal with soft sand luggas, occasional screes of lava rock and break-downs. However, a four-wheel-drive vehicle is nonetheless strongly recommended, with an extra spare tyre. And in remote areas, it is a good idea to travel in convoy. In addition, road conditions should be checked en route with the police and game department authorities.

We describe this safari in a clockwise direction, starting at Nyahuru-ru (Thomson's Falls) and rejoining the Mount Kenya circuit at Nanyu-ki. The trip can, of course, be reversed. There is little in the way of quality accommodations on the way—only at Maralal, Loyengalani and Marsabit—so it is essential that individual travelers carry tents, as well as adequate food, water and gasoline. The motoring organizations —try the AA—or experienced tour operators in Nairobi will advise on what precisely should be taken.

Allowing side excursions, including a visit to Sibiloi National Park on the east shore of the lake, the circuit could well involve 1,500 km. (930 miles) and take a minimum of seven days. It is an arduous "Jour-ney to the Jade Sea," but author and naturalist John Hillaby, among many others, considers it the most interesting and romantic safari in Kenya.

Marmanet

Shortly after Nyahururu, the murram road passes through the south-ern fringe of the Marmanet Forest, into which there are two possible deviations to the left. The forest contains mainly red cedars (or giant juniper), a hard wood, impervious to insects, and used extensively for building and making pencils. According to thirsty travelers, the trees have a strong smell, similar to gin and tonic.

Beyond the forest is a stretch of rich, well-watered ranch country extending to Rumuruti, which, though little more than a road junction serving the local farms, has a pleasant country club, a Post Office and police post. North from Rumuruti, the road runs parallel to the eastern edge of the Rift Valley, cutting through dry bush towards Maralal.

Ninety-six km. (60 miles) north of Nyahururu is a road off to the left, the D370, which leads down the eastern escarpment of the Rift Valley to Lake Baringo. Continuing on, however, the road passes the village of Sakuta Lol Marmar, where herds of cattle are brought to a series of large pools, and heads to Kisima.

The Mathews Range

At Kisima, it is possible to cut short the journey north and return to the main Mount Kenya circuit by taking a right turn. This is the main northern route across the Samburu National Reserve and to

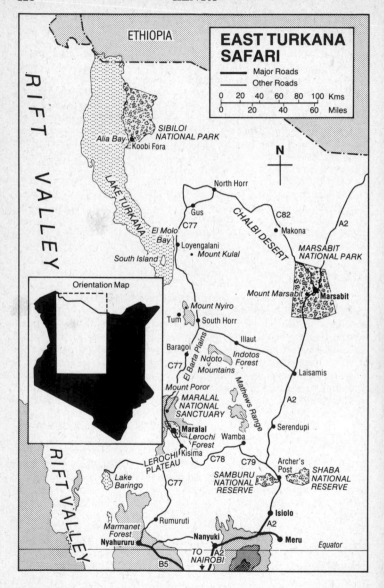

EAST TURKANA SAFARI

— Major Roads
— Other Roads

0 20 40 60 80 100 Kms
0 20 40 60 Miles

ETHIOPIA

RIFT VALLEY

SIBILOI NATIONAL PARK

Alia Bay
Koobi Fora

LAKE TURKANA

El Molo Bay

Loyengalani *Mount Kulal*

South Island

North Horr

Gus

C77

C82

Makona

A2

CHALBI DESERT

MARSABIT NATIONAL PARK

Mount Marsabit

Marsabit

Mount Nyiro

Tum South Horr

Illaut

Baragoi

Ndoto Mountains

Indotos Forest

Laisamis

C77

El Barta Plains

Mount Poror

MARALAL NATIONAL SANCTUARY

Maralal

Lerochi Forest

Kisima

Mathews Range

A2

Serendupi

Wamba

C78

C79

Archer's Post

SHABA NATIONAL RESERVE

LEROCHI PLATEAU

SAMBURU NATIONAL RESERVE

Lake Baringo

C77

RIFT VALLEY

Marmanet Forest

Rumuruti

Nyahururu

Nanyuki

TO NAIROBI

A2

Isiolo

Meru

Equator

B5

Orientation Map

Isiolo. The good murram road winds first over impressive volcanic hills and then across the arid northern plains towards Wamba in the foothills of the Mathews Range. Just before Wamba, the road forks right to weave between the lower hills of the range, passes Mount Lolokwe on the left and joins the A2 highway 24 km. (15 miles) north of Archer's Post.

The Mathews Range, named by Teleki after a helpful General—Sir Lloyd Mathews, then Commander-in-Chief of the Sultan's army in Zanzibar—is a little-explored mountain area, densely forested and full of game. It is accessible in parts to four-wheel-drive vehicles, but it is best to take a local guide or, ideally, a professional hunter.

Maralal

From Kisima, on the main route north, it is a 19-km. (12 miles) drive past the Lerochi Forest on the right to Maralal, an attractive trading center set in hills and attracting Samburu from miles around for cattle trading and general palaver. The area around the township is a game sanctuary. A modest tourist lodge on the outskirts has a strategically-placed waterhole for relaxed game-viewing from the verandah. Camping may be possible on private farms.

Maralal itself is a district headquarters for the Samburu with administrative offices, a police post, various agricultural and veterinary institutions and a forestry department section, where permission may be obtained for camping on Mount Kulal and elsewhere further north. There are *dukas* on the main street for final provisioning for the onward safari. Food, water and gasoline should be checked here as there are few opportunities to replenish stocks later en route to Marsabit. Minor mechanical repairs can also be undertaken at the service stations. Occasionally, the local authorities at Maralal will be able to arrange camel or donkey safaris for visitors (at very moderate rates) if the animals are available.

The Samburu

The Samburu are close relatives of the Masai, and speak the same language—Maa. The two peoples probably divided about 200 years ago, and the name Samburu, meaning Butterfly People, which the Masai gave the break-away group, dates from this split.

Not surprisingly, the way of life and style of dress of the Samburu are very similar to those of the Masai. In addition, the men of the tribe may not marry until they have completed a series of "graduation" ceremonies, and until this time they are under the control of the firestick elders who train them in tribal traditions and disciplines. This training does not finish until the men are around 30. Thereafter, however, polygamy is generally practised by the men.

Lerochi Plateau

With the services of a local guide, an interesting diversion is possible to the gamelands of the Lerochi Plateau and, eventually, to Losiolo, considered one of the most spectacular Rift views in Kenya and well worth the rigors of the detour. It stands at about 2,470 meters (8,100 ft.), with a fine view over the moonscape of the valley floor to the eastern wall of the Elgeyo-Marakwet escarpment. An alternative route to Losiolo is north from Maralal, then west at Poror.

North of the township, the road—the C77—worsens and begins a gentle descent to the scrub desert of the Northern Frontier District. In the hills around Poror are sizeable herds of the shy lesser kudu antelope, which very occasionally, usually in the evenings, may be seen from the road, silhouetted on a bush-covered cairn of rock.

Beyond, on the El Barta plains before Baragoi, it is more likely that you will be able to see wildlife from your vehicle—particularly Grevy's zebra and Beisa oryx. Baragoi is little more than a mission station and an airstrip, and only an intermittent source of gasoline and food. In the old days, it was a fairly important Samburu meeting place with wells that could usually be relied on even in the worst drought.

North of Baragoi, the land is dry, featureless scrub, enlivened only occasionally by large herds of grazing camels.

The Ndotos

Another circuit return to Samburu is possible via a right turn just before South Horr. This is definitely for four-wheel-drive vehicles only, but it passes through the scenic and seldom-visited Ndoto Mountains and Indotos Forest around Illaut. A short deviation on this route to Laisamis on the Marsabit–Samburu road takes in an outstandingly attractive mission station (and airstrip) at Ngoronet, set high in the Ndotos and replete with wildlife, including elephant.

Mount Nyiro

Back on the main route north, you come to the oasis of South Horr, 135 km. (85 miles) from Maralal. It is a tiny mission settlement by the side of a clear stream running down from nearby Mount Nyiro (2,831 meters, 9,285 ft.). There's an interesting detour from here, for four-wheel-drive vehicles only, along a track south of Mount Nyiro which leads to a small village and forest department camp in a lovely watered valley called Tum. If a guide has been collected from South Horr, a hard trek is possible across the Nyiro massif, avoiding the peaks. This is a scenic excursion through glades and ridges which affords views of Lake Turkana. Buffalo, and possibly greater kudu as well, may be seen on the way back to the Horr Valley, where hikers can pick up their vehicles, sent round from Tum.

Lake Turkana

South Horr is the gateway to Lake Turkana. A narrow valley leads to a ridge where Teleki and his party first gazed down at the 3,978-sq.-km. (1,535-sq.-mile) expanse of the Jade Sea. They were all but dropping from thirst and exhaustion, but were ecstatic at the sight and managed to scramble down the formidably-sharp lava barrier of the Serima escarpment to the edge of the lake. But the shimmering invitation of the water, as von Hohnel reported, proved deceptive: "The beautiful water stretched away before us, clear as crystal. The men rushed down shouting but soon returned in bitter disappointment; the water was brackish. What a betrayal!"

Since then the lake has acquired a reputation among travelers of being skittish at best, and outright bad-tempered and malevolent at worst. According to popular belief, the lake will exact a price on anyone intruding on its splendid isolation. Indeed, it is notorious for sudden storms which cut up the otherwise plate-glass surface, wrecking many tranquil lake crossings. On a British expedition led by Sir Vivian Fuchs, two of the party took a small boat onto the lake—no trace of them was ever found.

Mount Kulal lies to the right of the road, standing sentinel at the southeast tip of the lake, and apparently the source of these sudden storms. The mountain stands at the center of an area of low pressure which sucks in the coastal monsoon and becomes, in effect, a giant wind tunnel. Kulal itself is split down the middle and heavily eroded. It is possible to climb to its 2,294-meter (6,525-ft.) summit, but, so far as is known, the knife-edge ridge between the two peaks has never been crossed. There are forest guides available and possible accommodations in forest department huts if prior permission has been obtained from Maralal. On the lower slopes there is a thriving African Inland Church mission which will provide excursion advice and directions.

At the Serima escarpment, back on the main route, the road splits. To the left is an extremely rough descent to the lakeside opposite South Island; to the right, a stony but more easily negotiated track running west of Kulal and along the Balesa Kulal, the latter a sand river—except during flash floods—where local people dig for water. Those in saloon cars will find this section very difficult; it should be approached slowly and carefully to avoid losing a sump on the large lava rocks. In the past, the missions in the area have added considerably to their project funds by providing an anything-but-gratis breakdown service.

The road eventually arrives at Loyengalani, an oasis of palms around a bubbling spring, which erupts in the middle of the swimming pool. This is the luxurious culmination of a long and dusty safari for those who can afford it—a bathe in the warm clear water of the full-service Oasis Lodge pool, followed by a supper of lake fish and a comfortable bed. The lodge also operates a few boats, and big game fishing enthusiasts regularly fly into the Loyangalani airstrip for tournaments or a few hours' casual fishing for giant Nile perch, tilapia and tiger fish. Fishing is also organized from the western shore of the lake at Fergusson's Gulf, and at Eliye Springs.

The perch is the largest freshwater fish in the world. Records in Kenya are imprecise, but appear to be 112 kg. (246 lb.) for men and 75.35 kg. (166 lb.) for women, taken by trolling a 22–36 kg. (50–80 lb.) line. Tilapia up to eight kg. (18 lb.) have been caught, though the abundant tiger fish, which can be landed with light tackle, provide probably the best fight.

A rare mutation of the Nile perch, weighing in at 32 kg. (72 lb.) or more, comes in a bright golden color and resembles nothing so much as a giant goldfish.

El Molo

From the mission and police post at Loyengalani, the route continues north. Take the track to the left leading to El Molo Bay and Lorian Island, both boasting sheltered camp sites and the fascination of Kenya's smallest, and much-studied, tribe. There are less than a hundred of these distinctive El Molo peoples. Perhaps it is not surprising in view of their numbers, but they now appear to be on the point of integrating with the neighboring Samburu.

From El Molo and Lorian Island, the main road turns east and inland to a steep escarpment of loose stones. Once this (unmarked) Khamaed escarpment has been climbed, the road is flat and easily negotiable, leading to an unsigned fork: left to Alia Bay, right to North Horr.

Sibiloi National Park

The track to the temporary headquarters of the new Sibiloi National Park at Alia Bay is still difficult to follow, and offers a bumpy four-hour drive, strictly for four-wheel-drive vehicles only. Plans are afoot to improve the road, and make it the main access to the Park, but in the meantime the best way to get there is by boat (about 75 nautical miles) or by light aircraft.

The Park is still undeveloped for tourists, and is currently noted mainly for the Koobi Fora fossil site of early man. (The Koobi Fora museum here documents the evolution of man; it can only be visited by applying first to the National Museum of Kenya in Nairobi).

Wildlife in the region includes Grevy's zebra, Somali ostrich, gerenuk, Beisa onyx and a sub-species of topi (Tiang).

The Chalbi Desert

From the fork beyond the Khamaed escarpment, the track continuing straight on is stony but passable, and leads to an oasis with the unlikely name of Gus. This is a popular Rendille watering place where, in the right season, it is possible to find herds of 1,000 or more camels.

From Gus, the track seems to disappear in a desert of hard-packed volcanic dust. In the absence of tyre tracks or road to follow, the driver merely aims northeast, until the landmark for North Horr is sighted: a small hill named Dabandabli, which lies to the north of the tiny outpost.

This is principally a mission settlement and clinic among thick clumps of palms and numerous wells. Its particular interest are the large flocks of sand grouse which fly in the mornings and evening. They spend little time at the water, however, having been made wary by a history of shotgun blasts from visiting sportsmen.

Outside the settlement, the road bends sharply southeast and heads towards Marsabit, though the road itself is not always easy to find, and it may be necessary to ask for directions at the police post. And once discovered the track then loses itself again in another part of the Chalbi, but this time within sight of the eastern edge. This is a series of lava ridges in front of Tulu Dimtu and the distant Huri Hills close to the Ethiopian border.

You'll find frequent columns of Boran and Rendille stockmen, leading their skinny herds to some predetermined and remote grazing. A Boran caravan conveys an almost biblical impression, with their flowing white beards and semitic features. The Rendille, on the other hand, are unmistakably African, with bead decoration and little else above the waist. The Rendille are friendly and open to offers from a visitor-photographer. The cheerful trade of *shillingi*—candy for the children, mirrors for the women, and tobacco for the men—is advised since it is offensive to "steal" a picture.

At the edge of the desert, at Maikona, there is a small village and mission, no more than a glimmer of tin roofs from the distance. From here to Marsabit, the landscape is bare flat lava plain, grazed occasionally by Grevy's zebra, oryx and Grant's gazelle.

The Gofs

Three km. (two miles) before Mount Marsabit, a track leads off left for a worthwhile detour to one of the area's numerous *gofs,* local parlance for the craters which pockmark the flatland surrounding Marsabit.

This one is Gof Redo, about a mile wide and 200 meters (655 ft.) deep. It is practically forested with euphorbia, a cactus-like plant resembling a Hebrew candelabra with a blindingly-white sap known as "wolf's milk." It is also noted for eagles, which strike from perches on the crater walls, and strong updraughts, the latter thoroughly enjoyed by the swallows, which streak out into the crater like fighter planes, and by tour guides, who will grab a visitor's hat, hurl it into the crater and watch the victim's face as it sails back like a boomerang. Lesser kudu and, sometimes, rhino congregate on the crater floor.

Marsabit

Marsabit town is a district administrative center, county council headquarters, police post and general meeting place for wanderers from all over the vast northern region. The town boasts gasoline stations, stores, and the equivalent of friendly English pubs.

A well-signposted road leads up the 1,702-meter (5,585 ft.) mountain overlooking the town to Marsabit National Park, the freak 592-sq. km. (230-sq. miles) mist forest, renowned for its big-tusked elephant and other forest wildlife. We describe the park in more detail in the *National Park* section. Acceptable tourist accommodations are available in the Park at Marsabit Lodge, which overlooks a crater lake at Sokorte Dika.

Short excursions from Marsabit town are to three picturesque Rendille and Boran wells: Olandoola, eight km. (five miles) towards Isiolo; Saganta, where the Boran form a human chain to bring up water from the depths; and Korkum, near Kargi, an 80-km. (50-mile) trip east of Olandoola.

The main route from Marsabit back to Nanyuki and home is the all-weather A2 highway, stretching across the Kaisut desert. From Marsabit, the road passes the mission of Logaloga and reaches a bridge across the Milgis Lugga, which until recently would hold travelers for days during flash floods.

Laisamis

Shortly after the bridge, you come to the village of Laisamis, where, it is said, the phrase, "are you married, or do you live in Kenya?" originated after a certain English lord, on learning of his wife's infidelity, dispatched himself during a hunting trip in 1910. His wife later married the handsome white hunter. Less romantically, Laisamis is a possible refreshment stop and the turn off for the scenic excursion to Ngoronet and the Ndoto mountains. This area also includes the newly-gazetted Losai National Reserve.

South of Laisamis there is another bridge, this one over the Merille Lugga, which runs from the Mathews Range (to the west) through a series of gorges and past a thriving vermiculite mine.

Beyond the Merille Lugga, the road continues through Serendupi to the impressive, slab-like mountain of Ololokwe, announcing the impending junction with the main Samburu–Meru route and civilization.

COLOBUS MONKEY

MOMBASA AND THE SOUTH COAST

Mombasa has been accustomed to entertaining visitors, friendly and otherwise, since the site was first heard of in the *Guide to the Erythraean Sea (Periplus Maris Erythraei),* an important Roman mariner's manual of the 1st century B.C. It retains a clearly evident tradition of hospitality today in spite of the most recent foreign invasion—a comparative mass of tourists, since about 1960.

It is fundamentally an ancient port that has been modernized, and a popular stopover for visitors who enjoy the casual good humor of the people, the diversions and entertainments of the city and the sunny, steam-bath atmosphere.

The ambience is Swahili, a cultural amalgam of mainly Arab, Judaean and Bantu African over the past 2,000 years. But there is also a strong European influence, introduced by the Portuguese and, later, by the British.

Discovering Mombasa

Mombasa is a 13 sq. km. (five sq. miles) coral island, flanked by two creeks, Tudor and Kilindini, which provide its natural harbors, and joined to the mainland by the Makupa causeway.

The Old Town grew up beside the northern (Tudor) inlet, but when the harbor's capacity became overstretched as trade grew in the early part of this century, it was spared demolition and redevelopment and the new port was built in the deeper waters of Kilindini on the southern side of the island. So the traditional waterfront area remains as a period piece Arab settlement and a major tourist attraction.

The area is a maze of narrow streets and passages, many impassable to motor traffic, between Arab houses with overhanging balconies and carved doorways. Goldsmiths and silversmiths are the traditional craftsmen of the Old Town, but other traders conduct substantial import-export business despite the unpretentious appearance of their shop fronts.

At the Old Harbor is a square containing the Customs House, fish market and several shops specializing in carpets, chests and brassware brought by dhow from the Persian Gulf. A short distance away is a shop selling non-alcohol based perfumes, presumably for the teetotal Moslem women of the town.

In the harbor there are usually small coastal dhows from Lamu and Somalia at anchor, trading in fruit, dried fish and similar commodities. It is only in the December to April season of the *kaskazi* (northern) trade winds that the large ocean-going booms and sambuks from further afield can be seen. Nowadays, these amount to little more than a picturesque remnant of the dhow fleets of the heyday of the slave trade and ivory plunder, and most of them have diesel engines to supplement their traditional lateen sails.

But even in the quieter months there is plenty to see at the Old Harbor, with fishermen, stevedores and sailors, unconsciously photogenic, and perhaps a dhow Nakhoda offering cups of sweet black coffee in a drawn-out discussion over the purchase of a Persian carpet or a Zanzibar sea chest.

Nearby is the bulk of Fort Jesus, constructed in 1593 by the Portuguese, on a coral ridge guarding the passage to the old harbor. The fort was the scene of many bloody battles between the Portuguese and their various enemies; perhaps the most famous of which was a 33-month siege ending in 1698 with the capture of the 12 remaining defenders only a day before reinforcements arrived. The fort is now a

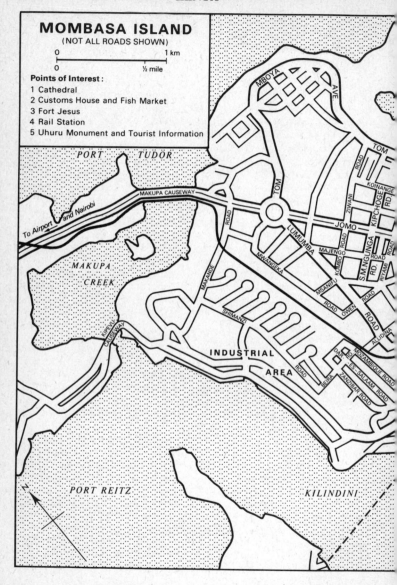

MOMBASA ISLAND
(NOT ALL ROADS SHOWN)

Points of Interest:
1 Cathedral
2 Customs House and Fish Market
3 Fort Jesus
4 Rail Station
5 Uhuru Monument and Tourist Information

museum of coastal antiquities, with a fine exhibit of ceramics and carved doors. It is administered by the National Museum of Kenya, charging a nominal entrance fee.

There is less of tourist interest outside the Old Town. These newer areas of the city reflect Mombasa's rapid expansion in the 20th century, especially after 1930 when the town spilled beyond the confines of the island and onto the mainland.

Along Digo Road are religious buildings of many sects; churches, mosques and Hindu temples. There are administrative buildings dating from early colonial days; street markets for souvenirs, fruit and colorful cloth; and a jostle of pavement vendors of coffee, coconut milk, roasted maize and cassava. By contrast, there are also new office blocks and modern shops stocking a limited range of imported goods.

Moi Avenue links the old and new port areas, and supports most of the travel and shipping agencies, local tour operators, a good selection of curio shops, and the better hotels, bars and restaurants. The highway is spanned by the city landmark of four crossed elephant tusks (actually made of steel), constructed to commemorate the visit of Princess Elizabeth (now, of course, Queen Elizabeth II), in 1952. They locate Mombasa's efficient Visitor Information Bureau and nearby is a pleasant park in which stands the national *Uhuru* (Freedom) monument.

Mombasa is essentially unhurried and casual, and visitors are soon as entirely relaxed as the residents. The right clothes are cool cotton prints, such as the *kikoi* sarong, or *kitenge* shirts and dresses, or the unexpectedly elegant *kanzus,* bought perhaps after a haggle with the laconic (and experienced) shopkeepers of Biashara (Bazaar) Street. For the energetic, Mombasa offers a range of sports, including golf, tennis and all types of water sports, with deep-sea fishing a particular specialty.

At night the city shakes off its lazy daytime air and offers visitors a lively nightlife, from relatively sophisticated dining and dancing at smart beach hotels to the less salubrious atmosphere of strip clubs and sailors' bars. The casino is a relatively recent addition and is found at the Oceanic Hotel on Mama Ngina Drive.

A wide variety of food is available in Arab, Chinese, Indian, Pakistani and European styles. Seafood is usually plentiful and inexpensive.

The city hotels have seen better days and are not as stylish as the best of the beach palaces, but they are generally comfortable and reasonably priced, if a little noisy.

The island itself has no extensive leisure beaches, but the coast north and south of the island is only a short distance away.

Getting Out of Town

Excursions further afield to Tsavo National Park and the Shimba Hills National Reserve are easily arranged through local tour operators or car hire firms. A number of sightseeing trips in the immediate vicinity of Mombasa may interest some visitors (see also the Ocean Safari chapter).

Just over Nyali Bridge towards the north coast is Freretown, the site of one of the oldest churches in East Africa. The settlement was founded for freed slaves by Sir Bartle Frere in the 1870s and many of their descendants still live there.

A right turn off Nyali Bridge leads to a memorial to Dr. Ludwig Krapf, the first Christian missionary (after the Portuguese), and the graves of his young family who died of the fever here in 1844. Nearby is Prince's Park extending round to Mackenzie Point. This was land donated to Mombasa for recreation by the British Dukes of Gloucester and Windsor, and is used once a year for the Mombasa agricultural show.

Straight ahead from the bridge is Nyali Estate, the city's best garden suburb, offering a fine beach, a sports club, a 12-hole golf course, and three of the finest hotels in Kenya.

Another excursion is to the workshop of the Wakamba carvers, situated 100 meters or so along the Port Reitz airport road where it branches from the main Nairobi road at Changamwe. Here are produced many of the sculptured wooden animals on sale in the middle of the town, but the showroom also contains some unusual pieces well worth looking at.

At Mazeras, about 20 km. (12 miles) along the Nairobi road, are the small municipal botanical gardens which contain a wide range of tropical shrubs, flowers and trees, many of which are, in time, used to beautify the city streets, parks and public places.

The mission stations of Rabai and Ribe, established by Krapf and Rebmann in the mid-19th century and rich in historical associations, are situated a few kilometers inland. Near Mariakani, 15 km. (nine miles) further on, the traditional *kaya* or stockaded settlement of the Giriama tribe can be visited with a guide.

THE SOUTH COAST

South of Mombasa lies some of the best coastline in Kenya and a tarred road, the A14, runs close by until reaching the Tanzanian border at Lungalunga. Two main excursions by way of this road for visitors staying in the Mombasa area are to the Shimba Hills National Reserve and the Kisite–Mpunguti Marine National Park.

With its wide, white sandy beaches and turquoise sea this coast has long been a popular location for beach holidays. But although once quiet and unspoiled, over the past 15 years it has been extensively developed for the tourist industry which has served mainly European demand for stay-put packaged beach holidays. This expansion of hotel beds has been confined to the area of Diani, a 20 km. (12 mile) stretch of fine coral sand.

From a luxury base hotel at Diani it is possible to undertake all worthwhile side excursions—to the Jadini Forest, the Shimba Hills or the Kisite–Mpunguti Marine National Park—as day trips. There is also an all-weather airstrip at Ukunda, near Diani, from where there is fast and direct access by light aircraft to the inland game parks.

Shelly Beach

Immediately after crossing Kilindini Creek on the Likoni ferry, there is a sharp left turn to Shelly Beach, where there is a pleasant, inexpensive hotel; the attractive Timbwani campsite and a Children's Holiday Resort, a group of simple family cottages established by a former Liwali of Mombasa, Sir Ali bin Salim. It is possible to scuba dive on the reef, which is exposed for a considerable distance at low tide; but the area does suffer from being close to Mombasa.

The main road runs on through the villages of Ngombeni and Waa, where there are high and wild coral cliffs and interesting bat caves accessible at low tide. Then, after an extensive coconut plantation, a sandy track leads to Tiwi beach. Although there is no formal hotel here, a cottage-style lodge with restaurant and bar is popular and inexpensive, as is the variety of attractive beach bungalows that can be rented. The campsite at Tiwi is among the most popular on the coast.

A short walk along the beach southwards is the mouth of the Mwachema River at Kongo (also accessible by track from Diani police station). There is an old, well-preserved mosque at this first dhow anchorage south of Mombasa. The site is well shaded with baobabs and is a good picnic site.

Diani Beach

This starts at Kongo and is said to be the finest beach in the country. It is certainly the most developed tourist area on the south coast. Its hotels, established campsites and private villas are served by a tarmac access spur from the main A14 coast road. However, with less than a dozen hotels along its 20-km. (12 miles) length, it can hardly be said to be overcrowded. There are proposals for a major resort village development in the area, and already it is becoming more sophisticated, with a casino and a few nightclubs. The hotels provide good food and accommodations; facilities for water sports, local excursions and a reasonable range of evening entertainment.

The beach at Diani is well shaded with pandanus palms and casuarina, the sea is turquoise blue and clean, offering ideal conditions for snorkelling and scuba diving on the outer reef. Jadini Forest, which lies behind the southern end of the beach, is still—despite some signs of human incursions—a largely unspoiled natural woodland, alive with birds and, especially, butterflies. Of the fauna, the most interesting are the black and white colobus monkeys. The forest makes a worthwhile walking excursion from the Diani beach hotels, or a picnic stop off the main route to the many unspoiled beaches further south.

Shimoni

There are no hotels off the main road between Diani and Shimoni, but for those who like isolation from the main tourist scene, there are plenty of attractive palm-shaded sites on which to pitch a tent; for example, at the fishing village of Kinondo, a Mazrui sheikh's 19th-century refuge at Gazi; and at Msambweni, where an old stone ruin is believed by archeologists to be the remains of a slave pen. The beach at Msambweni is particularly fine and almost unknown to visitors.

Further south—and almost on the Tanzanian border—is the village of Shimoni, now perhaps the most popular big game-fishing spot on the Kenya coast. The Pemba Channel Fishing Club offers inexpensive thatched banda-style accommodations, a restaurant, swimming pool, and fishing expeditions in season between 1 August and 31 March. The area is particularly noted for marlin (between December and March) and, beyond the reef, tuna and mako shark. The newly-opened Shimoni Reef Fishing Lodge offers accommodations in six comfortable cottages, with restaurant, bar and lounge built out of an old Arab trader's house. The Lodge specializes in deep-sea fishing and operates expeditions to the nearby Kisite-Mpunguti Marine National Park in converted Arab dhows and glass-bottomed boats, where the goggling is among the finest on the Kenya coast. The area is also well-known for dolphins.

In the Pemba Channel, four km. (two miles) off Shimoni, and beyond the ancient settlement of Wasini Island, is a series of coral gardens, established in October 1973 as the offshore Kisite Mpunguti Marine National Park. However, until the park is developed, together with adjacent accommodations and ocean excursion facilities, a visit to the Kisite Mpunguti coral gardens is for the enterprising, if not intrepid, visitor. This applies also to excursions further south to Vanga on the Tanzanian border, which is totally undeveloped for tourists.

PRACTICAL INFORMATION FOR MOMBASA AND THE SOUTH COAST

ARRIVING AT MOMBASA. Moi International Airport, though able to receive widebodied jets, is still a small-city airport. It offers all the same essential services as Nairobi airport—information desks, car hire offices, hotel-booking agencies—but on a reduced scale.

Transfer to town is by taxi or mini-buses operated by the larger beach hotels. Note, however, that most of the best Mombasa hotels are relatively widely dispersed and are located off the island on the beaches immediately to the north and south.

DIANI

Hotels

Leisure Lodge (E), Box 84383, Diani Beach (tel. Diani 2011). Facing the beach and landscaped with marvelous skill. Elegant rooms, casino, and cave-bar with disco.

Leopard Beach (E), Box 34, Ukunda (tel. Diani 2111). On the beach; excitingly-designed. Great service and pools with a difference.

Robinson Baobab (E), Box 32, Ukunda (tel. Diani 2026/7). Fine hotel high on a coral cliff. Huge grounds and magnificent beach. Many facilities.

Diani Reef (M), Box 35, Ukunda (tel. Diani 2175/6/7).

Diani Sea Lodge (M), Box 37, Ukunda (tel. Diani 2060).

Golden Beach (M), Box 31, Ukunda (tel. Diani 2172).

Jardini Beach and **Africana Sea Lodge** (M), Box 84616, Mombasa (tel. Diani 2021/5). Side-by-side complex of regular hotel and African village. Both with bars, restaurants, sports and gardens.

Nomad Beach Hotel (M), Box 1, Ukunda (tel. Diani 2155). Tented establishment on Diani beach.

Trade Winds (M), Box 8, Ukunda (tel. Diani 2016/2116). Reservations: African Tours and Hotels, Box 30471, Nairobi (tel. 336858). Recommended for slightly oldfashioned and relaxed charm. Many facilities.

Two Fishes (M), Box 23, Ukunda (tel. Diani 2101/2037). Reservations: African Tours and Hotels, Box 30471, Nairobi (tel. 336858). Designed and landscaped to very high standard. Efficient service.

Restaurants

The majority of the better restaurants are in the various hotels. Of them, the following two are of particular interest:

Makaa (Charcoal) Grill. Elegant grillroom shared between the Jardini Beach and Africana Sea Lodge on Diani beach.

Nomad, tel. 2155. African thatch *(makuti)* beachcomber-style restaurant in the Nomad Hotel. Seafood specialties imaginatively prepared.

MOMBASA

Hotels

Outrigger (E), Ras Liwatoni Rd., Box 84231 (tel. 20822). Good view of the harbor. Fine pool. Convenient location by the Yacht Club.

New Carlton (M), Moi Ave., Box 86779 (tel. 23776). Old-fashioned hotel; attractive bar.

Oceanic (M), Mbuyuni Rd., Box 90371 (tel. 311191/314892). Fair-sized hotel with casino, disco and goodish restaurant. Located on the Kilindini cliffs; convenient for golf and beach.

Castle (I), Moi Ave., Box 84231 (tel. 23403). Old-established hotel. Excellent restaurant, reasonably-priced. No pool.

The Manor (I), Nyerere Ave., Box 84851 (tel. 21822). Old, established hotel in the center of Mombasa, opposite the Catholic Cathedral. Restaurant, bars, terrace and parking.

Restaurants

Capri, Ambalal House, Nkrumah Rd., Box 90574 (tel. 311156). International menu with the slant on seafood; airconditioned. Reasonable snack meals in the attached *Hunter's Bar.*

Coral Grill Room, Oceanic Hotel. Standard international menu; snacks available till late to keep the casino's customers happy.

Mistral, Moi Ave., Box 83118 (tel. 24911). Fan-cooled spot with cocktail bar offering reasonable international food.

Tamarind, Cement Silos Rd., Box 85785 (tel. 471747). Just over the Nyali Bridge and probably the best restaurant in Kenya. Moorish decor and great view over the creek to Mombasa help set the atmosphere for superb seafood specialties. Expensive.

NYALI

For Hotels and Restaurants in Nyali see *Practical Information* for *Ocean Safari Circuit.*

SHIMONI

For Hotels in Shimoni see *Park Data* for *Marine National Parks.*

WASINI

Wasini Restaurant (tel. Mombasa 311970). On Wasini Island, close to the Tanzania border, and reached by small dhow. Excellent seafood served Swahili-style (mostly in coconut milk).

 TRANSPORTATION. The railway station, for an old-fashioned up-country safari, is located in the center of Mombasa, as are the bus and taxi facilities for the beaches and beyond, both north and south of Mombasa.

LION

OCEAN SAFARI CIRCUIT

This is the main game-safari and beach holiday circuit, described in an anti-clockwise direction from Nairobi. The route can, however, be reversed and otherwise varied constantly. For instance, many tours go directly down the Mombasa road to Tsavo (West) National Park, cutting out the loop to Amboseli; and Tsavo (East) is often treated as an excursion from Mtito Andei or Voi, avoiding the long murram road on the Sala Gate–Malindi route described here as part of the main circuit. Many tours originate at Mombasa where Moi Airport has been expanded to take the big jets.

There are a number of diversions possible from the main road route, either for places of special interest, or short cuts such as the dry-weather Mombasa by-pass at Mariakani. Each worthwhile excursion or deviation is briefly covered as it occurs on the route.

The circuit is detailed, of course, as a road route, though it is possible to take an interesting and comfortable sleeper train ride part of the way, from Nairobi to Mombasa. All the major tourist centers are accessible by chartered light aircraft from Nairobi, Mombasa or Malindi, and there are scheduled Kenya Airways services to and from Nairobi, Mombasa and Malindi. The main circuit covers possibly 1,600 km. (995 miles)—with a generous allowance for game runs—and the minimum duration should be about seven days if it is to be at all comfortable.

It is the most historic of the main Kenya tourist circuits, covering the old slave caravan and European explorer trails, running parallel to the eventful Mombasa–Lake Victoria railway, and touching dhow ports with a 2,000-year history of trade with Arabia and the East.

To Amboseli

Just outside the city limits of Nairobi, southeast on the all-tar Mombasa road, is the Mombasa Road Gate to Nairobi Park (right) and a few km. beyond, a left turn to Nairobi's Jomo Kenyatta International Airport. A few miles further, at the end of the park boundary, the circuit loops right (southwest) off the Mombasa road at Athi River for 130 km. (80 miles) of fine paved highway to the Tanzania border at Namanga, from where the main entrance to Amboseli National Park is reached.

Athi township is small but important to Nairobi, a result of its Kenya Meat Commission factory and a large cement works. The name derives from a now extinct tribe of dwarf bushmen hunters whom the Kamba people called *Aathi*. Nearby are the Lukenya cliffs, under the lee of the Mua Hills, which is a favorite practice ground for rock climbers. Immediately past Athi is the dry pasture heartland of the Masai. Plains' game traditionally share the grazing with the cattle and zebra; giraffe and gazelle are often seen by the roadside.

At Kajiado, the headquarters of the Masai district of the same name, the railway line which serves the Magadi soda factory crosses the road and there is a large hospital. Five km. (three miles) further on, Kenya Marble Quarries is signposted to the right and can be reached along 12 km. (seven miles) of track into the Toroko valley.

After the Kajiado township the road starts to wind between gentle hills and the grass plains are replaced by thicker thornbush country until Namanga is reached, overshadowed by the squat bulk of Ol Doinyo Orok mountain (2,526 meters, 8,285 ft.). There are two small settlements along the way which act as trading posts for the Masai, who are often to be seen on the roadside.

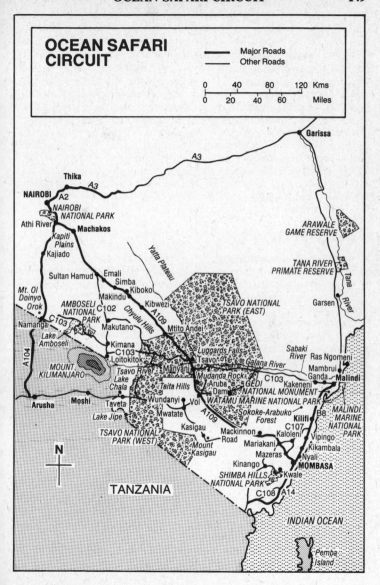

OCEAN SAFARI
CIRCUIT

Major Roads
Other Roads

| 0 | 40 | 80 | 120 | Kms |
| 0 | 20 | 40 | 60 | Miles |

Garissa

A3

Thika
NAIROBI A3
A2
NAIROBI
NATIONAL PARK
Athi River Machakos
Kapiti
Plains
Kajiado
Sultan Hamud Emali
Simba
Mt. Ol Makindu Kiboko
Doinyo C102
Orok AMBOSELI Kibwezi
NATIONAL
C103 PARK Makutano Mtito Andei
Namanga Kimana
Lake C103
Amboseli Loitokitok
A104 Tsavo River Manyani
MOUNT Lake
KILIMANJARO Chala
Arusha Moshi Taveta Wundanyi
Lake Jipe Mwatate
TSAVO NATIONAL
PARK (WEST) Kasigau
Mount
Kasigau

Yatta Plateau

TSAVO NATIONAL
PARK (EAST)

ARAWALE
GAME RESERVE

TANA RIVER
PRIMATE RESERVE

Garsen

Luggards Falls
Tsavo Galana River
Mudanda Rock
Aruba GEDI
Dam NATIONAL MONUMENT
WATAMU MARINE NATIONAL PARK
Vol Sokoke-Arabuko
A109 Forest
Mackinnon Kaloleni
Road Mariakani
Mazeras
Kinango
SHIMBA HILLS Kwale
NATIONAL PARK
C108 A14

Sabaki
River Ras Ngomeni
Mambrui
Ganda Malindi
Kakeneni
C103
MALINDI
MARINE
Kilifi B8 NATIONAL
PARK
C107
Vipingo
Kikambala
Nyali
MOMBASA

Chyulu Hills
A109
Taita Hills

N

TANZANIA

INDIAN OCEAN

Pemba
Island

Namanga

This is a small border market town which makes a good break in the journey before continuing to Amboseli. Petrol is available at two service stations which also perform minor repairs, and refreshments can either be taken at a service station cafe or in the cool and colorful garden of the Namanga River Hotel. There is also what amounts to a small market of Masai stalls selling souvenirs and beadwork.

The border and the road to Arusha are now open after many years of being closed, but the circuit bears left just before the border checkpoint. From here it is 80 flat, dry, dusty kilometers (50 miles) to Ol Tukai, the Park headquarters, center for game runs around Lake Amboseli and location for many of Hollywood's Africa epics, including *Where No Vultures Fly* and *The Snows of Kilimanjaro*—usually only visible in the early mornings and evenings.

Amboseli

The Lake Road detour, signposted right about 15 km. (nine miles) before Ol Tukai, is an alternative to the main track for those who want to get straight into the main wildlife concentration at the usually dry salt basin. This route is extremely dusty for most of the year, and subject to strange shimmering mirages. It should certainly not be attempted when wet.

Until recently, the Masai shared the pocket sanctuary with the wild animals, but have now moved out to new watering points whose construction was financed partly by the New York Zoological Society. Amboseli is also a popular tourist park with easily visible big cats, elephant and plains game strikingly set against a backdrop of Kilimanjaro.

The twin pressures of cattle grazing and heavy visitor use were becoming too much for the delicate ecosystem in the late '60s. It was accordingly raised from Reserve to National Park status in 1973. The more stringent regulations involved help ensure the regeneration of the grassland wildlife habitat.

To Tsavo

The route to Tsavo West heads east out of the Park from Ol Tukai and skirts the lower slopes of Kilimanjaro to a T-junction near Kimana, after 35 km. (22 miles) and turns right.

The colorful Masai market at Loitokitok, where Kenya's Outward-bound School is situated, is an interesting diversion along this road, but

The Triumphal Elephant Tusk Arch on the way in to
Mombasa; *below,* Lamu's colorful market.

The intriguing architecture of Salt Lick Lodge, based on native huts and providing good views over the Nature Reserve.

Above, the skyline of old Mombasa; *below,* the 16th-century Portuguese Fort Jesus, one of Mombasa's main sights.

Part of the famous Treetops Lodge, overlooking the
wildlife of Aberdare National Park.

the main circuit is left off the road to the village about five km. (three miles) from the junction. This is a new, wide, all-weather murram road, straight to the Chyulu Gate of Tsavo (West) National Park—just over 105 km. (65 miles) from O1 Tukai. Just before this gate is a spectacular black lava flow from the volcano of Shaitani ("devil" in Swahili), at the southern edge of the Chyulu Hills, which is believed to have erupted within the last two to three hundred years. The lava appears abruptly as a high black wall of impassable melted rock, but nevertheless the road presents an easy traverse.

An alternative and much slower route—allow six–seven hours from O1 Tukai to Kilaguni Lodge—leaves northeast from Amboseli, crosses the pipeline road leading to Emali at Makutano and winds up into the Chyulu Hills. This route should only be taken in a four-wheeled vehicle. Following their wooded crests for miles, the track provides spectacular views to the east towards the Yatta Plateau (believed to be the longest lava flow in the world) and west towards Kilimanjaro. The hills, which are volcanic and geologically young, are the source of the Mzima Springs in the Park. Their unspoiled beauty makes a visit worthwhile, but Chyulu is also a conservation area and harbors a good quantity of game, including rhino and buffalo. Descending the south end of the hills the road passes Shaitani and rejoins the shorter route at the Chyulu Gate.

The track from this gate leads directly to Kilaguni Lodge, one of the best of Kenya's safari hotels in terms of comfort and wildlife spectacle at a natural waterhole. The usual access to Tsavo West is from the Mombasa road, at the halfway Mtito Andei Gate or, coming up from the coast, at the Tsavo Gate.

Tsavo West

Kilaguni is at the center of the most developed game circuit section of the 20,720 sq. km. (8,000 sq. miles) park, and is perhaps Kenya's most magnificent wilderness. (See page 204.) It is known principally (and controversially) as elephant territory but most of the East African predators, primates, plains' game, birds, aquatic mammals and reptiles are represented in force. Tsavo West (about 7,000 sq. km., 2,702 sq. miles) and Tsavo East (c. 13,000 sq. km., 5,018 sq. miles) are two separate administrative units, but since the game disregards the boundaries, it is gazetted as one park—as big as Wales and one of the largest tracts of land anywhere in the world to have been set aside as the exclusive province of wild animals.

The landscape is totally unspoiled, often beautiful and occasionally wondrous—as at Mzima Springs, where millions of gallons of crystal-clear water daily flow over resident hippo and crocodile.

Apart from Kilaguni, there is the other first-class, full-service Ngulia Lodge, and two pleasant do-it-yourself camps, one at Kitani and the other in the Ngulia valley.

Kitani lies on the exit route to the Voi-Taveta road and there is a choice of three gates.

The Mbuyuni gate is nearest to Taveta (24 km., 15 miles) and the Kenya–Tanzania border, from where a paved road leads to Moshi and Arusha. Nearby Lake Chala is a worthwhile detour off this road and can be reached by turning north shortly before Taveta, on a reasonable track which, after about 14 km. (nine miles), reaches the village of Chala. A left turn just before the village leads to the rim of this beautiful crater lake, and a footpath inside the crater to a ramshackle jetty—a relic of a naval survey party. Nowadays it is used by local fishermen who fish precariously from makeshift rafts, ignoring the crocodiles.

The Murka Gate is further east along the main road and gives access to the southern sector of Tsavo West where, although the roads are maintained, there are no accommodations facilities, except simple self-service at Lake Jipe.

A possible diversion in this area is to Lake Jipe which can be reached through Tsavo Park (West), or by driving south from Taveta through Jipe Sisal Estate. The lake lies under the North Pare mountains and is about 50 sq. km. (19 sq. miles) in area, including adjacent swamps. The north end has been developed for commercial fishing, but the south end inside the park provides slightly alkaline water for large numbers of animals and birds.

The Maktau Gate is nearest to Voi, and is the most convenient exit for those wishing to visit the Taita hills.

Taita Hills

After the dusty drive through the park, the Hilton's striking and luxurious Taita Hills Lodge provides an opportunity for refreshment or a comfortable stopover before moving on to the coast. A few kilometers from this hotel, which has been built in the style of an old German fort, is the associated Salt Lick Lodge, a series of attractive rondavels built on stilts overlooking a game waterhole near the Bura river. The hotel has leased some land as a private game sanctuary.

Close to Mwatate the road becomes tarmac and at the village, a new tarmac road winds up to Wundanyi in the Taitas.

These fertile hills are in sharp contrast to the dry surrounding country, and are intensively cultivated. The Taita people have always been friendly to visitors and the area was one of the first to attract missionary activity (from nearby, Johann Rebmann first saw Kilimanjaro). The Taita also provided supplies and porters for many early caravans.

There are excellent views of the surrounding countryside, and it is possible to walk up the summits of Vuna and Yale; other peaks require rock-climbing skills. There are no tourist-style accommodations in the hills.

Voi

From Mwatate it is roughly 40 km. (25 miles) on to the junction with the main Nairobi–Mombasa road at Voi, which is a main access to Tsavo (East) through a gate close to the Park HQ. An alternative rough and difficult route to the Mombasa highway passes from Mwatate southeast to Kasigau, an attractive isolated peak, and back to join the main highway at Mackinnon Road. But this should only be attempted by those who insist on avoiding tarmac at all costs and prefer the eventful solitude of bush trails.

Voi has a frontier-town look about it, with a dusty main street flanked by unpretentious stores. Until recently it was an essential rest-stop on the Mombasa Road, but today the broad tarmac sweeps past in a wide arc and leaves the town more or less to the residents. The nearest hotel is the luxury Voi Safari Lodge just inside Tsavo (East).

From Voi, the main highway leads east through a region which in pioneering days was called Taru Desert, a bleak arid area dreaded by early travelers. Occasionally there was water at the Bachuma Wells, but otherwise the foot-trekkers had to climb 350 meters (1,150 ft.) up Mount Maungu (or Marungu) to a permanent rock pool. In those days there were no clearly defined tracks, but in 1883 the wealthy British ship-owner Sir William Mackinnon brought in steam rollers and built a road at his own expense. His main work camp is now a truck stop at Mackinnon Road.

Thereafter, the route moves in to the coastal belt, and the featureless country becomes greener until the first palms announce the imminence of the Indian Ocean. Cultivation replaces charcoal-burning as the local *modus vivendi* and the land becomes more populated. The increasing heat and humidity encourages a change to more casual clothes, particularly the colorful sarong of the Kenya coast known as the *kikoi.*

There is a major crossroads at Mariakani, the Kamba word for "arrows." The crossroads is thus a permanent reminder of their battles with the raiding Masai in the 1830s for possession of the waterholes in the area. To the right a good murram road runs due south through Kinango and Kwale to Tanzania. This is a main access route to the Shimba Hills National Park.

Off to the left at Mariakani the C107 murram road via Kaloleni bypasses Mombasa and joins the main road to Malindi just south of Kilifi. This is a dry-weather route and may be closed to all traffic during the rains. It runs through the seldom-visited agricultural hinterland of the Giriama people, noted for their friendliness and entertaining dances.

Back on the main route at Mazeras, just before a long winding escarpment down to Mombasa, is a small botanical garden run by the Mombasa Municipal Council. Nearby is an old ivory-trading market at Kwa Jomvu, where Arab and Asian merchants once exchanged beads for tusks with the Kamba hunters; today it is a roadside tropical-fruit market.

The Coast North of Mombasa

Ahead at Changamwe (and Moi International Airport), the sea is visible. From here it is a short run to Makupa Causeway and the noise and bazaar-bustle of Mombasa Island. The Island itself has no extensive sandy beaches, but on the coastline north and south of Mombasa there is a succession of them. Some are developed for tourists, with first-class hotel, cottage or camp-site facilities, but it is always possible to find a secluded spot, shaded by casuarina or palm trees, with safe swimming and the opportunity for snorkeling inshore of the main reef. The entire beach-line is freely available for public use, though in places it may be difficult to find an access track without crossing private land. But the "natives" are friendly, and almost always offer an informal right of way to a pleasant approach.

The circuit exit from Mombasa Island is via a new toll bridge which offers a fine photographic view back to the old town and ahead to Kisauni and the largest watersports center on the coast. The road straight ahead from Nyali Bridge leads to the Nyali Estate, the smartest of Mombasa's garden suburbs with one of the finest palm beaches on the coast. There is a 12-hole golf course with fairways running alongside the beach, facilities for other sports at the Nyali Club, as well as some of the resort's best hotels.

For the purpose of this main Ocean Safari Circuit, Nyali is bypassed on a left turn immediately after the bridge. The main B8 road is paved all the 119 km. (74 miles) to Malindi. Shortly after the turn off is Freretown which has a church built in commemoration of a freed slave settlement founded by Sir Bartle Frere who negotiated an end of regional slavery with the Sultan of Zanzibar in 1873.

Just beyond the village is a turning to Bamburi Beach, site of the President's holiday State House, and the public Kenyatta Beach 2. This has today been developed and has a large parking lot and changing rooms. There are some hotels in this area catering mainly for package tourism, and several beach cottages for rent. There is also the Bamburi Cement Company behind the road, which rather spoils the scenery.

Just north of Bamburi is the smarter, up-market beach of Shanzu, with hotels distinguished for their striking architecture. Shanzu is rated the best strip of clean white sand between Nyali and Watamu. There are attractive trees running its length, swimming is possible at all tides and the reef is particularly good for coral and fish.

Above Shanzu is Mtwapa Creek, an extensive inlet with areas of mangrove, used for bird watching cruises and water skiing. It is crossed via a toll bridge which, perhaps regretably, has replaced a picturesque old "singing" ferry where travelers used to be hand hauled across by a regular glee club of workers. A kilometer or so beyond the bridge is a track to 15th-century ruins partly excavated in 1972, known as Jumba la Mtwana, the slave master's house. Almost on the beach are the remains of a large mosque and a tomb. Close by is the main settlement, yet to be cleared of thick bush.

The next developed resort beach, a few kilometers north, is Kikambala which has a palm fringed shoreline in the classic postcard style. There are a number of economy hotels and cottages on the beach.

Although there are beaches between here and Watamu, there are few hotels on any of them and Kikambala at present effectively marks the limit of the developed beaches which look to Mombasa rather than Malindi for their services.

Kilifi

The main coast road continues north through extensive sisal plantations at Vipingo to Kilifi Creek. This section is relatively heavily populated. There are cheerful Giriama women in their bustled skirts and men in *kikois* gathered under cashew or mango trees or at impromptu roadside markets along the way.

Mnarani village on the south side of the creek contains some hard-to-find ruins. Nearby is the Mnarani Club—a luxurious hotel which specializes in deep sea fishing and other water sports.

Cruises up the creek are extremely popular, especially among bird watchers who head deep into the inlet for a spectacular colony of migratory carmine bee eaters. The creek is crossed by a 24-hour, free, motor-ferry service. There are often queues at public holidays. Those traveling north can take the chance to visit the serpentarium by the side of the road. Southbound travelers are diverted only by cheerful urchins selling nuts and mangoes for a few cents.

From Kilifi north of the creek the road passes through the fringes of the Sokoke-Arabuko Forest, rich with natural rubber and other indigenous trees, butterflies and birds. It is the last remaining large natural forest area on the north coast. Several tracks lead from the main road to Sokoke and it is well worth taking a little time to explore them and enjoy watching the birds or the shy forest mammals such as the yellow-rumped elephant shrew.

Watamu

Skirting Mida Creek (invisible from the road) the route goes off to the right after 40 km. (25 miles) by a paved road all the way to Gedi and Watamu. Watamu is an idyllic spot for a restful holiday. The beach is glistening white coral sand on the shores of three beautiful bays (Watamu, Turtle and the Blue Lagoon). Swimming is possible at all tides and the water is clear and teeming with colorful fish, since the whole area is inside a marine reserve, and most of it also within the fully-protected Watamu Marine National Park. The emphasis here is on water sports of all kinds, from casual viewing of the coral gardens in glass-bottomed boats to deep-sea fishing, sailing and water skiing. It is also possible to go bird watching in Mida creek or scuba diving in underwater caves, the home of friendly giant grouper (rock cod). Snake safaris or oyster collecting are alternative pastimes at Mida.

With four hotels (and several local bars in Watamu village), there is no shortage of entertainment and Malindi is only 15 minutes away by car for those who feel they need further variety.

Gedi

A popular morning or late afternoon diversion from the Malindi and Watamu hotels is a visit to the local equivalent of Pompeii—the 45-acre ruined town of Gedi. This, with Fort Jesus in Mombasa, was the odd man out of the Kenya national parks system, but is now more logically administered by the National Museum of Kenya.

It is the remains of a prosperous Afro-Arab (Swahili) settlement of medieval origin, complete with a palace, large mosque, three pillar tombs and about a dozen town houses so far excavated. The palace features an audience court, with a bench of justice situated at the east end so that the presidents of the court would be shaded from the morning sun while the accused sweltered before them. The Great Mosque is typical early Kenyan, with a north-south main hall of prayer and a pointed arch in the north wall indicating the direction of Mecca. Chinese and Persian pottery has been unearthed as evidence that Gedi was inhabited in the thirteenth century. A tomb is dated 1399 and the place was obviously prosperous for a century afterwards. Some calamity clearly befell the town in the mid 1500s and Gedi was suddenly abandoned and never reoccupied to the same extent. It could have been the plague or a punitive sacking by the Portuguese, or an invasion of

Zimba cannibals from the south or the fierce Galla from the north—no one knows for sure. There is no evidence of life in the town after 1625.

Around the ruins is a fine old forest of great interest to naturalists, with numerous monkeys, small antelope and the yellow-rumped elephant shrew. Butterflies and birds are prolific, among them a rare swift which nests in the town's disused wells.

Malindi

From the Gedi–Watamu turn-off it is eight km. (five miles) to Malindi airport and a further eight km. to the town itself.

Historically, Malindi is an Arab colonial trading and administrative center. Today it is almost exclusively a tourist resort. Closely juxtaposed are simple Swahili dwellings and western-style hotels; graceful dhows and ski boats; donkeys and smart safari cars; Moslem and Christian; Swahili and a babble of foreign tongues. Everywhere the traditional exists side by side with the new and the unconventional in a happy atmosphere of easy going relaxation.

The town itself is architecturally undistinguished, but nonetheless picturesque. Palm thatched and whitewashed houses jostle together with shops and stalls, surrounding a village green complete with war memorial. The market and fish market by the harbor are colorful scenes of activity; the new mosque stands beside two 15th-century pillar tombs and a church of the same age is nearby. Further away is the Vasco da Gama pillar, surmounted by a cross of Lisbon stone brought by the explorer himself.

To the north of the town, Malindi Bay stretches eight km. (five miles) from the boat-filled harbor towards the Sabaki (Galana) River; its shore is lined with good hotels near the town, deserted and peaceful further off. Fine silt from the river prevents coral growing here and the absence of a reef means a heavy surf rolling in from the Indian Ocean when wind and tide are right. August and September are the best months for belly-surfing.

On the south side of town Silversands Beach, dazzling white, reef sheltered and shaded by palms, is ideal for bathing, lazing and shell spotting. Fringed with holiday villas, the coral strand runs south from the Vasco da Gama pillar round Casuarina Point to Leopard Point and the boundary of the marine national park.

Not surprisingly, much leisure activity in this, Kenya's main beach resort, centers on the sea and water sports. Swimming is safe, although the bay currents should be given due consideration; the beaches are uncrowded for sunbathing or simple strolling and the more energetic can take their pick of water skiing, scuba diving, sailing or deep-sea fishing, arranged by the hotels or specialist firms in town.

Big game fishing has become a Malindi specialty. Its quality and variety have earned the town an international reputation and many special events are organized in the November to April season, including an international billfish competition. Alternatively, there are also shore-side sports available, such as golf, tennis and horse riding.

Other attractions include shopping for locally-made carvings, mats and baskets, *kangas, kikois* and *kanzus,* with plenty of opportunity for friendly bargaining with the vendors. The nightlife centers on the hotels but spills over into the town's bars for more local and esoteric interest. The hotels often provide the opportunity to watch Giriama tribal dancing and all offer a range of local excursions.

Excursions

Northwards, trips can be arranged to the Giriama village of Ganda, to Mambrui with its mosque and holy pillar tomb, to the secluded fishing village of Ras Ngomeni and the gourmet's desert island known as Robinson Island. Tour operators in Malindi also provide tailor-made local excursions or longer trips to Tsavo National Park and interest centers on the Tana–Lamu excursion safari. Kenya Airways operate from Malindi to Mombasa and Nairobi and there are two charter aircraft companies in Malindi both operating airbus services to Lamu at moderate rates. The budget conscious can hire taxis or catch a country bus.

To Tsavo East

It is possible to undertake an extended bush road circuit back to Nairobi via Lamu and Garissa, but the majority of tours either return via Mombasa or go directly across country to the Sala gate of Tsavo (East) National Park and on park tracks to the Mombasa road. The first colonial proconsul, Frederick, Lord Lugard, of the Imperial British East Africa Company, recommended this old slaving trail along the Galana River as potentially the best route to Machakos, the designated administrative center of the interior up to the Uganda border, then at Naivasha. He considered that camels were the most practical means of transport.

The advent of tourism has now led to the 120 km. (74 mile) Malindi–Sala gate road, the C103, being improved for all-weather access to Tsavo by motor vehicles. The road runs due west out of Malindi towards the small village of Ganda, and then passes through the northern tip of the Sokoke-Arabuko forest. As the track emerges from the Sokoke forest, for a few kilometers it follows the meandering course of the Sabaki River which becomes the Galana further upstream. Off to the left, just before the village of Kakoneni, is the bird sanctuary at Lake Jilore. The area is sparsely populated and the stunted tangle of commiphora bush, with its pungent camphor smell, is the chief feature of the landscape.

Tsavo East

This thick nyika scrub has been thinned out considerably by elephant at the approaches to the Park's Sala gate, and the land is bleak red ocher desert until the track reaches the gallery forest along the Galana. Just before the gate, there is a right turn to the new, luxury Crocodile Tented Camp.

From the Sala gate there is a choice of routes through the Park which eventually arrive at the various exits to the Mombasa highway. Left the track is signposted to Aruba Dam, 48 km. (30 miles) across arid thorn-bush country, from where the Voi river circuit can be followed along to the main Park gate and Lodge at Voi. Staying inside the Park and heading north from Voi toward the Manyani gate, the track passes Mudanda Rock where large concentrations of game are often seen.

Straight on from the Sala gate the track follows the banks of the Galana and, although passing through a few drifts, should be easily motorable in the dry season. After 59½ km. (37 miles) is Crocodile Point where rocks overlook a bend in the river which is a favorite haunt of these prehistoric reptiles. Just up-river from here are Lugard's Falls where the Galana flows through narrow gorges of strangely-shaped weathered rock. A junction left leads inland for 27 km. (17 miles) to a T-junction; right for Mudanda rock and the Manyani gate, left for Voi Lodge and gate.

From Voi, the route is 320 km. (198 miles) straight up the historic Mombasa road. Not long ago this was a perilous two days of motoring on soft sand or black-cotton slides, but now there is the all-asphalt A109 highway, straight and fast, and for this reason not without its hazards. Resident drivers tend to ignore the national 100 k.p.h. (62 m.p.h.) speed limit and, too often, either roll off into the bush or tangle with heavy haulage traffic.

After 19 km. (12 miles) the Manyani gate lies on the right and 11 km. (7 miles) further on the highway reaches the Tsavo river. Just before the bridge is the Maneater Motel, actually a service station with restaurant and rest facilities, but no accommodations. It was close by in 1898 that the "Man-Eaters of Tsavo," a couple of rapacious and hungry lions, harassed the builders of the railway and consumed several dozen of the workforce before being hunted down.

The Tsavo River is bridged after Manyani, and from the river there are 50 km. (31 miles) of flat bush and baobab country to Mtito Andei

(Kikamba for "the forest of eagles" or "vultures"). This is the principal refreshment and refuelling stop on the road, almost exactly halfway between Mombasa and Nairobi.

It offers a number of garages, an AA service station, wayside cafes and a full-service hotel, the Tsavo Inn. Mtito is also the main access to Kilaguni in Tsavo West.

Just outside the town is a 16 km. (ten mile) murram track off to the right, leading to the luxury Tsavo Safaris Camp on the banks of the Athi River.

Further up the highway is a region called Kikumbulyu, which was the field headquarters for Kenya's first Christian missionary, the German Ludwig Krapf. He moved there from Mombasa in 1844 in search of the "shining thing" or *Kinyaa,* as the Kamba call the snow-capped mountain far to the northwest. Another Kikamba version is that Kinyaa means ostrich—the black and white mountain. However, Krapf later wrote the word in the Italo-Swiss fashion as Kegnia, eventually anglicized as Kenya.

Kibwezi is the region's only evident settlement on the road. It has its place in history and in the recent memory of motorists as a treacherous stretch of black swamp, but today is hardly more than a fleeting refuelling stop. Its name probably derives from the *kikwezi* coins, brought in by 19th-century traders from the coast, although it was Scottish finance which finally put the township on the early map of Kenya. In 1891 Sir William Mackinnon founded the Scottish Industrial Mission, the first up-country school and hospital, superintended by the legendary medical missionary Dr. Moffat, who helped fight off rampant malaria in the area.

Two oddities of the area are the scatterbug, which group together and pretend to be a cluster of flowers, and a river which erupts from under lava rock through the roots of massive trees.

Makindu (palm trees) is recognized by a colorful minareted Sikh mosque on the side of the road. It is now a ghost town, but was once a huge rail-construction camp and, in 1899, a relief station for a famine which decimated the Kamba. The free issue of Indian rice at the time is still commemorated in local folk song.

From Makindu to Kiboko is an area of former wildlife which, until recently, was known as Hunter's Park in tribute to John (J.A.) Hunter, the sportsman and author-raconteur of the perils of the bush. The custom was that no professional hunter would raise a gun in the area as a mark of respect for the mentor of them all.

Kiboko (hippo in Swahili) started as a tsetse control station and is now a popular tourist stopover at a full-service lodge, set among shady acacias along the Kiboko River. Hunter's Lodge has developed its own game-viewing circuit westwards towards the Chyulu hills.

Birds and butterflies are the attraction of Simba Springs further on, a swampy area which takes its name from an early caravan stop called Kampi ya Simba, the camp of the lions.

At Emali there is a left turn to an all-weather murram road leading to the Leme Boit Gate of Amboseli National Park. Sultan Hamud is by-passed by the main road, but is a sizeable border township between Kamba and Masai country. It was named after the Sultan of Zanzibar who took a train ride to the spot—then the railhead—in 1898. Off the road, beyond the township, are the hills of Mukaa and Kilungu, where the Kamba have vast areas of cultivation; and Kima Station, where a man-eating lion hunted its human hunters, pulling one of them out of a railway carriage and carting him off.

From Sultan Hamud, the highway travels across the plain before gaining height to a range of hills through which it twists and turns. They make a pleasant change of scenery, with good vegetation and shambas growing maize on both sides of the road. Then it is plains again, this time the Kapiti, which were once covered with game but are now giant cattle ranches.

At Athi River the highway dips past the Kenya Meat Commission on the left and Tannery on the right to cross the river. It then passes on the left the road to Amboseli and Arusha, where the circuit began, before making the short run into Nairobi.

PRACTICAL INFORMATION FOR THE NORTH COAST

For Hotels and Restaurants in Malindi and Watamu, see *Park Data* for *Marine National Parks*.

BAMBURI BEACH

Hotels

Kenya Beach (E), Box 90663, Mombasa (tel. 485821). Reservations: African Safari Club, Box 46020, Nairobi (tel. 28760). Superbly-designed hotel linked to the Bahari and Silver Beach hotels.

Severin Sea Lodge (E), Box 82169, Mombasa (tel. 485001). Plenty to do in this unpressurized hotel.

Neptune Beach (E), Box 82169, Mombasa (tel. 485001). Affiliated to the Severin Sea Lodge.

Bamburi Beach (M), Box 83966, Mombasa (tel. 485611/3). Friendly and informal coast hotel. Good value for families; good service.

Ocean View (M), Box 81127, Mombasa (tel. 485601). Reservations: Repotel, Box 46527, Nairobi (tel. 27828).

Plaza Hotel (M), Box 88299, Mombasa (tel. 485321). Attractive gardens and huge pool in good new hotel. Airconditioning throughout.

KIKAMBALA

Hotels

Sun n' Sand (M), Box 2, Kikambala (tel. Kikambala 8). Reservations: Repotel, Box 46527, Nairobi (tel. 27828). Relaxed and peaceful spot, with very attractive local craft features. Good family hotel.

Whispering Palms (M), PO Kikambala (tel. Kikambala 5). Reservations: African Tours and Hotels, Box 30471, Nairobi (tel. 336858). Busy spot with plenty of activities available: tennis, pools, mini-golf, disco, etc.

Restaurant

Le Pichet, Kikambala Beach (tel. 48592). Rated one of the top three coast restaurants. French seafood specialties.

KILIFI

Hotels

Mnarani Club (M), Box 81443, Mombasa (tel. Kilifi 18). Reservations: African Tours and Hotels, Box 30471, Nairobi (tel. 336858). Excellent hotel with wide range of nautical activities.

Seahorse (M), Box 70, Kilifi (tel. 90). Reservations: Box 67868, Nairobi (tel. 338599). Another water-oriented spot, but this time with tents too. Fine for an adventurous family holiday.

Restaurant

Seahorse Restaurant and Boat Grill, (tel. 90/64). International fare in the more formal Seahorse; definitely more casual in the breezy and open Boat Grill, the boat being the prow of a dhow serving as a bar.

NYALI

Hotels

Bahari Beach (E), Box 81443, Mombasa (tel. 471603). Reservations: African Safari Club, Box 46020, Nairobi (28760). Pool, good beach, fine swimming; fishing boats available.

Mombasa Beach (E), Box 90414, Mombasa (tel. 471861). Reservations: African Tours and Hotels, Box 30471, Nairobi (tel. 336858). Magnificent and well-looked after grounds of around 20 acres. Good restaurant and many activities available.

Nyali Beach (E), Box 90581, Mombasa (tel. 471551). Reservations: Block Hotels, Box 47557, Nairobi (tel. 331635/22869). About the largest hotel on the coast. Wide range of activities—beach and otherwise—and a number of restaurants.

Reef (E), Box 82234, Mombasa (tel. 471771). Attractive and spacious hotel, with gardens, pool, tennis.

Silver Beach (E), Box 81443, Mombasa (tel. 471471). A slightly more expansive off-shoot of the Bahari Beach (see above). Very attractive grounds.

Restaurants

All the better restaurants are in the beach hotels. Among the best are the **Bistro Mchana** (tel. 471551), with French specialties, and the **Mvita Grill;** both in the Nyali Beach Hotel.

SHANZU

Hotels

Serena Beach (E), Box 90352, Mombasa (tel. 485721/4). Reservations: Serena Lodges and Hotels, Box 48690, Nairobi (tel. 338656). Rated very highly by those in the know; with attractively ethnic decor. Can be crowded.

Dolphin (M), Box 81443, Mombasa (tel. 485801). Reservations: African Safari Club, Box 46020, Nairobi (tel. 28760). Excellent cliff-top location, with fine views. Many water-oriented activities.

Restaurant

Le Joli Coin, Box 83402, Mombasa (tel. 485633). Almost in the sea. Seafood French style.

EGYPTIAN GOOSE

THE LOWER TANA RIVER AND LAMU

The Tana is Kenya's largest river—600 km. (372 miles) as the crow flies, or 1,012 km. (628 miles) counting every bend. It starts as tumbling streams on the slopes of Mount Kenya and the Aberdares, converges into a wide and powerful torrent east of these mountains and then matures into a slow and sinuous river for the lower half of its course. Here it dissects a vast and wild area of eastern Kenya where, from the air, the fertile ribbon makes a vivid contrast with the parched bushland stretching to the horizon on every side.

Nowhere is this more apparent than in the remote Kora Game Reserve, 130 km. (80 miles) from Garissa, where the Tana emerges from the violence of its middle section to reach the arid plains of its lower course. This is one of the most desolate yet starkly beautiful places in the country, but strictly for the connoisseur of wilderness. It is here that George Adamson continues his *Born Free* work of rehabilitating tame lions into the wild. He and his brother Terence have cut a considerable number of tracks in the reserve and it is possible to drive out of the southwest corner of the reserve into Kitui district and rejoin the Garissa–Nairobi road near Ngomeni.

As a newly-created game reserve, wildlife numbers at Kora are rapidly recovering from a long history of illegal hunting. Elephant, lion, lesser kudu and waterbuck are all to be seen. The river is outstandingly photogenic here and hippo and crocodiles are plentiful.

South of Kora the country is endless dry bush dominated by several prickly species of acacia trees and gnarled commiphora. Arid though it is, this country is extensively used by both wildlife and domestic stock, whenever water is within reach. While some animals do not need to drink as they obtain sufficient moisture from their leaf diet, most others, including cattle, have to drink regularly. As the puddles dry up after the rain, the river becomes increasingly the focus for both man and beast.

The nomadic Somali and Orma peoples have adapted to the requirements of this environment and move large distances in search of ephemeral pools and grazing, but where they are settled there is often overgrazing and soil erosion. This is sadly in evidence around Garissa.

There are more than 100 distinct tribes of the Somali in two groups. They are Hamites and are all Moslems. The Kenyan Somali are intelligent, adaptable people, fiercely independent and proud. Boys are initiated in large groups of up to 50, usually around eight years of age. The girls have to go through a unique and frankly rather barbaric initiation ceremony in which they are infibulated—a practice not carried out by any other group in East Africa.

In modern Kenya many Somalis have become successful traders, especially in the more remote and difficult areas. Most of them are still cattle herders, keeping large numbers of cows, sheep and goats.

The Orma are close relatives, but live mostly south of the Tana. Like other Hamites they are cattle herders, but are more settled than nomadic. They also keep some sheep and large numbers of goats. The men are tall and dress in brightly colored cloths. Men and women have long thin bones and the fine-featured women wear large numbers of bracelets on their arms and legs.

Garissa

A safari in this area could be centered in the town of Garissa, although there are no accommodations suitable for tourists. Camping is, of course, possible out of town on the river banks.

Garissa is the administrative headquarters of the North Eastern Province, once part of the old Northern Frontier District (NFD). The administrative boundaries were changed in the 1960s and the area east of the Tana and north all the way up to the Ethiopian border became the North Eastern Province. However, Garissa still exudes a frontier spirit and it has been the main military base for a border dispute with Somalia, known as the Shifta Troubles.

The Somali people dominate the whole of the North Eastern Province which immediately adjoins the Republic of Somalia. Clusters of their rough grass huts surrounded by cattle and camels are a common sight on the north and eastern side of the river, but in contrast with the crude exteriors of their dwellings, their carved and woven artefacts are some of the finest in Kenya. Their head-rest stools are particularly well made.

Craftsmen also still produce a deceptive weapon called a sword stick. This looks like a leatherbound walking stick, but the handle can be pulled out to reveal a sharp blade of up to two feet in length. A permit must be obtained from the local District Commissioner to be legally in possession of one of these.

Around Garissa, agricultural people are increasingly in evidence along the river banks. They are the Korakora and, below Nanigi, the various sub tribes of the Pokomo, the latter being Bantu people allied to the coastal tribes and different in every respect from their neighbors and historic enemies, the Somali and Galla.

Their land is far too dry to grow crops on rainfall alone and they are completely dependent on the river for their livelihood. They cut dugout canoes from the forest to move from one village to the next or to catch fish in the river. The moisture of the riverbanks supports their staple crop of bananas and the floods provide standing water and nutrients for rice and maize. However, the river is an unpredictable life giver and floods can as easily destroy as nurture crops.

South of Garissa, the arid bush continues, but below Hola the country becomes greener, the result of its proximity to the coast and its higher rainfall. This is one of the best wildlife areas in the country with several unique attractions.

On the east bank of the river around Hola and stretching in a band across to the Somali border is the only home of the Hunter's antelope, a hartebeest but with lyre horns. Little is yet known about this animal but it is easily seen around Ijara on the road from Garissa to Lamu. A game reserve has been gazetted for its protection named (in Somali) Arawale.

The river is a barrier to the distribution of some other antelopes as well, such as the Peter's (Grant's) gazelle which is only found on the west bank and the oribi which is restricted to the east bank in this part

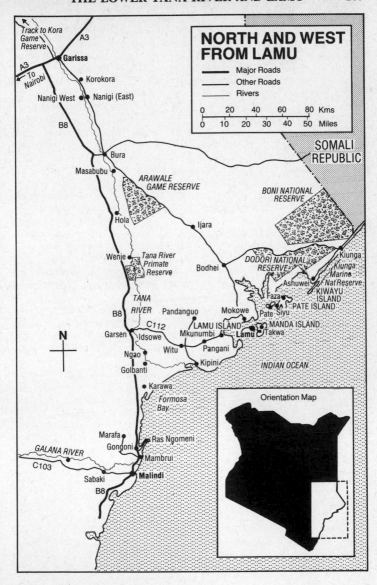

NORTH AND WEST FROM LAMU

— Major Roads
— Other Roads
— Rivers

| 0 | 20 | 40 | 60 | 80 | Kms |
| 0 | 10 | 20 | 30 | 40 | 50 | Miles |

SOMALI REPUBLIC

Track to Kora Game Reserve

A3

Garissa

A3
To Nairobi

Korokora

Nanigi West   Nanigi (East)

B8

Bura

Masabubu

ARAWALE GAME RESERVE

BONI NATIONAL RESERVE

Hola

Ijara

Wenje

Tana River Primate Reserve

Bodhei

DODORI NATIONAL RESERVE

Kiunga

Kiunga Marine Nat Reserve

Ashuwei

KIWAYU ISLAND

TANA RIVER

Faza

B8

Pandanguo

Mokowe

Pate   Siyu

PATE ISLAND

C112

LAMU ISLAND

MANDA ISLAND

Garsen   Idsowe

Mkunumbi   Lamu   Takwa

N

Ngao

Witu

Pangani

Golbanti

Kipini

INDIAN OCEAN

Karawa

Formosa Bay

Orientation Map

Marafa

Ras Ngomeni

GALANA RIVER

Gongoni

Mambrui

C103

Sabaki

Malindi

B8

of Kenya. As well as being a barrier to wildlife, the river also provides a habitat for several forest species. Of particular interest are the Tana river varieties of red colobus and crested mangabey monkeys. Both of these species are found predominantly in West Africa and their presence in the gallery forests of the lower Tana is evidence of extensive forest belts across East Africa in earlier times. The populations of both species, however, are restricted to a strip of 60 km. (37 miles) between the villages of Wenje and Garsen, and their future is severely threatened by destruction of the forest by Pokomo agriculture. The destruction was particularly acute during the Shifta troubles when all the Pokomo on the east bank left their homes and had to start new farms on the safety of the west bank.

The Tana River Primate Reserve has been formed near Wenje to conserve the best of their remaining habitat. Recent studies have shown that both the red colobus and crested mangabey monkeys are well adapted to life in the complex forests. The mangabey, for example, can feed on fruit in the trees or insects on the ground, and alter their social organization accordingly. The availability of these foods is as variable as the crops of the Pokomo and the species owes its survival here and nowhere else in East Africa to these adaptations.

The new reserve is meant to feature guided walks in the forest which, helped by the abundance of other wildlife in the area and its proximity to Malindi, will eventually make it very attractive.

The southern limit of the rare monkeys' range is near Garsen, where the floodplain opens into a wide grassy delta extending in a triangle between Garsen, the present mouth, to the river at Kipini and an old mouth at Karawa. This is the main dry-season grazing land of the Galla and, to the south, the Orma.

Finally, the delta is an area of great historical interest, being one of the main routes into the interior of what is now Kenya before the construction of the Uganda railway at the turn of the century. Such famous explorers as Charles New, Karl Peters and the Denhardt brothers all hoped to reach the interior via the Tana. Their accounts are full of the horrors of mosquitoes, disease and floods.

All in all, the lower Tana and its basin is as genuine a remnant of old Africa as the traveler will find, with a fine heritage of wildlife, traditional life styles and history.

Up the Coast to Lamu

While the attraction of the Lower Tana area is based on a string of new—but as yet undeveloped—game reserves enclosing some of the best wildlife areas in the country in a tough frontier setting, the appeal of Lamu is of a subtle and historic culture, unspoilt beaches and a gentle climate. To reach Lamu after a safari through the arid hinterland is to reach an oasis presenting a relaxing and magnificent contrast to the tough journey that precedes it.

Some introductory comments are needed on transport in the area. The road up the coast from Malindi to Lamu is now all-weather murram the whole way except for a short section near Garsen. Unfortunately, this is a vital section as it crosses the floodplain of the Tana and may be impassable in the rainy seasons (check with the bus drivers in Malindi). Otherwise for most of the year, it is a reliable if somewhat rough road.

Most of the other roads in eastern Kenya are of sand or clay and can be treacherous in wet weather. They should only be attempted by rugged saloon cars in the dry season. However, since the climate is consistently hot and dry in all but the months of November, December and mid-March to mid-June there is ample opportunity to visit the region without fear of getting stuck.

Distances are considerable and both people and traffic sparse, so all visitors by road should take adequate quantities of gasoline, water and food for camping and be able to mend a puncture if necessary—an extra spare is a good idea.

North of Malindi, gasoline is always available at Garsen, Hola and Garissa and usually at Witu and Mokowe. A four-wheel-drive vehicle is helpful, but only essential in the dry seasons on the very rough road from Garissa to Kora Game Reserve, between Garba Tula and Meru National Park and on the road from Bodhei to Kiunga where the sand ruts are too deep to drive without high ground clearance. The main disadvantage of saloon cars is their low ground clearance; however, since the roads are essentially sandy, rather than rocky as in northern Kenya, damage is seldom worse than a broken silencer.

The bus service from Malindi to Lamu is inexpensive, around Shs. 40/-, and takes about five hours. Alternatively there are several mini-bus services which ply the route daily and two air charter companies in Malindi operate a frequent air-taxi service. At around Shs. 400/-return, the flight is good value and gives a clear introduction to the tortuous outline of the coast around Lamu, otherwise quite disorientating on the ground. Air travel is an alternative means of getting to other parts of the area and any of the charter companies will fly to established air strips.

As the Tana River and North Eastern Game Reserves become developed with tented camp facilities, this will become an increasingly attractive proposition.

One final means of getting to Lamu is by persuading the captain (*nanhoda*) of a coastal dhow to take on passengers from Mombasa.

This is rated by some as the most interesting and relaxing way to travel to the far north coast, but it is not easy to arrange the trip.

Since northeastern Kenya, apart from Lamu, is not opened up for easy access, the majority of our route description is intended for the independent visitor traveling by car.

Malindi to Garsen

The 225 km. (140 miles) road to Lamu leads north from Malindi and crosses the Sabaki river over a suspension bridge. This river is known inland as the Galana and its major upstream tributary is the Athi river. Five km. (three miles) on is the turning to Mambrui which, unlike Malindi, is strongly Moslem in character. It has a fine mosque and pillar tomb and access to a vast expanse of beach stretching up a spit of sand dunes known as Ras Ngomeni. This is worth remembering when flooding of the Sabaki coupled with a northeasterly wind turn Malindi Bay brownish with silt.

An alternative access to this beach is a turning five km. (three miles) beyond Mambrui which leads to the village of Ngomeni and also to the San Marco rocket launching pad. This installation is run by the Italian Space Administration and consists of two platforms one km. out to sea. A number of satellites have been launched from here and launches are a spectacular sight, particularly at night.

A worthwhile deviation at this point is to Marafa or Hell's Kitchen, reached by a left turn from the Malindi–Lamu road two km. after the Mambrui turning. After about 30 km. (18 miles) of rough road, a right turn at the village of Marafa leads to a gorge on the left, full of spectacularly eroded rock pinnacles and strikingly-colored cliffs.

Beyond Gongoni the road runs to the coast before turning inland and passing through a belt of coastal thicket for some 40 km. (24 miles), where there is a possible side excursion for anyone particularly interested in the Tana delta region.

The turn off is signposted to the village of Terasaa, an entirely new settlement built to serve the less accessible but older villages of Golbanti and Ngao. Golbanti was the site of a Methodist mission station set up in 1885 by Thomas Wakefield. One year later it was raided by Masai and the incumbent missionary, the Reverend Houghton, his wife and 11 others were killed. The fact that the Masai could raid as far as this is an indication of their farflung power at the time. The rival German Lutheran missionaries established themselves at nearby Ngao and built an impressive and defensible house on top of a hill in the village in 1893, now used by the doctor in charge of the hospital.

The local Pokomo are a coastal tribe, probably driven inland ahead of the invading Galla around 1200. They have been in their present area, centered on Hola, ever since. Like other Bantu the Pokomo are mainly farmers and grow millet, maize and other crops in the fertile land on the banks of the Tana.

The main Malindi–Lamu route (B8), five km. (three miles) before Garsen, climbs over a small hill which affords the only view in the whole lower Tana basin—a hazy vista of endless dry bush country broken only by the green ribbon of the river. To the right, over the hill, is an old pill-box built during the war against an expected Italian invasion from Ethiopia.

At the bottom of the hill is a turning to the village of Idsowe (four km.—two miles—in towards the river). This is a typical village of the lower "Malachini" or Christian Pokomo, only remarkable for a famous heron breeding ground on a nearby lake. If the river floods in May the whole delta supports a huge number of waterbirds and many species of heron breed on this lake in June and July. Idsowe can also be reached from Garsen on a good and shorter track along the south bank of the Tana.

Garsen

The town of Garsen itself is an important local trading center, often crowded with Waldei Gabbra (Somalis), Orma and Pokomo people. It is exactly halfway to Lamu and a good place to buy a soda and sit and watch the scene. It is also the take-off point for a direct cross-country return to Nairobi via Garissa.

Back on the the Lamu route (now C112) the road crosses the Tana on a ferry and then covers eight km. (five miles) of floodplain on a raised road. This is the black-cotton soil section which can be impassable after rain for saloon cars.

The road then crosses a larger area of grassland maintained by the river floods and used extensively as a dry season grazing area by the Somali and Orma herdsmen. Depending on the season, waterbirds and topi are also common here. Much of the grassland, however, is created by forest burning and this can be seen by taking a short diversion left to Wema, five km. (three miles) beyond the ferry. Here there are many scattered forest patches, remnants of a much larger area. The road leaves the floodplain at a bridge called Lango la Simba (Lion's Gate) and enters a woodland thicket zone again.

Just beyond the small, picturesque township of Witu is a possible diversion to Kipini, 20 km. (12 miles) away on the coast. It is now a dilapidated fishing village on the mouth of the Tana, but formerly the district headquarters before it was moved to Hola. Like Witu, the village is Swahili in character with stone-walled houses and *makuti* (coconut thatch) roofing. The river outlet to the sea dates only from the 1860s when the Sultan of Witu had a canal dug at Belazoni between the old course of the river and a small stream called the Ozi, which flowed into the sea at Kipini. During a flood in 1892 the river adopted this as its main course and the old course has largely silted up.

The canal was the site of another enterprise, the Belazoni Estate, which was founded in 1906. An eccentric Englishman, Percy Petley, was one of the managers. The Estate produced a wide variety of crops, including rubber, until it went bust in 1931 with the depression.

As a district headquarters Kipini acquired notoriety through the suicides there of three administrators, and the old District Commissioner's house is supposed to be haunted. Certainly the village has a sultry, jaded and very romantic atmosphere.

A track leads along the coast to the east and there are several old Swahili ruins, the best being at Ras Ya Mwana, ten km. (six miles) from Kipini. This is a fine coastline, almost entirely devoid of habitation, with camping only for visitors who go out of their way to find the place.

Beyond Witu, the main road passes through the edge of Witu forest, once much more extensive. The surrounding area is now mostly parkland of doum palm and bush, interspersed with grassy *ziwas*—shallow depressions which flood during the rains. Baboons, topi and elephant are numerous in this area, today named the Pandanguo Game Reserve.

At Mkunumbi the road turns inland for some distance to swing round the creeks and mangrove swamps that lace the area. Eventually the sea is reached again, two km. beyond Mokowe. Here travelers must take a boat across to the island of Lamu. Cars may be left at the jetty where a watchman guards them (for which service he should be tipped). Alternatively they can be left at a park behind the garage in the village of Mokowe or sometimes at the police station. But since both of these car parks are two km. (one mile) from the jetty, a lift must be begged if there is much baggage to carry. Security in the jetty park has varied in the past, but cars and their contents are probably reasonably safe. However, no chances should be taken with valuables and it is probably worth taking as much with you as you can into Lamu.

The cost of chartering a boat to Lamu island is negotiable, but should not cost more than Shs. 30/- each for a party of over six people.

The Lamu Archipelago

Lamu and the neighboring islands on the far north of Kenya's coastline have become a fashionable destination for trendy tourists. The port of Lamu is the only substantial survivor of an urban civilization which has existed at least 1,000 years on the coast. It retains an almost unspoilt 18th-century look and life style, and once access is fully developed, will become one of Kenya's premier visitor attractions.

Settlements in the archipelago were first noted in the *Periplus Maris Erythraei,* a 1st-century B.C. mariner's handbook—an invaluable record although sadly anonymous—but no evidence of habitation has yet been excavated earlier than the 9th century. The settlements of Weyuni and Hedabu are, by tradition, 7th century but, according to latest archeological research, are no older than the 13th century. Hedabu, once the principal township, was finally engulfed by sand dunes around 500 years ago. These same shifting sands are now threatening Shela, a picturesque village and tourist beach at the southern tip of the island.

Lamu Town

In Lamu town itself, the oldest of 29 island mosques is the Pwani whose qibla dates back to 1370. The Friday Mosque was established in 1511, but almost all other buildings are late-18th-century. Very little architectural development has taken place since this time, and the narrow cloistered town plan and Arab-style structures are intact.

Lamu was a thriving port by 1505, when it surrendered to the Portuguese invaders. It managed to avoid involvement in the ensuing wars between the colonists and neighboring island and city states, but there were frequent troubles between Lamu and the sultanates of Mombasa, Zanzibar and Pate (pronounced as in the French *paté*), the dominant island port to the north. The town was then surrounded by a defensive wall, and according to Portuguese historian, Duarte Barbosa, its Arab inhabitants were constantly skirmishing with their African neighbors.

At this time, the Lamu economy was slave based. Like most other states in the archipelago, its production was mainly grains and fruits, and its exports ambergris, mangrove poles, turtle shells, rhino horn and ivory. These highly profitable commodities were sent out on dhows to Yemen, Arabia, the Persian Gulf and, on the reverse trade winds, southeast to India.

During the 17th century, the nomadic Galla invaded from the north and sacked most of the coastal settlements, except those located on islands. The effect of this was migration to Lamu, and the other islands of Pate, Siyu and Faza, all of which developed rapidly with Pate preeminent by the 18th century. Culture flourished at this time; a great tradition of poetry was developed, architecturally ambitious houses built, some of them with hot-and-cold plumbing systems which made European ablutions primitive by comparison. Clothing was elegant and jewelery ornate, with gold and silver cloth woven in Lamu, where furniture inlaid with silver and ivory was also produced.

Paradise was not complete, however, because for two generations the two island states warred with each other until peace was finally settled in 1813 when the people of Lamu defeated an army of the Nabhani of Pate at the battle of Shela. From then on, Lamu began its golden age which lasted more or less until 1873 when the British forced the Sultan of Zanzibar to sign an anti-slaving pact. The Royal Navy patrolled the coast, and prevented the Sultan's attempt at slipping dhow shipments of slaves past the blockade from Kilwa to Lamu. By 1897, there were less than 10,000 slaves on the island and ten years later slavery was abolished once and for all. The cheap labor on which Lamu's prosperity depended was gone and the island plunged into decline.

Among the early tourists to the island at around this time was Henry Morton Stanley who, according to legend, distributed small gold American dollars which still circulate in the area. A few years later, the Germans moved in to establish a short-lived protectorate around Witu on the mainland. They opened the Lamu post office, the first German Post Office to be established outside Germany. For 70 years, Lamu merely jogged along, isolated from developments within the new British East African Protectorate and later the Kenya Colony. Western technological progress and industrial progress touched Lamu hardly at all. Even today, the island is still largely remote from the modern age. Needless to say, this remoteness is the principal factor in its unique charm.

In 1962, shortly before Kenya's independence, Lamu's economy began to rally, principally from a new role as shipper of Somali cattle to Mombasa. Tourism arrived in 1967 with an initial eight beds at the Peponi (Happiness) Hotel at Shela. Since then two more first-class hotels have been built and scores of lodging houses opened by the local people offering accommodations at unbelievably low rates to itinerant young visitors. The government set up an administration on the island for the district which has stimulated agricultural and fisheries development.

Communication with the island is also being improved, with the up-grading of the Malindi–Mokowe road and of airstrips on adjacent Manda Island and mainland Mokowe. Lamu now looks set to emerge from its doldrum age and from its position as an antique outpost of the Kenya Republic.

For the moment, however, the old-world ambience remains as a major visitor attraction. The approach to the town is still exclusively by sea—usually by creaking diesel-powered launches from the road-head at Mokowe or a jetty close to the light aircraft strip on Manda Island. A strong sea wall runs the length of the town, decorated in many places with black defunct cannon. Many of the buildings facing the sea are pillared or castellated, or with verandahs in Arab/Swahili style. Behind them is a maze of narrow streets no wider than the span of a donkey cart—the only Lamu haulage vehicle apart from boats.

Inset in the unbroken lines of tall buildings are heavy ornately-carved timbered doors and shuttered windows which, unfortunately, preclude a glimpse of the often attractive courtyard gardens inside. The tiny shops in the alleyways are always thronged with strollers—the men in white full-length *khanzus* and *kofia* caps and the women almost all in black purdah, (*bui-bui* in Swahili).

Close to the Boma (District Commissioner's office) is the excellent Lamu museum and the attractive Petley's Inn on the seafront. Just behind is the main town square and market, dominated by a "Beau Geste" fort. This was built in 1821 and is now a national penitentiary. Behind this, on rising ground, are some of the larger houses of the town, many of which span the streets to create mysterious areas of light and dark. These give way to a mosaic of Swahili mud-and-wattle houses, roofed with makuti thatch, leading to the viewpoint summit of the hill on which is located the town hospital.

The beach tourism sector of Lamu is at Shela village where the Peponi Hotel is situated at the beginning of a 12-km. (seven-mile) beach of uninterrupted, empty foreshore, flanked by high dunes. The normal approach from Lamu is by "boat" taxi. Across the channel on Manda Island is the Ras Kitau Hotel, the most recent tourist development. Both hotels offer facilities for fishing, water skiing, and snorkeling, as well as expeditions to Pate, Siyu and Faza.

At the end of Shela beach is the sleepy village of Kipungani, noted for its mango orchards and two old mosques. On the nearest settlement to the mainland is Matondoni, whose people are particularly friendly and addicted to music and dance festivals.

These celebrations, or *ziaras,* give a special importance to Lamu in the Moslem world. The most important of them is the Maulidi al Nebi (Birthday of the Prophet) which occurs shortly after Easter. Thousands of pilgrims from East and North Africa, Arabia and the Persian Gulf inundate the town for the event. They sing and dance in the square before the principal Riyadh Mosque, and there is impressive evening worship under the stars.

Among the many other attractions of Lamu are its splendid and characteristic souvenirs: jewelry, brass-bound and carved chests, model dhows, and Swahili furniture—sometimes of ebony inlaid with ivory—abound.

Excursions from Lamu

There is a ferry which offers a regular service around the islands. Hotels or private entrepreneurs also rent crewed boats.

Pate Island is 30 km. (18 miles) northeast of Lamu, and the ruined towns of Faza and Siyu, which also has a well-preserved fort, can both be visited at any tide.

The town of Pate itself is more difficult to reach. On the right tide it is possible to land there, but otherwise it means a long, albeit fascinating, hike from a landing stage on the southern end of the island.

On Manda are the ruins of a village dating from the 16th and 17th centuries called Takwa, similar in interest and preservation to Gedi. The ruins of Manda town at the north end of the island are completely overgrown and buried, but archeological work has determined this to be the oldest (9th century) settlement on the Kenyan coast. There is sometimes game on Manda Island and elephant have been known to swim across from the mainland, where the consolidation of Pandanguo Game Reserve is now being undertaken.

Northeast from Lamu, inland from the sea, are the Dodori and Boni National Reserves and the newly-gazetted Kiunga Marine National Park, extra attractions which will undoubtedly add to an already magnificent Lamu holiday destination.

Northeast from Lamu

Most visitors will probably return directly to Malindi from Lamu, but for the more intrepid there is a road right to the Somali border at Kiunga. It may be closed for security reasons, or the rains, so check at Mokowe police post. However, if it is open the road runs a lovely 120 km. (74 miles) to Kiunga from the village of Bodhei up to the Dodori and Boni National Reserves and Kiunga Marine National Park on the coast. It is a sand road and totally without services, passing through only one or two small villages of the Boni people. Until recently the Boni lived as hunter-gatherers in this wild area of forest and thicket.

The Boni National Reserve is a large waterless and isolated bush area running along the Somali border. At the moment visitors are not encouraged to visit it until it is more developed. The heartland of this primeval forest is, however, rich in wildlife though this is not easily seen because of the thick vegetation. Signs of elephant in particular are abundant.

The track eventually climbs over the Mundane Range, a low ridge of ancient sand dunes, and the sea comes into sight.

Kiunga is a charming village with an old District Officer's house perched on a coral headland. It is inhabited by the Bajun, an island people of obscure origin, although with clear Bantu-Arab characteristics. Some members of the group claim Persian ancestry. They are all strict Moslems. Men do all the manual work—many of them are fishermen—and the women are expected to stay at home. They have a strong musical tradition, an unusual feature of which is that women often play instruments at festivals. A mellifluous one played by the men is the *zuzmari,* or Swahili oboe.

The Bajun are attractive people, the women wearing long flowing robes of black material, the men white *khanzus.* Their village harbor is protected by a string of raised coral islands one km. off the present coastline. These are important breeding grounds for seabirds which nest there between July and October. The Kiunga Marine National Park comprises extensive coral gardens of spectacular beauty, attracting myriads of brightly-colored fish. The park lies within the reef and fish, corals and shells are entirely protected, but licenced local fishermen can operate inside the surrounding reserve.

North of Kiunga a track goes up to the Somalian border, just beyond Shakani. There is positively no access to Somalia at this point.

Shakani has some 400-year-old tombs marked with large pillars. South of Kiunga the track follows the coast down past ruins at Omwe and Ashuwei, ending at the bay of Kokoni opposite Kiwayu Island. This is a fine place for camping and a small Castaways Lodge offers gourmet seafood and some accommodations in a beautiful, remote location.

Cross-Country Return to Nairobi

The route first backtracks from Kiunga to Bodhei above Lamu, and then passes into a thick woodland zone, an extension of the true Boni forest to the east. This area is dissected with numerous paths cut through the woodland, all dating from the 1960s when British Petroleum were prospecting for oil.

Just before Ijara the road emerges quite suddenly onto an area of wide open grassland which extends a considerable distance north towards Bura. There is no equivalent vegetation zone on the west bank of the river and this is the only habitat of the Hunter's antelope. Beyond this, the Arawale Game Reserve has been gazetted between Masabubu and Hola, primarily for the conservation of the Hunter's antelope.

After passing the police post at Bura, the vegetation becomes dry semi-desert bush similar to that on the west bank. Somalis and their stock are much in evidence here and game is not as abundant in the area as it used to be.

The route continues north 94 km. (58 miles) to Garissa, from where the A3 speeds back to Nairobi (400 km., 248 miles).

PRACTICAL INFORMATION FOR LAMU

HOTELS. In Lamu Town: Petley's Inn (I–M), Box 4 (tel. 48 and 107). 11 double rooms, all with shower. Full board. Book direct. The first hotel at Lamu, Petley's overlooks the harbor and retains its character. Attractive snack bar in the adjoining garden.

Mohamed Lali (I), Box 115 (tel. 139). Two traditional Arab houses to let in the old town. Flower-filled courtyards. Self-catering. Book direct.

New Mahrus Hotel (I), Box 25. 36 rooms, 13 with shower, toilet and balcony. Near the market and the old fort. Hotel also owns a private Arab house for rent. Self-catering for lunch and dinner. Book direct.

At Shela Village: Peponi Hotel (E), Box 24 (tel. 29). A connoisseur's hotel, well-located 3 km. (2 miles) from Lamu Town facing Manda Island. All rooms self-contained with shower, balcony, ocean views. Lovely gardens, excellent cuisine, shop. Big-game fishing, water sports, excursions to neighboring islands available. Advance booking essential.

Shela Rest House (I), Box 10 (tel. 132 or 193). Large two-story Arab house with two apartments, each with two double bedrooms, shower, and kitchen. Self-catering; meals provided at extra charge. Good for families. Book ahead.

On Manda Island: Ras Kitau Beach Hotel (M). Comfortable self-contained rooms with all facilities, facing Shela. Dining room, bar, lounge, shop. Quieter than Peponi, with a beautiful, almost deserted beach shaded by baobab trees. Good goggling nearby. Daily boat service to Lamu Town. Deep sea fishing and excursions arranged. Full board.

RESTAURANTS. The Equator. Best place to eat in Lamu. On the waterfront, run by long-time resident Ron Partridge. Excellent cuisine in Swahili-style decorated restaurant. Try the smoked sailfish or delicious crayfish. Specialty is crêpes topped with sesame seeds and served with wild forest honey.

Peponi Hotel. Civilized cuisine in a Moorish setting. A Danish-German proprietress, Vera Korschen, prepares superb seafood for well-known migrants. Pricey, though.

Petley's Inn is also recommended for excellent fare. Moderate.

HOW TO GET THERE. By Air: Regular flights to Manda airstrip from Mombasa and daily service by *Air Kenya/Sunbird* from Wilson Airport (Nairobi) to Manda airstrip. **By Road:** Mombasa/Malindi/Mokowe coastal road (dry season only), or cross-country to Nairobi. Check conditions first; four-wheel drive vehicles recommended.

HYENA

NATIONAL PARKS AND GAME RESERVES

There are, at the moment, nearly 40 parks and reserves in Kenya of which perhaps some two dozen could be said to be properly established in terms of their access and facilities for tourists. Four of these sites are marine parks protecting sections of inshore ocean and coral reefs. The remainder cover an area of over 35,000 sq. km. (13,514 sq. miles), equivalent to six percent of Kenya's total land-mass. National Parks are reserved exclusively for wildlife and tourism; National and Forest Reserves are open to limited, controlled use by the local population.

Park Pointers

All the main parks and reserves can be visited in a normal, sturdy passenger car with the exception of Sibiloi on the eastern shore of Lake

Turkana. A safari there should be made with a four-wheel-drive, high-clearance vehicle, carrying spares and supplies of food, water and gasoline. At times during the rainy seasons, access and park roads may be impassable, especially in the mountain areas. A check should be made with the Automobile Association (A.A.) in Nairobi or with the Kenya Police, although up-to-date reports are not always available. Generally the main circuit tracks in the parks and reserves are all-weather earth or gravel, and are often in better condition than the access roads.

The best time for viewing animals in the parks is during the dry periods when the game animals, widely dispersed in the wet seasons, concentrate around the main sources of permanent water—which are usually those areas developed for visitors. As a general rule there are two wet seasons over much of the country, the short rains in October–November and the long rains in April–June, so the ideal timing of a visit would be in either August–September or January–March.

Maps and guides are available for the country as a whole, and for most of the parks and reserves. However, stocks tend to run out at safari lodges, so the advice is to buy them before your trip at Nairobi or Mombasa.

There are fairly stringent rules and regulations governing visits to the parks and reserves; many of them standard, others specific to a particular area. The rules are mostly commonsense, designed to safeguard both visitors and the sanctuaries.

We have logged details of park accommodations in the *Park Data* sections at the end of each park entry. They vary from the spectacularly luxurious to the simple—sometimes tented camps. Do-it-yourself lodges (often simple timber cottages or thatched bandas) are also available in the larger sanctuaries. In these, only the basics are provided, and visitors are required to bring their own food, bedding, etc. Bookings are generally made with the Park/Reserve authorities on a first come, first served basis.

Camping is perfectly safe, provided the rules are carefully observed. Sites are designated by the wardens, and many are supplied with water, toilets, firewood, and occasionally, service staff.

Entrance fees for the land parks and reserves, at time of writing, were—Sh.1/-per child (under 12); Shs.30/-per adult; Shs.25/-per vehicle up to five seats; Shs.40/-per vehicle of six to 13 seats; Shs.50/-for an aircraft.

Marine parks run at Shs. 20/-per day for an adult; Shs.2/50 for a child under 12.

Season tickets are available for all parks and reserves, but are for Kenya residents only.

Access is usually from 6 A.M.–6 P.M.

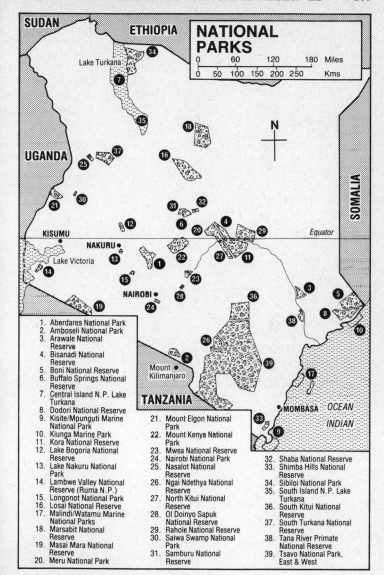

NATIONAL PARKS

| 0 | | 60 | | 120 | | 180 | Miles |
| 0 | 50 | 100 | 150 | 200 | 250 | | Kms |

N

SUDAN
ETHIOPIA
Lake Turkana
UGANDA
KISUMU
NAKURU
Lake Victoria
NAIROBI
TANZANIA
Mount Kilimanjaro
SOMALIA
Equator
MOMBASA
OCEAN
INDIAN

1. Aberdares National Park
2. Amboseli National Park
3. Arawale National Reserve
4. Bisanadi National Reserve
5. Boni National Reserve
6. Buffalo Springs National Reserve
7. Central Island N.P. Lake Turkana
8. Dodori National Reserve
9. Kisite/Mpunguti Marine National Park
10. Kiunga Marine Park
11. Kora National Reserve
12. Lake Bogoria National Reserve
13. Lake Nakuru National Park
14. Lambwe Valley National Reserve (Ruma N.P.)
15. Longonot National Park
16. Losai National Reserve
17. Malindi/Watamu Marine National Parks
18. Marsabit National Reserve
19. Masai Mara National Reserve
20. Meru National Park

21. Mount Elgon National Park
22. Mount Kenya National Park
23. Mwea National Reserve
24. Nairobi National Park
25. Nasalot National Reserve
26. Ngai Ndethya National Reserve
27. North Kitui National Reserve
28. Ol Doinyo Sapuk National Reserve
29. Rahole National Reserve
30. Saiwa Swamp National Park
31. Samburu National Reserve

32. Shaba National Reserve
33. Shimba Hills National Reserve
34. Sibiloi National Park
35. South Island N.P. Lake Turkana
36. South Kitui National Reserve
37. South Turkana National Reserve
38. Tana River Primate National Reserve
39. Tsavo National Park, East & West

AMBOSELI NATIONAL PARK

Amboseli lies close to Kenya's border with Tanzania, due south of Nairobi. The Park takes its name from Lake Amboseli, which for the most part is a dry, flat, saline bed, only 1,190 meters (3,904 ft.) above sea-level. Just 40 km. (25 miles) to the south is Kilimanjaro, the highest mountain in Africa. The main peaks are snow-capped Kibo (Uhuro Peak) at 5,894 meters (19,340 ft.) and Mawenzi at 5,050 meters (16,900 ft.), which tower five km. (three miles) above the plain of Amboseli completely dominating the scenery and surely provide the finest and most photogenic backdrop to any wildlife sanctuary in Africa. But even more important to the Park is that the mountain provides a fresh water run-off, mostly subterranean, which feeds the springs and swamps at the center of the Park and attracts a permanent concentration of wildlife.

Kilimanjaro, like other big mountains, often has its head in the clouds for much of the day and the best opportunities for clear views of the peaks are in the early morning and late afternoon. It is also the best time for spotting game animals, which seek shade in the heat of the day; so those classical photographs of animals grazing in front of the majestic Kilimanjaro are most likely to be taken on the early morning or evening game runs.

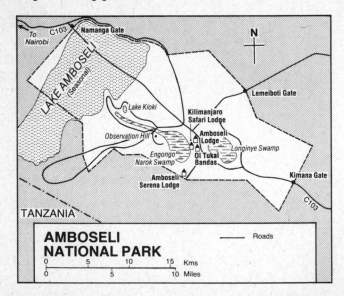

AMBOSELI
NATIONAL PARK

Until the early 1970s Amboseli was part of a much larger game reserve covering 3,200 sq. km. (1,235 sq. miles), administered by the Masai and also shared by them for the grazing of cattle. A program of water bore-holes enabled more widespread grazing of Masai stock and the core of the reserve around the swamp area of Ol Tukai was then made a National Park, exclusive to wildlife. It covers an area of only 380 sq. km. (145 sq. miles) but embraces a wide range of habitats from dense swampland, through acacia woodland to thorn-bush and open plain.

The ecology of the Park is much more delicate than most of Kenya's game sanctuaries and could easily be upset. In the 1950s an unexplained rising of the underground brackish water table had the effect of enlarging the swamps and killing numbers of fine yellow-barked acacias. Much of the plain is able to support only a few sparse saline grasses on its grey dusty bed, but these are important to the grazing of the game and visitors should be careful not to drive away from established tracks as this can damage the grass, which may take years to recover.

Game is abundant in and around the central swamp areas with a wide variety viewed easily in the course of a short game run. There are large numbers of wildebeest, zebra, buffalo, impala and both Grant's and Thomson's gazelle, all of which help support a good number of resident lion, some cheetah and a few leopard. The Park's elephant herd is recovering well from the poaching onslaught of a few years ago and is to be found most days cooling-off in the swamp-waters. The black rhino, for which the Park was once famous, suffered even more from poaching but although reduced to a handful, they have begun to breed well again and are often seen browsing the bushland to the east of Ol Tukai.

The bird life of Amboseli is particularly rich with over 420 species recorded, 47 of them raptors. A wide variety of water birds can be seen around the swamps, some of the most attractive being the resident saddle-bill storks. The very local Taveta golden weaver is common near the lodges although it is still comparatively rare outside Amboseli.

Ostrich and bustard can often be seen on the plains; the buffalo and rhino carry both species of oxpeckers, while the elephants carry egrets. The beautiful crowned crane is common and in the dry season the sandgrouse make an interesting spectacle when they arrive at watering places in communities of several hundred.

PARK DATA

DIRECTIONS. From Nairobi, travel south for 164 km. (102 miles) to the border town of Namanga, then turn left for the 80 km. (50 miles) to the Park

Center at Ol Tukai. Alternatively, head east from Nairobi on the Mombasa highway for 125 km. (78 miles) to Emali, then turn right on to the Loitokitok road for 66 km. (41 miles) before another right turn to Ol Tukai, 30 km. (19 miles).

ACCOMMODATIONS. There are five first class lodges, three at the center of the Park and two on the eastern perimeter. In addition, there are thatched self-help banda cottages.

Amboseli Lodge. Reservations: Kilimanjaro Safari Club, P.O. Box 30139, Nairobi (tel. 338888). Pleasant and popular place in the central area of the park facing the mountain. The longest established lodge in the park. Large pool.

Amboseli Serena Lodge. Reservations: Serena Lodges & Hotels, P.O. Box 48690, Nairobi (tel. 338656). A deluxe lodge with many attractive design features in the Masai style. Good pool and good birdwatching in the lovely gardens. Faces a stream often visited by elephant. In the central area of the park.

Kilimanjaro Buffalo Lodge. Reservations: P.O. Box 72630, Nairobi (tel. 336088). A new and luxurious lodge built in traditional African style with makuti thatched chalets, situated 15 km. (10 miles) east of the central park area at the junction of the C.102 Loitokitok/Emali road to Nairobi. Lovely garden, large pool, and the bar overlooks a waterhole visited by game at night.

Kilimanjaro Safari Lodge. Also owned and managed by Kilimanjaro Safari Club. Reservations as for Amboseli Lodge above. Situated under acacia trees a short distance from Amboseli Lodge in the central area of the park, facing the mountain.

Kimana Safari Lodge. Reservations: P.O. Box 43817, Nairobi (tel. 742731). A new and attractive lodge situated overlooking the Kimana river. Plenty of character and good fishing. Situated 15 km. (10 miles) from the central park area just off the Loitokitok/Emali road to Nairobi, near the turn-off for Kilaguni Lodge in Tsavo Park West.

Ol Tukai Bandas. Reservations: Nomads Kenya Ltd., P.O. Box 24793, Nairobi (tel. 331826). Thatched, self-help cottages. Crockery and cooking utensils are provided, bedding can be hired, but take your own food. Originally built as film crew accommodations by Paramount Pictures.

Campsites. Located at the edge of the woodland near the Serena Lodge but there are no facilities. They are very popular at times so it is best to book through the Game Department in Nairobi.

LAKE NAKURU NATIONAL PARK

Lake Nakuru was first made a National Park in 1961, but the Park was enlarged in 1974 to include the immediate hinterland and a substantial area south of the lake, so that it now covers 200 sq. km. (77 sq. miles). Though the level of the lake is subject to considerable fluctuations depending on rainfall (these changes may be part of a continuing pattern over a much longer period), at the moment the area of the lake is about 40 sq. km. (25 sq. miles).

Nakuru is one of a series of shallow alkaline lakes which have formed on the floor of the rift valley and lies just south of the equator, at an altitude of 1,758 meters (5,767 ft.). The town of Nakuru is three km. (two miles) to the north of the lake on the lower slopes of Mount Menengai, an extinct volcano whose rim rises 514 meters (1,700 ft.) above the lake and encloses one of the world's largest craters, some 11 km. (seven miles) across.

The Park is renowned for its birdlife and the lake itself has been termed "the greatest bird spectacle on earth" by Roger Tory Peterson, one of the world's leading ornithologists, for its huge concentration of lesser flamingos which at times form a pink fringe around the blue waters of the lake. Estimates have put the number of flamingos as high as one million in an exceptional year but it can vary considerably, and likewise the spectacle. Although the reasons for this variation are uncertain it is thought they relate to the delicately balanced food cycle of the flamingos, which might be disturbed by changes in the water level, and possibly pollution.

But it should not be thought that the attractions of the Park are overly dependent upon the size of the flamingo population, for there are over 400 other species of bird resident here, including large numbers of darters, cormorants and white pelicans. In addition there are 50 mammal species to be found in the different habitats around the lake shore.

The Lake

Three seasonal rivers flow into the lake but there is no outlet, so hundreds of years of evaporation of the waters have increased the mineral content considerably. Most plant species are unable to survive this highly alkaline medium, but certain microscopic algae thrive under these conditions and they provide food for both the flamingo and the fish, which are able to filter the algae out of the water. The lesser flamingo feed mainly in the shallow water near the shore, thousands of them forming a startling pink ribbon along the lake shore. The greater flamingo occur in smaller numbers and generally feed slightly away from the shore in deeper water. The fish, which were originally introduced in to the lake as an anti-mosquito measure, are of one species only, *Tilapia grahami.* They are, however, abundant and support a large number and variety of fish-eating birds—pelicans, cormorants, darters, grebes, spoonbills, fish eagles, storks, ibis and several different herons.

Neither flamingos nor pelicans breed at Lake Nakuru, but there is a large colony of white-necked cormorants and African darters at the mouth of the Njoro River, where birds breed actively most of the year. The pelicans also use the Njoro for washing off the soda from the lake. The fresh waters of the Njoro and a series of springs along the north shore of the lake provide a contrasting habitat to the highly alkaline lake. A large variety of bird species is found in the vicinity of the fresh water and, particularly during the European winter, large numbers of migrant waders and ducks concentrate in these areas. The fresh water is much less turgid than the lake water and herons and kingfishers prefer these areas for fishing. The resident hippo spend most of the day in the waters by the fresh springs but come onshore to graze at night.

Waders, avocets and stilts feed along the shore in the shallows and their numbers are greatly increased during the European winter months by migrant species. A variety of plovers is also resident at the lake and can be found nesting on the mud flats between June and August.

An all weather road completely encircles the lake, off which there are numerous tracks down to the lakeshore where parking areas are provided. Visitors should not attempt to drive too close to the lake's edge as the salt encrusted shoreline conceals very soft mud; instead it is best to leave your vehicle and walk along the shore, being careful not to startle the large flocks of birds.

On entering the Park by the main gate the road leading straight on follows the western shore of the lake, from which off to the left is the track to the mouth of the Njoro river, then tracks to a wide, open shoreline. The road going left from the main gate travels around the north shore, from which off to the right are tracks to "Hippo Point", then a number of observation hides.

Grasslands, Bushland and Forest

To the east the lake is bounded by rocky hills which are covered with a fascinating forest of strange "Candelabra" trees (Euphorbia) which is probably the best of its kind in Kenya. A rocky escarpment known as "Baboon Rocks" is to be found on the western shore and offers a superb view over the lake. Baboons are frequently seen in these areas and the little rodent-like rock hyrax is common. Antelope found here include the sure-footed klipspringer and Chanler's reedbuck; the rocks are also the home of that elusive predator, the leopard—which is apparently increasing in number.

There are open grasslands running down to the lake on its northern and southern shores. The coarse spiky grass on the immediate shore and the lusher grass further inland provide grazing for herds of Defassa waterbuck, impala, Thomson's gazelle and Bohor reedbuck. It is probably the only place in Kenya where these reedbuck can be seen in large numbers.

Birds found in this habitat range from minute larks and ground nesting plovers, to the graceful crowned cranes, secretary birds and the comical waddling ground hornbills. Rodents are common, especially in the dry seasons, and a variety of birds of prey frequent both this area and the bush and forest regions of the Park.

Away from the lake's edge the grassland merges into Tarconanthus scrub and this provides yet another habitat for the animals of the Park. Birds found here include shrikes, rollers and coucals, and among the mammals are zebra, warthog, Grant's gazelle and jackal.

Fairly extensive tracts of yellow-barked thorn trees *(Acacia xanthophloea)* on the eastern shore and south of the lake provide a habitat for vervet and colobus monkeys, and cover for the more secretive bush buck and Kirk's dikdik. Between 300 and 400 buffalo inhabit the Park—most likely to be seen in the forest areas at dawn or dusk. Colorful waxbills, sunbirds, hoopoes and chats are well represented in the forest as well as larger birds of prey such as the magnificent long-crested hawk eagle and fish eagles. In the southwestern corner of the Park there is also an olive tree forest which is sometimes found to shelter a rhinoceros.

PARK DATA

DIRECTIONS. Nakuru town lies in the rift valley northwest of Nairobi, 156 km. (97 miles) along the new A104 highway, and the Park is just three km. (two miles) due south of the town, left from the main street.

ACCOMMODATIONS. There are two comfortable lodges within the Park.
Lake Nakuru Lodge. Reservations: P.O. Box 561, Nakuru (tel. Elmenteita 5Y6 and 5Y9). A farmhouse on the park boundary and now converted into a lodge. Guests stay in the main lodge building or in surrounding cottages. Good pool.
Lion Hill Camp. Reservations: Repotel, P.O.Box 46527, Nairobi (tel. 27828). Accommodations mainly in permanent safari tents, very comfortable, with electricity, hot and cold running water, showers and flush toilets. On the slopes of Lion Hill, with good views over the lake.
Midland Hotel. In Nakuru town (tel. Nakuru 41277).
Lake Baringo Lodge. Reservations: Block Hotels, P.O. Box 47557, Nairobi (tel. 22860 and 335807). 121 km. (75 miles) north of Nakuru on tarmac all the way. A first rate lodge in beautiful grounds, on the edge of Lake Baringo.

Thomson's Falls Lodge. Reservations: P.O.Box 38, Nyahururu (tel. 6). 65 km. (40 miles) northeast of Nakuru, at Nyahururu, once known as Thomson's Falls. Friendly place with period charm. Comfortable cottages, log fires at night.

Campsites. There are three campsites within the park boundaries, all with toilet facilities, water and firewood.

MASAI MARA GAME RESERVE

The Reserve is effectively an extension into Kenya of Tanzania's great Serengeti National Park and lies along their common border, 249 km. (155 miles) west of Nairobi. It is considered by many people to be the best of Kenya's wildlife sanctuaries, where plains-game can still be found in the great numbers once common to much of the country, and which in turn support a large population of predators.

Established in 1961 the 'Mara', as it is known, covers an area of 1,800 sq. km. (695 sq. miles) and is under the control of the local district authority who have divided it into two parts. In the outer regions of the Reserve the land is shared by the Masai who graze their cattle alongside the wildlife—and take their chance with the lions. But in the south, in the area around Keekorok Lodge is an inner reserve of ap-

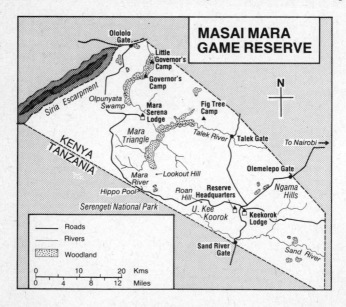

proximately 500 sq. km. (193 sq. miles) which is treated as a National Park, with no settlement or grazing allowed, although unlike most parks, vehicles are permitted to leave the tracks to approach game.

The landscape of the Mara is for the most part one of gently rolling savannah grasslands stretching to the horizon, intersected by the dark green veins of rich acacia woodland which occupy the banks of the Reserve's two main rivers, the Mara and Talek, and their many seasonal tributaries. It is less arid and much greener than most parks, benefitting from the more humid conditions of the Lake Victoria region and an altitude of 1,650 meters (5,412 ft.) which combine to produce a more temperate climate.

Amongst the rolling grasslands of the Reserve many species of plains animals are to be found throughout the year, including herds of buffalo, wildebeest, hartebeest, impala, zebra and gazelle, and often number hundreds at a time. Common to Mara but not often found elsewhere in Kenya are large herds of topi, which are related to hartebeest but of darker and more distinctive colouring, and a small colony of rare roan antelope is to be found in the western section of the Reserve near the Siria escarpment—but not at the misleadingly named Roan Hill near Keekorok Lodge.

Dense thickets of thorn bush sometimes reveal a browsing black rhino and large numbers of Masai giraffe and elephant are to be seen, usually near to the riverine woodland. The Mara river, which bisects the Reserve, has a very prolific population of hippo which often gather in numbers of 50 or more in the larger pools to be found at intervals along its length. Crocodile also frequent the banks and sandspits.

But it is perhaps the predators that visitors come to see most of all in Mara, and with so much food around it is no surprise that the Reserve hosts the country's largest population of lion. Indeed it is renowned for its large prides which often number between 20 and 30 and are not difficult to find, particularly with the help of a local ranger. The open country is, of course, ideal for the cheetah which is present in good numbers and the less glamorous hunting dogs, jackals and hyenas are also frequently encountered on the open plains.

For the ornithologist the variety and interest is equally diverse. 53 species of raptors alone have been recorded; on the plains a variety of bustard may be seen along with the strutting secretary birds. The riverine forests have their own species including the beautiful Ross's turaco, recognised by the flash of its scarlet wings through the trees.

As if all these wildlife attractions of the Mara were not enough, it has one more exceptional offering - the annual migration of zebra and wildebeest from the Serengeti. Every year, around July, hundreds of thousands thunder across the border in columns which stretch for miles to feed on the grasslands of the Reserve. On reaching the Mara river they hurl themselves into the fast flowing waters which claim thousands of victims as they struggle to cross to the lush grazing of the Mara Triangle.

PARK DATA

DIRECTIONS. From Nairobi follow the old Nairobi road, B3, for the 56 km. (35 miles) to the foot of the rift escarpment, then left across the valley floor for the 90 km. (56 miles) to Narok. From Narok the B3 continues in murram to Sotik but after 17 km. (11 miles) the road forks, whence left leads to the centre of the Reserve and Keekorok, 90 km. (56 miles). Straight on, then left after 42 km. (26 miles) at Ngorengore leads to the northern area of the Reserve and Governors, Mara Buffalo, Kichwa Tembo and Mara River tented lodges.

ACCOMMODATIONS. There are two excellent lodges and four tented camps in the Reserve, and additionally, four tented camps on the periphery.
In the Reserve:
Keekorok Lodge. Reservations: Block Hotels, P.O. Box 47557, Nairobi (tel. 22860, 335807). Extremely comfortable, well run, and highly recommended. Airstrip alongside the lodge. Balloon safaris available. Good pool. It is rated among the best in Kenya for comfort, service and cuisine, but can be noisy.
Mara Serena Lodge. Reservations: Serena Lodges & Hotels, P.O. Box 48960, Nairobi (tel. 338656/7). Newer, and occupying a hilltop site with vast views over the Mara Triangle and Mara river. The architecture is styled on a Masai engkang (village), and the interior decor makes effective use of Masai motifs. Traditional dancing performed after dinner each evening. The lodge has a good pool and the colorful gardens attract countless species of birds. All weather airstrip nearby.
Fig Tree Camp. Reservations: P.O. Box 67868 Nairobi (tel. 21439, 20592). Situated near the Talek Gate on the eastern side of the Reserve. Somewhat simpler than the others.
Governor's Camp and Little Governor's Camp. Reservations: P.O.Box 48217, Nairobi (tel. 331871, 331041). Reckoned to be the best of several privately-operated luxury tented camps on the Mara river in the northwest corner of the Reserve. These two adjacent superb old-style safari camps are accessible by air and maintain safari vehicles for game runs throughout the Reserve. Both of them offer first-class comfort and cuisine.
Mara Sarova Camp. Reservations: Sarova Hotels, P.O. Box 30680, Nairobi (tel. 333233). A new luxury camp in the central Keekorok area.
Tented camps on the periphery:
Cottar's Camp. Reservations: Nairobi Travel Center, P.O. Box 41178, Nairobi (tel. 27930, 27939). Very comfortable camp situated under giant fig trees by a natural spring, not far from the Olemelepo Gate. Safari vehicles supplied for game runs and escorted foot safaris also available.
Kichwa Tembo Camp. Reservations: Signet Hotels, P.O. Box 59749, Nairobi (tel. 338656). Excellent camp in the northwest corner just outside the Reserve

boundary near the Olololo Gate. Airstrip. Foot safaris available. First-class cuisine.

Mara Buffalo Camp. Reservations: Repotel, P.O. Box 46527, Nairobi (tel. 27828). Very comfortable camp overlooking the Mara river.

Mara River Camp. Reservations: Bookings Ltd., P.O. Box 20106, Nairobi (tel. 25255). Downstream from Mara Buffalo Camp, also situated overlooking the river.

Campsites. There are several in the outer Reserve, some located outside the Talek gate along the river. There are no facilities so campers must be self-sufficient and prior booking must be made through the Game Department in Nairobi.

MARSABIT NATIONAL PARK

Marsabit is one of Kenya's more remote national parks, situated 273 km. (170 miles) north of Isiolo and surrounded by deserts—the Dida Galgalla (north), the Koroli (west) and Kaisut (south and east). Its 592 sq. km. (230 sq. miles) consist largely of forested mountain which rises over 1,500 meters (5,000 ft.) and is able to generate sufficient moisture to support this welcome oasis in the middle of such a hostile wilderness.

The area is pitted with spectacular volcanic craters which sometimes fill to form seasonal lakes. The best-known of these is Lake Paradise, where the Americans Martin and Osa Johnson spent four years in the '20s writing about and filming what was then their private paradise. The lake is almost circular, about two km. (one mile) in diameter and ringed with a bright green marsh and grass before the curtain forest. It attracts varied bird life, especially coots for which a one-time hunter on Marsabit had an interesting recipe. The secret, he wrote, is to boil the coot together with a brick in a large pot for six hours—then throw away the bird and eat the brick!

Below Lake Paradise is a rocky pool named "Boculi" after a fine old gun-bearer of the Johnsons. This, like the big lake, is a popular watering place for elephant, buffalo and kudu.

Animals found in the Park include buffalo, lion, leopard, caracal, striped hyena, reticulated giraffe and aard wolf, but are often difficult to spot in the thick forest. Probably the main wildlife attraction, though, are the herd of greater kudu with their heavily spiralled horns, and magnificent elephant which have a reputation for very large tusks, often weighing over 45 kg. (100 lbs).

Until a few years ago the Park was the undisputed kingdom of "Ahmed", a big-tusked bull elephant who became the symbol of wildlife conservation in Kenya. This giant was a great attraction for Marsabit—he was a loner, fairly tolerant of human admirers and occasionally over-friendly—when for instance he would walk into town to sample someone's vegetable garden. He was immensely popular locally, nationally and internationally and was endowed with special life-time protection by decree of President Kenyatta and given a permanent honor guard of rangers. Since his death in 1974 Ahmed has stood, ignominiously stuffed, in the courtyard of Nairobi Museum.

Ornithologist John Williams estimates there are 52 species of raptors among the birds of the mountain, including the lammergeier on the cliffs of the largest crater, or "gof", which is called Gof Bongole.

PARK DATA

DIRECTIONS. From Isiolo on the A2, Ethiopian Highway, it is a tortuous 275 km. (170 miles) north to this mountain refuge.

ACCOMMODATIONS. Marsabit Lodge. P.O.Box 45, Marsabit (tel.44). Reservations: African Tours and Hotels, P.O.Box 30471, Nairobi (tel. 336858). Well-run and popular locale on the edge of Lake Paradise.
Marsabit Tented Lodge. Reservations: P.O.Box 14982, Nairobi (tel. 7742926).

Campsites. There is a public campsite near Lake Paradise.

MERU NATIONAL PARK

Meru National Park is 1,554 sq. km. (600 sq. miles) of unspoilt wilderness lying 95 km. (60 miles) to the northeast of Mount Kenya, at the beginning of the flat, arid bushland which stretches to the coast. It is perhaps best known for its association with "Elsa", the lioness in *Born Free,* and the Adamsons who reintroduced her to the wild here and for many years afterwards continued their studies of both lion and cheetah in the Park.

Although it straddles the equator in a generally hot, dry area, the Park's northwestern perimeter is in the foothills of the Nyambeni range which receives a very high rainfall. This feeds a dozen permanent streams and rivers which flow through the Park. To the south it is bounded by the Ura and Tana rivers and in the east by the Murera and Rojewero rivers, along whose banks stand rich woodland of acacia, fig and palm trees, alive with parrots and vervet monkeys.

The easterly flow of the Rojewero river from the Nyambeni hills divides the Park into two areas of contrasting topography. To the north are open grazing plains with light acacia woodland, cut through by numerous river courses running down from the hills and sprouting Doum palms. It is in these areas that the Park's main concentrations of game are to be found, including many of the main species and a number characteristic of the northern areas, such as reticulated giraffe, Somail ostrich, Beisa oryx and the occasional Grevy's zebra.

Unique to Meru is a handful of white rhino which are not native to the country, and were in fact introduced here from South Africa a few years ago. They comprise of two, small family groups and are closely guarded by the rangers in the area of the Park's Headquarters. So used to man's presence have they become that on request the Rangers will escort visitors on foot to within a few yards—an opportunity not to be missed. The unguarded black rhino is more likely to be encountered on the plains a few miles to the west of the Headquarter's though they are elusive.

In the area of the Meru Mulika Lodge and toward the Murera gate are a number of swamps where a large part of the Park's herd of 4,000 buffalo are often to be found. It is also a favorite with the elephants who cross over the plain to cool-off here and take mud baths.

To the south of the Rojewero river the country is completely different, being arid and dusty, covered in thick thornbush and disected by numerous sand luggas. The area is home to the long-necked gerenuk which feeds from thorn bushes by standing on its hind legs, and the timid lesser kudu with its magnificent horns, and which is plentiful toward the Tana river.

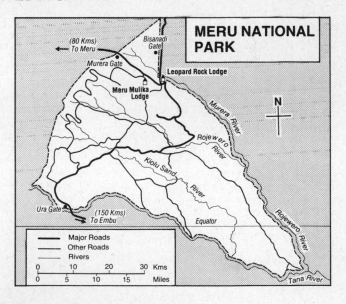

MERU NATIONAL PARK

(80 Kms) To Meru

Bisanadi Gate

Murera Gate

Leopard Rock Lodge

Meru Mulika Lodge

Murera River

N

Rojewero River

Kiolu Sand River

Ura Gate

(150 Kms) To Embu

Equator

Rojewero River

Tana River

Major Roads
Other Roads
Rivers

0   10   20   30   Kms
0   5   10   15   Miles

At the south eastern corner of the Park near the confluence of the Rojewero and the Tana rivers are the Adamson Falls where the Tana cascades through a surrealist confusion of quartzite and granite rocks weathered into strange shapes. The Tana is a good place to see hippo and crocodile although they are also to be found in many of the Park's other rivers.

Species of birds in Meru number over 300 and are particularly colorful, with parrots in the forests, and kingfishers and herons by the many rivers. Hornbills of many kinds are plentiful while the white-throated bee eater is often seen perched on the very end of a branch of thorn bush.

A good network of tracks covers the Park and uses the marker-post system for identification purposes in conjunction with the very good official park map. The tracks are generally well maintained and pose little problem for a sturdy saloon in the dry season, but in the wet season—apart from the main tracks—a four-wheel-drive vehicle is recommended for negotiating the numerous river crossings and muddy drifts.

In the northwest of the Park the tracks take the form of a series of long thin loops parallel to the course of the numerous rivers and enclosing the main swamps and areas of plain. The plains surrounding the Park Headquarters are also criss-crossed with a network of good tracks. South of the Rojewero the few tracks stretch out to the Ura and Tana rivers and although it is a long dusty haul—24 km. (15 miles) each way—it is well worth the effort: early morning or late afternoon being best when the equatorial sun is least oppressive and the shy lesser kudu and gerenuk venture from the shady bush.

PARK DATA

DIRECTIONS. There are two main access routes to the Park from Nairobi. The first is via Meru town which is best reached by the A2 highway through Nanyuki, 294 km. (183 miles). A tarmac road, C91, then runs for 48 km. (30 miles) into the Nyambeni range of hills to Maua, just before which a track off left travels the remaining 25 km. (16 miles) to the Murera gate. An alternative and more direct route from the Capital takes the easterly route around Mount Kenya, via the town of Embu, 138 km. (86 miles). From Embu take the Meru road, forking right after 19 km. (12 miles), for nearly 80 km. (50 miles) before a well signposted turning off right to the Ura gate—another 64 km. (40 miles). From this gate it is a further 48 km. (30 miles) to Meru Mulika Lodge or Leopard Rock Self-Service Bandas.

ACCOMMODATIONS. Isaak Walton Inn. P.O.Box 1, Embu (tel. 28). In Embu, on the route from Nairobi. Attractive gardens. Trout fishing available—a permit must be obtained from the warden.

Leopard Rock Self-Service Bandas. Reservations: A.A. Travel Ltd., P.O. Box 14982, Nairobi (tel. 742926). Comfortable cottage-style accommodations under acacia trees overlooking a stream. Crockery and cooking utensils provided, bedding can be hired, bring your own food. Situated a short distance from Meru Mulika Lodge.

Meru Mulika Lodge. Reservations: African Tours & Hotels, P.O. Box 30471, Nairobi (tel. 336858). A full service lodge, attractively designed and built of interesting local materials. Situated overlooking Mulika swamp a short distance from the Murera Gate entrance to the park. Good concentrations of elephant, buffalo, zebra and other game animals are easily seen from the terrace of the lodge.

Pig and Whistle Hotel. P.O.Box 1218, Meru (tel. 20688). In the center of Meru township.

Campsites. Authorised campsites have been designated by the warden at Park Headquarters. Nominal fees. The main site, close to the Headquarters, has modest facilities and a few, simple bandas.

VISITOR ADVICE. Owing to the remoteness of the Park, it is recommended that visitors schedule at least two days in the Park, including a night's stop-over.

Although the days are normally warm, evenings and nights can sometimes be chilly, especially April to August; it is advisable to bring suitable warm clothes.

Anti-malarial precautions should be taken and campers should bring mosquito nets.

Visitors are advised not to swim in the rivers as there are crocodile in all of them.

Vehicles should carry a good selection of tools and spares as well as water and petrol reserves.

NAIROBI NATIONAL PARK

The most striking feature of Nairobi National Park is not some unusual geological formation, nor a group of rare animals, but that it is here at all. For the Park's 114 sq. km. (44 sq. miles) begin just eight km. (five miles) from the centre of this bustling city of over one million people, a wedge of wild Africa thrusting into the suburbs and industrial areas of its southern outskirts. For visitors staying in Nairobi it is literally just a few minutes down the road and a visit should not be missed.

The Park is fenced on its western boundary where it borders the residential suburbs of Karen and Langata, and on its northeastern boundary which fronts the main Mombasa highway across which lie the airport and the city's industrial area. Otherwise it is open to the migration of game from the Athi plains and the Kitengela and Ngong Conservation Areas, to the south of the capital.

The topography is principally of open plain which gently slopes from the west and is broken into ridges and valleys by numerous seasonal rivers running southeast into the Mbagathi/Athi River. These are often steep and rocky with richer vegetation than the surrounding plain, including strands of acacia woodland. The permanent Mbagathi/Athi river is attended by a rich forest of yellow acacia on its journey through the Park, and in the west it runs through a steep gorge where rocky outcrops are reputed to be a favorite haunt of leopard.

In the extreme west a low ridge is covered in a highland forest of hardwoods which is home to herds of bush-buck and impala as well as some of the Park's baboons. Impala Point, at the edge of the ridge, makes a good vantage point from which to view the Park and to scan the plains with binoculars for concentrations of game or vehicles grouped around an important find.

At various points in the Park the courses of seasonal streams have been blocked to create dams of various sizes. Besides providing a better distribution of permanent water for the game they also create another, different habitat which proves attractive to certain types of bird, some of which were not found in the Park previously.

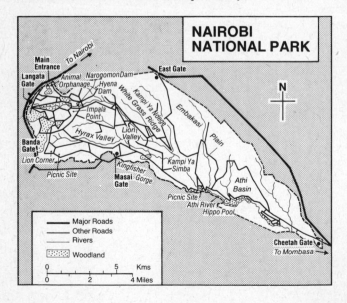

Despite its urban location and small area, the Park contains many of the main species of game to be found elsewhere in Kenya, but with the notable absence of elephant for whom it is much too confined. Plains game are particularly well represented with zebra, wildebeest, Coke's hartebeest, eland, impala and both Grant's and Thomson's gazelle. Scampering warthogs and arrogantly strutting ostriches are also common on the open plains.

Larger game includes Masai giraffe which browse much of the woodland, and the occasional black rhino, sometimes found in the light bush around the forest area. Predators are one of the Park's main attractions with lion present in reasonable numbers, and cheetah are also to be found stalking the game on the plains: the rangers keep a careful note of their movements and so it is worth asking advice of the best area to try. Crocodile and hippo are present in the larger pools of the Mbagathi/Athi river and can be viewed from a nature trail in the eastern section of the Park.

Birdlife is equally varied with native species supplemented by migrants at certain times of year, mainly March–April. Eagles, hawks and buzzards are much in evidence as are those scavengers the vulture and marabou stork, which are often seen gathered around the waterholes. Herons, Egyptian geese, crowned cranes and yellow-bill storks are also seen around the dams and marshes, whilst elsewhere weaverbirds and sunbirds are common.

The Park has a very comprehensive network of all-weather trails suitable for saloon cars, which are well signposted at junctions and clearly marked on the official map. However, visitors should not expect colorful place names such as "lion corner" or "leopard cliff" to be necessarily indicative of current residents. The best time of day for game viewing, as with other Parks, is early morning or late afternoon when the animals are most active.

Beside the Park's main entrance on the Langata road is the animal orphanage. Opened in 1963 its objective is to shelter animals which are strays, orphaned or sick until they can be reintroduced to their natural habitat. It strongly protests at being labelled a zoo but many of the animals are permanent residents and the inclusion of non-native species —including tigers—does nothing to support these protests. Nonetheless, it offers the opportunity for visitors to see more closely some of the animals they have, or have not, encountered on the open plains, and few miss the opportunity to photograph the resident leopard lazing in the branches of a tree.

PARK DATA

DIRECTIONS. For the main entrance take the Uhuru highway in the direction of Mombasa and just after the football stadium turn right along Langata Road, signposted Nairobi National Park, past Nairobi Dam, Wilson Airport and the army barracks. Alternatively, access can be gained from the Mombasa road gate; continue on the Uhuru highway until a signposted right turn just after the drive-in cinema.

SAMBURU–ISIOLO–SHABA GAME RESERVES

These three Reserves are grouped together around the Uaso Nyiro river where the foothills of Mount Kenya end, and the hot, arid lands of Kenya's Northern Province begin. For all practical purposes the Samburu and Isiolo Reserves are treated as one and they lie to the west of the Great North Road (A2) at Archer's Post. Shaba Reserve, more recently formed in 1974, is found to the east of the road opposite the Isiolo Reserve.

The Samburu–Isiolo Reserves together cover an area of 337 sq. km. (130 sq. miles) and are divided by the Uaso Nyiro (brown water) river which can be crossed within the Reserve by a bridge just upstream from Samburu Lodge. For the most part the country is semi-arid plain covered in thorn bush with a few open grazing areas, but contrasting sharply is the thick band of rich woodland which accompanies the river through the Reserve. The landscape to the north is also in striking contrast, with the rugged granite outcrop of Mount Lolokwe standing as giant sentinel and changing hue as the sun slowly sinks.

For such a small area the Reserve sustains a surprising number and variety of game year round, made possible by the long stretch of permanent river waters. It is in the area of the river, with its thick blanket of acacias and doum palms, that many of the animals are to be found, including the Reserve's herd of elephant which now numbers over 100. Numerous hippo and crocodile can be seen in the river and the best place for viewing the latter is from the terrace bar at Samburu Lodge. This overlooks a wide stretch of river whose shallows and banks are home to dozens of crocodile which often leave the river to bask alongside the terrace; it really isn't unusual here to slake the thirst of the afternoon's game-run eyeball-to-eyeball with a croc.

Another permanent source of water is found at Buffalo Springs in the east of Isiolo, where waters probably originating on Mount Kenya surface to form a series of clear pools. In addition to some visitors who take the opportunity to cool-off, the springs attract game from the nearby grazing plains and a constant stream of birds. The swamp area between the springs and the nearby river is also a good area for viewing wildlife.

Buffalo, impala, waterbuck, gazelle and common zebra are all to be found here but there are also additional species, found only in the northern areas, which constitute one of the Reserve's main attractions: these include reticulated giraffe, the blue-necked Somali ostrich and the rare Grevy's zebra whose fine pin-striped skin is highly prized. Beisa oryx are also present, and it is probably the best place to view the long-necked gerenuk which are plentiful here. The main predators can also be seen, including the elusive leopard which frequents the woodland near Samburu Lodge, lured by baited platforms.

Over 300 species of bird inhabit the Reserve and amongst a good variety of eagle the Martial is not uncommon. The red-rumped buffalo weaver and red-billed hornbill abound and characteristic of the area are large flocks of rich-blue vulturine guinea-fowl.

The Reserve is extensively tracked both north and south of the river but the more rewarding runs are often along the course of the river itself. In the north, downriver from the bridge, there is good access to the river bank. To the south, the "Lower river circuit" and "Upper river circuit" are well marked and cover a variety of habitat from thorn-bush to Doum palm. In the southeast Buffalo Springs, the river lookout, the swamplands and the grazing lands behind can all be taken in during a run of a few miles and this is probably the best area for viewing reticulated giraffe and Beisa oryx.

The Shaba Reserve comprises 130 sq. km. (50 sq. miles) of similar terrain on the southern bank of the river, but although rich in wildlife it is not as yet as well provided with tracks. Sadly, it was here in 1980 that Joy Adamson was killed during what was to be her final "Born Free" experiment with the leopard Penny.

PARK DATA

DIRECTIONS. From Nairobi take the A2 highway north to Nanyuki, then over the shoulder of Mount Kenya to Isiolo, a distance of 290 km. (180 miles). From Isiolo continue on the A2, now loosely surfaced in stone, for 26 km. (16 miles) where signposted left is the Ngare Mara gate to the Samburu–Isiolo Reserves. Continuing on the main highway a few miles further, off left is the Buffalo Springs gate and to the right the entrance to Shaba.

ACCOMMODATIONS. Buffalo Springs Tented Lodge. Reservations: African Tours & Hotels, P.O. Box 30471, Nairobi (tel. 336858). Situated further downstream in the Buffalo Springs Reserve on the south bank of the Uaso Nyiro river. This is an especially good area for beisa oryx and a variety of game animals attracted to the swampy grass near Buffalo Springs. Cheetah frequently seen here.

Samburu Lodge. Reservations: Block Hotels, P.O. Box 47557, Nairobi (tel. 22860/335807). Built of local stone and mountain cedar and with an international reputation for comfort, cuisine and wildlife spectacle. Traditional Samburu dancing performed daily. Swimming pool. Situated overlooking the Uaso Nyiro river.

Samburu River Lodge. Reservations: Signet Hotels, P.O. Box 59749, Nairobi (tel. 335900, 335807, 21318). A short distance upstream from Samburu Lodge, also overlooking the Uaso Nyiro river. Slightly more remote and peaceful, and with a good swimming pool. Especially noted as a birdwatching locale.

Shaba Tented Camp. Reservations: Bookings Ltd., P.O. Box 20106, Nairobi (tel. 25255). Dining room and bar built of local materials. Hot and cold showers, washing facilities and toilets attached to each spacious, insect-proof tent. Natural swimming pool. A really delightful get-away-from-it-all place. Four-wheel-drive safari vehicles advisable in this somewhat rugged area.

Campsites. Campsites are also available. Check with the Warden at the Samburu Reserve headquarters. Check also with Nairobi tour operators on the possibility of fully-serviced accommodations at non-permanent luxury tented camps which may be operated in any one of the three reserves.

THE SHIMBA HILLS NATIONAL RESERVE

The Reserve lies 24 km. (15 miles) south of Mombasa, and covers 192 sq. km. (74 sq. miles) of the Shimba range of hills. The landscape is almost park-like, consisting of green rolling hills patched with areas of ancient forest, and provides a welcome change of scenery for visitors staying in the coastal hotels.

The area was given reserve status to protect a herd of the beautiful sable antelope which are now rare in Kenya. They are easy to view in the Reserve, and most likely to be found in the area between Longo-Magandi forest and the Giriama Hill viewpoint. Another rare animal, the roan antelope, was transferred from a ranch near Thika in the late '60s and has become an additional wildlife attraction.

There are a few elephant in the Reserve, but they are fairly timid for some reason and tend to remain in the forests. Lion and leopard are present in small numbers but are rarely encountered. Other animals include buffalo, bushbuck, Bohor reedbuck and colobus monkeys. None of the large animals amounts to a deterrent to a nature walk anywhere in the Reserve, including the dense Makadara Forest section.

Birdlife is profuse and includes occasional clouds of carmine bee-eaters, palm nut vultures, Fischer's turacos, silvery-cheeked hornbills and spurfowl—in Swahili, *Kwale,* after which the district is named. Butterflies are a particular attraction, as are ground orchids, gladioli and other wild flowers decorating the meadowland.

PARK DATA

DIRECTIONS. From the tarmac coastal road take a turning inland on the C106 just north of Tiwi, clearly signposted to Kwale, the district capital. The main gate is found on the left, about a mile after passing through town.

Campsites. Camping is available in the Park.

SIBILOI NATIONAL PARK (Lake Turkana)

The Park was established in 1970 and lies along the northeastern shore of Lake Turkana from Alia Bay to within a few miles of the Ethiopian border. Its 1,554 sq. km. (600 sq. miles) consist of semi-desert and scrubland, and lacks any of the usual facilities of a national park, such as a track network or lodge accommodations.

The most important feature of the Park is the richness of its fossilised remains, and the area is often referred to as the "Cradle of Mankind". It was here that Richard Leakey discovered a skull of early man some 2½ million years old, which predates discoveries anywhere else in the world. The skull itself is now in the National Museum in Nairobi, but John Leakey—Richard's son—has recently opened a small museum at Koobi Fora, where there is a cast of the skull, many evolutionary exhibits, as well as geological specimens of the area and plant and animal life. The museum can only be visited on prior permission from the National Museum, Nairobi.

The area around the "1470" find is strewn with fossil fragments of Australopithecus and of the first tool-makers, as well as the huge mammals (including a three-toed predecessor of the horse) which roamed the prehistoric green hinterland of Lake Turkana. The fossils are left for visitors to see—but not to touch and there are heavy penalties for their removal without a license.

Excavation and classification of fossils is continuous at the Park and up-to-date information is available to the visitor at the National Museum in Nairobi.

For such a hostile environment there is a surprising variety of wildlife in the area. There are sizeable herds of the northern game species of oryx, topi and smaller antelope, and large crocodile and hippo populations at the shoreline. The Park is also remote enough for discerning and sometimes distinguished royal birdwatchers to relax and enjoy their hobby in a totally unspoiled technicolor seascape. There are many thousands of flamingo on Turkana as well as pelicans, gulls, waders, ducks and geese, and rarities such as black-tailed godwits and spotted redshanks. Between March and early May the lake is invaded by vast numbers of European migrant birds, especially wagtails and marsh sandpipers.

At present there are no formal gates to the Park and the rule is that prior arrangements for a visit should be made with the park authorities in Nairobi or at Marsabit or with the Sibiloi warden at Alia Bay. Entry may be restricted to four-wheel-drive vehicles carrying enough equipment and supplies, including gasoline, for a self-contained stay in the Park.

PARK DATA

DIRECTIONS. Access is best gained by air to landing strips at Alia Bay or Koobi Fora. By road it is an arduous journey which should not be attempted without four-wheel-drive vehicles, and even then it is advisable to travel in pairs. From Nairobi it is 724 km. (450 miles) via Nyahururu, Maralal, Loyangalani and North Horr—left turn for Alia Bay.

ACCOMMODATIONS. Oasis Lodge. Reservations: Thorn Tree Safaris, P.O.Box 42475, Nairobi (tel. 25641). The nearest visitor accommodations, at Loyangalani, by the lake. Boats, good fishing, hot springs.

Campsites. Camping is possible in the Park itself, by prior arrangement with the warden.

TSAVO NATIONAL PARK

Tsavo National Park is by far the largest of Kenya's wildlife sanctuaries and covers the astounding area of 20,720 sq. km. (8,000 sq. miles), greater than all of the country's other parks and reserves added together. It lies southeast of Nairobi just over halfway to the coast at Mombasa, and stretches 241 km. (150 miles) from the Tanzania border in the south to the dry semi-desert north of the Galana river.

The Park is divided into two sections, Tsavo East and Tsavo West. They are separated by the main Mombasa highway. Each park has its own headquarters, its own warden and field staff—and separate entry fees. But otherwise, they are treated as one unit. Although it was one of the first parks to be developed for tourism it is so large that much of it is still not easily accessible, and in Tsavo East some two thirds of its area, north of the Galana, is almost untouched and visited only with special permission.

Tsavo East is the least varied of the two sections, being mainly dry thornbush country, although in the developed area between the Galana and the Mombasa highway numerous seasonal river courses provide richer vegetation. The vegetation in this area was once much denser with a good covering of acacias, but the destructive action of too many

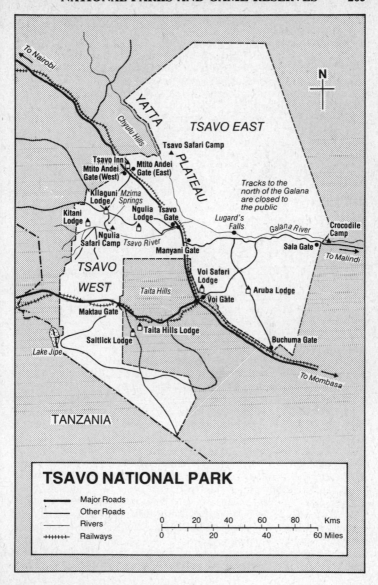

TSAVO NATIONAL PARK

	Major Roads
	Other Roads
	Rivers
+++++	Railways

0   20   40   60   80   Kms
0   20   40   60 Miles

elephants and a period of drought had a drastic affect. Fewer elephant and a more regular rainfall are now leading, thankfully, to its slow regeneration.

There are two outstanding physical features in the eastern section, the Yatta plateau and the Mudanda Rock. The Yatta plateau, which is only a couple of miles across, forms an impressive escarpment along the northern bank of the Galana river and is in fact an ancient lava flow which begins 322 km. (200 miles) away in the highlands near Nairobi. Mudanda Rock is a mile-long outcrop of rock just off the track leading between the Manyani and Voi gates, beside which is a waterhole formed by the collection of the rock's own run-off. In the dry season hundreds of elephant, buffalo and other game are often gathered here and the spectacle they present can be viewed from the flat top of the rock itself, reached by steps leading up the opposite face to the water-hole, from a parking area.

Tsavo West has a more diverse range of habitats than its eastern neighbour and is scenically much more interesting, which probably accounts for its greater popularity with visitors. Like Tsavo East it is divided into two by a permanent river, this time the Tsavo, with the area to the south consisting mainly of open savannah and bushland stretching the 80 km. (50 miles) to Lake Jipe on the Tanzanian border.

To the north of the Tsavo river the landscape stands in sharp contrast to the remainder of the Park, being an area of past volcanic activity. Here there are numerous hills and impressive rocky escarpments such as Ngulia and Ndawe which rise thousands of feet above the plain and are covered in thick woodland, a result of the extra rainfall generated by the hills. Many old volcanic cones have been eroded into smooth grassy hills but at Chaimu and Shetani activity has been recent enough to leave exposed the black cinder cones, around which there are marked nature trails for visitors.

In the northeastern corner of the Park lie the Chyulu Hills, an undulating chain of rounded peaks which provide a pretty backdrop to the Park and an interesting half-day visit. They too are of volcanic origin, being only a few thousand years old, and are riddled by a network of tunnels, some extending for several miles. The Shetani cone lies at the southern end of the range and activity here within the past 200 years has produced an extensive lava-flow which tumbles down the hillside for eight km. (five miles).

Mzima Springs are perhaps the most famous of Tsavo West's volcanic features and should certainly be on the itinerary of any visitor to the area. Here luxuriant vegetation surrounds large pools of clear spring water which surfaces at the rate of 50 million gallons a day, having travelled 48 km. (30 miles) along lava tunnels from the Chyulu Hills which form the catchment area. Some of the water is piped to Mombasa as part of the town's water supply, the rest flowing into the Tsavo river. Families of hippo laze in the pools and can even be observed underwater from an observation chamber sunk into the upper pool. Barbel fish and crocodiles are also found in the pools whilst vervet monkeys and numerous birds inhabit the surrounding woodland. A well marked nature trail leads around the pools but beware of crocodiles, and other animals which may be coming to drink.

A wide range of Kenya's wildlife is represented in Tsavo but easily the most dominant animal is the elephant which, although greatly reduced from earlier levels, still numbers more than 10,000 within the Park. Apart from large gatherings at certain times of the year at Mudanda Rock and Aruba dam they are perhaps most easily viewed at the waterholes of the main lodges, although game runs through the hilly country of Tsavo West usually encounter them—often as a "traffic hazard". Hippo are best viewed at Mzima Springs but are also present in the Tsavo and Galana rivers as are crocodile, and the best vantage point for the latter is at Crocodile Point in Tsavo East. The Park's black rhino population is the largest in Kenya despite a devastating period of poaching in the mid 70s, but they are very difficult to find in such a vast area.

Most of the species of plains game are present in large numbers, and in the eastern section there are in addition some of the dry country animals such as oryx, gerenuk and the magnificent lesser kudu. Lion and cheetah are numerous but difficult to spot in the good cover provided by much of the Park and visitors staying only a couple of days might be disappointed. In Tsavo West leopard are the subject of extensive research, with several animals being tracked by means of radio collars.

Birdlife is profuse, especially around the rivers and dams of the Park, with over 400 different species regularly noted; it also benefits from Tsavo being on a migration corridor from the coast.

Several species of starlings and weaver-birds abound along with hornbills which are always ready to take tea with guests at the Kilaguni Lodge. European and lilac-breasted rollers are common and there is a good variety of raptors, including the distinctive secretary-bird. Amongst water birds are herons and yellow-bill and saddle-bill storks.

Both sections of the Park have a good network of murram tracks in the developed areas between the rivers and the main Mombasa highway, being well signposted and numbered at junctions for reference to the Park maps. Many are passable throughout the year but some may be subject to closure in the wet seasons, so at these times it is best to seek advice from rangers.

In Tsavo East the tracks center on the Park Headquarters and the lodge at Voi, from which there are two major circuits. The most inter-

esting is the Galana river circuit which can include a visit to Mudanda
Rock before the 27 km. (17 mile) drive across the plains to the banks
of the Galana, where Lugard's Falls and Crocodile Point make interesting stopping points before the return journey via Rhino ridge. The Voi
river circuit takes in the riverine woodland and marsh of the seasonal
river eastward to Aruba before returning through light bush.

Central to the track network in Tsavo West is Kilaguni Lodge.
Eastward from the lodge, tracks with many interesting diversions wind
through the hills and escarpments to Ngulia Lodge and make a good
viewing circuit for elephant. South from Kilaguni, tracks lead to
Mzima and Poachers Lookout—where, from the top of a grassy volcanic hill, there are excellent views over the Park and toward Mount
Kilimanjaro. Further tracks then circuit both banks of the Tsavo river
and the adjacent grazing lands where plains game should be encountered.

PARK DATA

DIRECTIONS. Both sections of the Park are easily reached from Nairobi or
Mombasa by the main highway linking port with capital. Entrances to Tsavo
West are at Mtito Andei and Tsavo, respectively 241 km. (150 miles) and 290
km. (180 miles) from Nairobi. Tsavo East can be entered from the highway at
the Manyani gate, 11 km. (seven miles) further on, at Voi which is 331 km. (206
miles) from Nairobi—but only 151 km. (94 miles) from Mombasa, or at the
Buchuma gate, a further 48 km. (30 miles) still, at the southern corner of the
Park.

Another frequent approach to Tsavo West is from Amboseli, where a good
murram road leads across the plains to the Chyulu gate, near Kilaguni Lodge,
a distance of 105 km. (65 miles). Tsavo East is also often approached across
country, from Malindi following the route of the Galana to the Sala gate, 121
km. (75 miles).

ACCOMMODATIONS. Tsavo West. Hunter's Lodge. Reservations: P.O.
Box 30471, Nairobi (tel. 23285). At Kiboko on the main highway. A pleasant
hotel and a good stop for travelers between Nairobi and the coast.

Kilaguni Lodge. Reservations: African Tours and Hotels, P.O.Box 30471,
Nairobi (tel. 336858). Big, busy and bursting in season. One of Kenya's most
popular lodges, well sited above its own waterholes with distant views to the
Chyulu hills and Mount Kilimanjaro.

Kitani Lodge. Reservations: A.A. Travel Ltd, P.O.Box 14982, Nairobi (tel.
742926). Simple, self-help accommodations, close to the Tsavo river.

Ngulia Safari Camp. Reservations: A.A. Travel Ltd, P.O.Box 14982, Nairobi
(tel. 742926). Self-help accommodations, close to the main lodge. Built on
groups of rocks overlooking a waterhole which lies on a game trail.

Ngulia Safari Camp. Reservations: A.A. Travel Ltd, P.O.Box 14982, Nairobi (tel. 742926). Self-help accommodations, close to the main lodge. Built on groups of rocks overlooking a waterhole which lies on a game trail.

Ngulia Safari Lodge. Reservations: African Tours and Hotels, P.O.Box 30471, Nairobi (tel. 336858). Full-service lodge in the Park. Quiet; good for the serious visitor.

Salt Lick Lodge and **Taita Hills Lodge.** Reservations: Hilton Hotels International, P.O.Box 30624, Nairobi (tel. 334000). Two Hilton phantasmagorical creations which recall the glories of Hollywood spectaculars of days gone by. Outside the Park, off the Voi–Taveta road. Fancifully lavish in comparison to the surrounding wild, they are nevertheless very comfortable and fulfill their function admirably.

Tsavo Inn. Reservations: Kilimanjaro Safari Club, P.O.Box 30139, Nairobi (tel. 338888). Conveniently situated half-way between Nairobi and Mombasa at Mtito Andei opposite the main entrance gate to Tsavo West.

Tsavo East. Aruba Lodge. Reservations: P.O.Box 14982, Nairobi (tel. 742926). Self-help accommodations. Six thatched bandas on the shore of the dam, which is a favorite watering place for elephants.

Crocodile Tented Camp. Reservations: Repotel, P.O.Box 46527, Nairobi (tel. 27828). Close to the Sala gate and certainly worthy of its name.

Ndara Ranch. Reservations: P.O.Box 3, Voi (tel. 155) or, United Touring Company, P.O.Box 42196, Nairobi (tel. 331960). A private ranch providing safari cottages. Situated 15 km. (nine miles) south of Voi on the main Nairobi–Mombasa road, then turning west for two km. for the ranch. Plenty of game. Home cooking (steaks and seafood), good bar and swimming pool. Pleasant family atmosphere. Reasonably priced.

Tsavo Safaris. Reservations: Kilimanjaro Safari Club, P.O.Box 30139, Nairobi (tel. 338888). 30 km. (19 miles) east of Mtito Andei, overlooking the Athi river. Visitors are able to arrange trips into the restricted area from the camp.

Voi Safari Lodge. Reservations: African Tours and Hotels, P.O.Box 30471, Nairobi (tel. 336858). Full-service lodge, with ultra-modern features. Close to the main Voi gate. Very busy. Situated on a hilltop, with good views over the plain.

Campsites. In Tsavo West at the Mtito Andei, Chyulu and Mbuyuni gates, and at Voi gate and Aruba in Tsavo East; campsites have water and toilets.

THE MARINE NATIONAL PARKS

Kenya now has four areas of coastline designated marine National Parks or Reserves. The first to be established were the National Parks at Malindi and nearby Watamu in 1968, and they were followed in 1973 by the Kisite–Mpunguti Marine Park which lies offshore from Shimoni, close to the Tanzanian border. A more recent addition has been the

388 sq. km. (150 sq. miles) of the Kiunga National Marine Reserve which protects the most northern stretch of Kenya's coastline.

Snorkling amongst the reefs and coral gardens of these parks is permitted but fishing, spear or otherwise, is banned. Coral and shells are both protected items which should neither be damaged, nor removed from where they rest.

The best months of the year to enjoy diving in Kenya's marine parks are October through to March but they remain open all year round.

MALINDI AND WATAMU MARINE PARKS

The Malindi and Watamu Marine Parks were established in 1968 and were the first of their type in Africa. The two sanctuaries have a total area of 122 sq. km. (47 sq. miles) and lie off the tourist centers of Malindi and Turtle Bay (Watamu).

A marine national reserve envelops the parks from a point just south of Malindi town to below Watamu, extending seawards to the five km. (three mile) territorial limit. Included in the reserve is a large mangrove-tangled inlet known as Mida Creek and a narrow strip (only 30 meters wide) of mainland.

This part of the coast has some of the finest unspoiled white coral beaches in the world. Pandanus palms and wispy casuarina trees skirt the high water line and occasional headlands of dark limestone split the shore into bays, coves and lagoons each with its fringe of fine white sand. Just below the surface of the water are extensive coral reefs which blossom fully at night when the shy, sometimes phosphorescent polyps emerge from their hard limey shelters. Amongst this coral, is a profusion of colorful fish. A definitive survey of Kenya's reef has yet to be made and no-one knows how many species there are in these lagoons, or why some of the fish are so bizarre and so brightly patterned.

The recommended time to visit the reefs is at low tide. The fish at Watamu, for instance, have learned to expect visitors' arrival and crowd round the boats.

Malindi Marine Park

The Park, starting at its southern end, extends from Leopard Point to a spot just southwest of Sand Island, then northwards along Stork Passage to just beyond the tip of North Reef, and from there back to the beach at Chanoni Point. The coastline is an attractive coral sand beach, and low tide exposes more sand, broken by shallow pools and channels.

Between the shoreline and the two main reefs, North Reef and Barracuda Reef, runs Barracuda Channel. The water here is too deep for normal snorkeling, but the sandy bottom, with its rich growth of seaweed, harbors numerous shells, particularly the common spider conch, which may often be seen on the shallower edges of the channel.

Barracuda Reef lies on the shoreward side of North Reef. The lowest tides expose the tips of only a few coral heads, the rest of the reef showing as a smooth slick on the surface. The many varieties of fish and coral can be seen by the non-swimmer from the comfort of a glass-bottomed boat. However, for divers with face mask and flippers, there is a richer life still, under overhanging pieces of rock or coral.

The North Reef is the main reef, lying parallel to the shore for about two-thirds the length of the Park. Much of the reef is exposed at low tide, unlike Barracuda Reef. The southern end of the reef has a particular attraction for more adventurous swimmers. Here, at its outer edge, the bank of coral slopes away out into the depths of the channel, and the types of fish to be seen change dramatically, as the coral dwellers are invaded by the fish from the open sea. Kingfish and kole-kole sweep past the sloping face and back into the blue haze beyond. Unicorn fish steam haughtily away from the diver, large rock cod flip back into their coral holes and lobsters wave their long white feelers. Big turtles come to feed on the lower slopes, but on the whole they are shyer than the fish and soon paddle off when approached. It is an exciting and rewarding diving area within easy reach of the coral gardens where most of the hire boats anchor.

Watamu Marine Park

This Park is situated 22 km. (14 miles) south of Malindi, running from the mouth of Mida Creek at its southern end, then northwards to include Turtle Bay, its seaward boundary being the coastal reef.

There are small coral reefs here which lie parallel to the shore just inside the main channel. They are not exposed at low tide and their position is marked with buoys. The seabed is characterized by brain coral. It does not provide shelter for many of the small coral fish, which prefer to hide among the branches of madrepores, finger and staghorn. However, the charming anemone and clown fish are well represented as there are large numbers of sea anemones.

The northern end of the reefs away from the markers is perhaps more interesting than the rest. Down the edge of the channel the coral tends to grow in large boulders and spires, separated by stretches of sandy or weedy bottom. It is better to dive here rather than view from a boat so as to flip through a coral canyon in company with the various fish that live there.

Whale Island

This is a formidable, jagged island lying at the southern end of the Park. The "tail" is divided from the "body" by a narrow sandy cover, while the flat slope on the top of the island is sparsely covered with grass and low scrub. At low tide one can walk round the base, where there are occasional eels or sea urchins, and everywhere there is a scuttling retreat of brightly-colored rock crabs and agile marine lizards.

Tewa Caves

A spur of dark grey limestone coral runs out from the south shore across the mouth of the Mida Creek. The little reef rises only slightly above the water, and is completely covered at high tide. There are tunnels which run right under the reef, and in these underwater caves live a group of giant rock cod or groupers (*tewa* in Swahili). The larger ones are more than two meters (seven feet) long and weigh several hundred kilos. They must be one of the most exciting sights in either of the marine parks, although strictly speaking it is a sight reserved for experienced skin-divers, and only at slack tide. However, the novice can enjoy the spectacle providing a few simple rules are observed: have the right gear; go in a party of three; and swim with the current. The only other rule is . . . don't chase the tewa—they are quite easily frightened and may disappear for the rest of the day if upset.

Nearby Areas of Interest

Just outside the southern boundary of Watamu Marine National Park there is a very attractive bank of coral. It is quite narrow, deep on the offshore side but with some of the higher coral heads almost breaking the surface at low tide. It contains a considerable variety of coral, a fair share of both large and small fish, and numerous sea anemones. It also has some shells of which there are very few, if any, in the coral gardens. The lovely porcelain cowrie is quite common; it's usually found on the strange rubbery bathmats. As at Watamu, there is a brisk trade for the cleaner wrasse, with some stately batfish among their customers.

Mida Creek is an attractive, sheltered stretch of water within the marine reserve, lined with mangroves, backwaters and sandspits. Small islands provide resting places for a large number of water birds, both indigenous and migratory.

PARK DATA

DIRECTIONS. Malindi Marine Park lies offshore just south of the town itself. Watamu Marine Park is 16 km. (ten miles) further south at Turtle Bay, reached by a spur from the main Mombasa-Malindi road.

ACCOMMODATIONS. Malindi. Blue Marlin and **Lawfords.** Reservations: Jambo Hotels, P.O.Box 20, Malindi (tel. 20440). Adjoining hotels, located on the beach downtown. Friendly but can be very crowded.

Che Sale. Reservations: Signet Hotels, P.O.Box 59749, Nairobi (tel. 335900, 335807, 21318). We are putting this beach club in here, though it is an hour's drive from Malindi. It is a kind of Kenyan Shangri-La, with thatched cottages on the edge of the surf and around 24 km. (15 miles) of deserted beach to romp in. Season Aug. through Mar. but best from Dec. on. It has had its full share of jetset beachcombers. Gourmet food, watersports, deep sea fishing. Ideal for those wanting to get away from it all.

Driftwood Beach Club. Reservations: P.O.Box 63, Malindi (tel. 20155). South of the town, near the marine park. Used by up-country locals for family beach holidays and associated sports. The restaurant is good, ambitious but not pretentious.

Eden Roc. Reservations: P.O.Box 350, Malindi (tel. 20480). Comfortable, stylish and friendly.

Sindbad Hotel. P.O.Box 30, Malindi (tel. 7). Quiet, with stylish Arabic architecture.

Restaurant. Umande. Seafood and French cuisine. Malindi's leading restaurant. Located outside town, but provides transport from any hotel.

Watamu. Ocean Sports. P.O.Box 340, Malindi (tel. Watamu 8). Small, unpretentious and good value. Well-equipped for water sports in Turtle Bay and the Marine Park. More or less the local pub by the sea, but has good seafood specialties.

Turtle Bay. P.O.Box 453, Malindi (tel. Watamu 3). Tops for style in the resort. Lots of activities, including a diving school.

Watamu Beach. Reservations: African Safari Club, P.O.Box 46020, Nairobi (tel. 25228). Hotel tel. Watamu 1. Lots to ride, from horses to trimarans.

FACILITIES. Most of the hotels in the Malindi and Watamu area provide trips in glass-bottomed boats. These last about two-and-a-half hours over the low tide period and the charge depends on the facilities made available. The boat owners supply face masks and flippers.

For the serious scuba-diver, it is possible to obtain a boat on hire from one of a number of companies in Malindi operating water sports and boating services. A limited amount of diving equipment and underwater cameras are also available for hire.

KISITE–MPUNGUTI (SHIMONI) MARINE PARK

This is the third marine national park. It lies off Shimoni close to the Tanzanian border. It comprises four coral islets: Kisite, Mpunguti ya Chini (lower), Mpunguti ya Juu (upper) and a small outcrop, Jiwe la Jahazi. All of these islands are surrounded by gardens of fine coral.

Kisite, though furthest from Shimoni, is probably the most visited and normally has the best conditions for skin-diving. Clear water, a shallow reef and the Mpungutis afford Kisite a certain amount of protection from rough weather in the northeast monsoon. The reef is more exposed at low tide, and provides an ideal picnic place with shallow pools for the less adventurous.

During World War I, Kisite was used for target practice by ships of the two powers involved—notably the German battlecruiser *Konigsberg,* and up until a few years ago some of her great 40 cm. (16 inch) shells could be seen lying on the reef near the island.

The waters around Mpunguti ya Juu and to the east of Mpunguti ya Chini are really for the scuba diver, being considerably deeper than Kisite. Coral life is not so prolific, being more exposed to the weather and hence rough seas. These waters contain all the fish of the Kenya coast including sail fish and sometimes the large whale shark.

There is a noticeable difference between the fauna of the northern marine parks and Kisite, where soft corals abound and form a swaying and colorful garden as beautiful as any on the coast. Many of the fish are common, but occasionally a reef fish will be seen at Kisite which is rare or even unknown further north.

PARK DATA

DIRECTIONS. From Mombasa it is 85 km. (53 miles) south on the A14 heading toward Tanzania before a left turn, to Shimoni, just past Ramisi.

ACCOMMODATIONS. Pemba Channel Fishing Club, Box 54, Ukunda (tel. Msambweni 5Y2). At Shimoni, it has modern boats for trips to the Park. Center for deep-sea fishing. Friendly atmosphere. It is also possible to negotiate a ride in a *ngalawa* dugout with Shimoni and Wasini fishermen.

Shimoni Reef Fishing Lodge, Box 82234, Mombasa (tel. 471771), telex 21199, cables REEF. Cottage accommodations, restaurant, bar, lounge. Specializes in deep-sea fishing and excursions to the nearby Kisite–Mpunguti Marine National Park.

KIUNGA MARINE PARK

The latest of Kenya's marine parks. Its most fascinating coral formations center on the tiny islet of Kiu, a great attraction for the scuba enthusiast and reached by private boat from Kiwayuu Island or by boat from Lamu. It is situated south of the Somali border at Kiunga, between the Boni and Dodori National Reserves.

PARK DATA

ACCOMMODATIONS. On Lamu Island. Peponi Hotel. P.O.Box 24, Lamu (tel. Lamu 29). At Shela village, three km. (two miles) from Lamu town.
Petley's Inn. Reservations: Bunson Travel Services, P.O.Box 45456, Nairobi (tel. 25465). Hotel tel. Lamu 48. In Lamu town.

On Kiwayuu Island. Kiwayuu Island Lodge. Reservations: tel. Nairobi 21177, 20296.

Near Mkokoni. Kiwayuu Safari Village. Reservations: P.O.Box 48287, Nairobi (tel. 891381).

MOUNTAIN NATIONAL PARKS

Kenya has established three Mountain National Parks, all of which lie in the area generally known as the Kenya Highlands. This region, which lies to the north and west of Nairobi, has a complex geological history and was formed from the uplifting of the Earth's crust into a dome which then split down the middle to form the Great Rift Valley. Around the edge of this great tear in the crust, violent volcanic action produced great lava flows and giant volcanoes which today form the region's main mountain ranges.

Of the three parks Mount Elgon National Park is the smallest and occupies only a sliver of the eastern slope of the mountain, which straddles the Kenya/Uganda border. However, it does extend across the range of vegetation zones on major mountain slopes.

The other two Parks, Mount Kenya and the Aberdares, are only 80 km. (50 miles) apart and lie just a couple of hours' drive north of Nairobi. In both cases the Parks encompass the whole upper region of the massif, together with a few salients. They are also both surrounded by forest reserves which are well stocked with game, although this can be difficult to view except at one of the recognized mountain lodges.

The Parks were not set up primarily to protect game, but to provide recreation areas of high scenic, geological and botanical interest. There are no regular closed seasons but road conditions can become treacherous when it rains and it is always best to check first either with the Park's Headquarters or the A.A. in Nairobi. Temperatures below freezing are common at night so suitable warm clothing and bedding should be taken by those intending to camp, as well as a sound waterproof tent.

MOUNT KENYA NATIONAL PARK

Mount Kenya is a giant of a mountain which rises 3,048 meters (10,000 ft.) above the surrounding highland plateau and extends to some 80 km. (50 miles) in diameter. Although volcanic in origin it does not retain the smooth contours of many other volcanic mountains, but is instead crowned with two jagged, snow covered peaks: Batian (5,199 meters, 17,058 ft.) and Nelion (5,188 meters, 17,022 ft.). These and the smaller peaks nearby are the remaining volcanic plugs of the now eroded, but once massive, volcanic crater.

The lower slopes of the mountain are heavily cultivated particularly on the southern and eastern sides where high rainfall and rich volcanic soil support very intensive subsistence farming. Above there are dense rain forests of cedar, olive and podo which merge into a bamboo zone at around 2,440 meters (8,000 ft.). This in turn gives way to a belt of rosewood trees and giant St. John's wort before dying out at the heath zone at about 3,200 meters (10,500 ft.).

The National Park itself covers an area of 588 sq. km. (227 sq. miles) which, with the exception of two salients at the Naro Moru and Sirimon approaches, begins where the upper forest merges with the heath *(Erica arborea)* zone. (The *Erica arborea* is a weirdly-shaped bush often as large as a tree and covered with moss and lichen.) At 3,500 meters (11,480 ft.), the giant heather is replaced by open moorland covered in tussock grass and studded with many species of giant lobelia and groundsel growing to a height of 3 to 5 meters (10 to 17 ft.). The ground is covered in a rich profusion of everlasting helichrysums and alchemillas and interspersed with gladioli, delphiniums and "red-hot pokers."

An attractive feature of the mountain is its 32 small lakes and colorful tarns. Hall Tarn is superbly situated overlooking the Gorges Valley and Lake Michaelson far below. At the Curling Pond beneath the Lewis Glacier it is sometimes possible to skate.

The central area of peaks, scree slopes, glaciers and snowfields offers a great variety of climbing routes. These are of varying degrees of difficulty, but all the summit ascents call for high mountaineering skill and experience of rock, ice and snow techniques. Vast areas below the peaks are ideal for mountain walking and scrambling, and there are a number of subsidiary peaks and interesting glacier routes up to Point Lenana (4,986 meters, 16,358 ft.) which are suitable for visitors with little or no climbing experience.

The mountain has a wide variety of bird life ranging from the huge eagles to the delicate multi-colored sunbirds. Among the most distinctive species are the crowned eagles, mountain buzzard, Mackinder's owl, Jackson's francolin, the scarlet-tufted malachite and golden-winged sunbirds, and the mountain chat.

The forests below the moorlands contain an abundance of game animals, including elephant, rhino, buffalo, leopard, bongo antelope, bushbuck, several species of duiker, giant forest hog, colobus and Sykes' monkey.

Lions inhabit the moorlands; although they are not common. Eland are often seen on the northern and drier parts of the moorlands and zebra migrate from the lower plains. Leopard and wild dog are not uncommon in the peak zone and tracks of both have frequently been recorded in snow above 4,575 meters (15,010 ft.). Unquestionably these two predators find adequate and easy prey among the many varieties of rodent and rock hyrax in these high regions.

Several species of reptiles are found, among them the Hinds montane viper, exclusive to the Mount Kenya and Aberdare moorlands.

Several tracks for vehicles wind their way up the forested ridges, and two reach the moorlands—the Sirimon route extends to 3,965 meters (13,009 ft.) and the Timau Track to 4,209 meters (13,809 ft.), forming the highest roadhead in Africa. The quickest access to the peaks is via the Naro Moru track which reaches 3,050 meters (10,007 ft.) and stops immediately below the moorlands.

For Mount Kenya Park, all visitors must sign in at the Park entrance gates on the Naro Moru, Sirimon and Chogoria routes. Unaccompanied visitors are not permitted through the park gates on Mount Kenya, except for a day trip terminating at 4 P.M. For a longer stay on the mountain, there must be two or more people, as well as guides and porters, who may be booked at the Naro Moru River Lodge.

The Batian peak was first climbed in 1899 by Sir Halford Mackinder, but did not become well-known to mountaineers until Sir Eric Shipton made the second recorded ascent in 1929. There are now five established main routes to the summit, and nine minor ascents for the most skillful alpine mountaineers.

There are strict regulations governing a climb or over-night stay in the Park—all carefully thought out to safeguard the visitor from the obvious hazards of cold, tricky rock faces, wild animals, and mountain sickness—which the inexperienced climber might not expect but which is a possibility at altitudes above 4,000 meters (13,000 ft.). Climbers must register their intended route at Park Headquarters.

Central Kenya is subject to two rainy seasons per year. These periods are off seasons for climbing due to the wet conditions on the mountain and the accumulation of ice and snow on the peaks. Climbing is generally attempted only during the two dry seasons which occur in late December, January, February and early March, and again in July, August, September and early October. This is not to say that climbing is not possible during the off seasons, merely that approach conditions are difficult and the climbs are at least one grade harder and several hours longer. There have been very few successful ascents during the rains.

A variety of services is available from commercial establishments around the mountain; walking guides, porters, cooks, pack animals, tentage, climbing and camping equipment, food provisions, motor transport to the roadheads, and accommodations of various standards. Various high level huts, campsites and cabins are available for hire from the Mountain Club of Kenya, the Naro Moru River Lodge and the Parks Headquarters at Mweiga.

Kenya National Parks operate a mountain rescue service.

PARK DATA

DIRECTIONS. From Nairobi take the A2 via Thika to Naro Moru, 177 km. (110 miles), where a right turn leads to the Park Headquarters, and access via the Naro Moru track. The Sirimon track is off right a short distance beyond Nanyuki.

ACCOMMODATIONS. Meru Mount Kenya Lodge. Reservations: P.O.Box 60342, Nairobi (tel. 29539). Self-service accommodations on the eastern slopes of the mountain.

Mountain Lodge. Reservations: African Tours and Hotels, P.O.Box 30471, Nairobi (tel. 336858). Built on stilts, like Treetops, but with even more luxurious facilities. Correspondingly costly. Ground-level viewing room for close-up photography.

Mount Kenya Safari Club. Reservations: Intercontinental Hotel, P.O.Box 30353, Nairobi (tel. 335550). Hotel tel. Nanyuki 2141. Owned by millionaire Adnan Kashoggi, and definitely in the jetset range. The grounds include a nine-hole golf course. In a class of its own.

Naro Moru River Lodge. Reservations: Alliance Hotels, P.O.Box 49839, Nairobi (tel. 337501, 29961). Hotel tel. Naro Moru 23. A good base for visiting Mount Kenya. Just outside the township, and set in lovely wooded grounds on the banks of a river. Good fishing and birdwatching. Also has self-service cabins, bunkhouse and campsite, and from here climbers can hire guides, equipment and mountain huts.

Sportsman's Arms. Reservations: Repotel, P.O.Box 46527, Nairobi (tel. 27828). Hotel tel. Nanyuki 2057, 2717. A long-established and well-known country hotel.

Climbing Accommodations. Mountain Club huts may be booked at Naro Moru River Lodge (see above).
1 Top Hut, Australia, Two Tarn, Firmin and Kami Huts—Shs. 20/-.
2 Teleki, Klarwills, Liki North, Minto and Urumandi Huts—Shs. 2/- (club member), Shs. 5/- (non-member).
3 Porters huts (Klarwills and Kami)—No charge.

ABERDARE NATIONAL PARK

The Aberdare range of mountains stretches northward from Nairobi along the eastern flank of the Great Rift Valley. Between the two main peaks of Satima (4,000 meters, 13,120 ft.) in the north and Kinangop (3,906 meters, 12,816 ft.), 40 km. (25 miles) to the south, is an extensive plateau of open moorland.

The western slopes of the range constitute part of the rift valley wall and drop sharply to the Kinangop plateau. The eastern slopes are less steep and fall to the highland farming country which lies between the Aberdares and Mount Kenya, 80 km. (50 miles) to the east. The slopes of the range are covered in a thick forest of hardwoods.

The National Park covers an area of 590 sq. km. (228 sq. miles) consisting primarily of the moorland plateau, but extending down through the rain forest in the northeast in the area of the Treetops salient. It is an area of great scenic beauty, of rolling country covered in tussock grass, large areas of mixed giant heath and forested patches of rosewood and St. John's wort. Giant lobelias and groundsel are also found in sheltered valleys.

Streams of ice cold water thread their way across the moorland suddenly to disappear into valleys and ravines in a series of beautiful waterfalls. Most spectacular are the Gura and Karuru falls which lie on opposite sides of a deep valley, the Gura cascading almost 1,000 meters (3,280 ft.) without interruption whilst the Karuru falls in three steps. Easy access is afforded to the head of the Karuru falls and there are breathtaking views of the Gura across the valley. Other impressive falls are the Chaina falls, and the Cave waterfall—recently used as one of the sets for the film "Sheena—Queen of the Jungle."

The streams are stocked with rainbow, brown and American brook trout and fishing is permitted provided a current trout fishing license is held. There is no size limit and a generous bag is allowed, up to six fish per rod per day from each stream (fly fishing only). There are campsites and picnic areas close to the waterfalls on the Gura and Karuru rivers.

The Aberdares are well endowed with a great variety and quantity of wild animals, and despite the periodic cold and mist the plateau moorlands form a popular habitat. The western slopes of this range are relatively steep and not generally as attractive to game as the more gentle slopes of the eastern side. Elephants, buffalo, rhino, eland, bongo, waterbuck, bushbuck, reed buck, several species of duikers, suni, giant forest hog, bush pig, warthog, serval cat, leopard, lion, colobus and Sykes' monkeys, hyaena and wild dog, occur in varying numbers. Rhino—although recently heavily poached—are still fairly well represented on the plateau moorlands, and in the Treetops salient.

Early morning or evening drives offer the best chance of seeing game, and a careful lookout at the various roadside salt-licks, forest glades and open valleys should prove rewarding. If the visitor is particularly patient, he or she may be lucky enough to see some of the more elusive of the mountain dwellers such as the shy bongo antelope, the black leopard and the giant forest hog or even the crowned eagle hunting one of his favorite foods, the colobus monkey.

Black serval cat are not uncommon and are often seen on the open moors, usually hunting duiker, francolin, or rodents. Melanism (an unusually dark pigmentation) is a condition which is seen in these high altitude zones among leopards, serval cats, and some of the smaller predators and the Augur buzzard.

Rather disturbing are recent reports concerning the Park's lions, which, it seems, have become uncharacteristically aggressive toward humans. A number of serious injuries have occurred to people out in the open and visitors are cautioned against camping or straying too far from their vehicles without a ranger, until further notice.

The Park has a good network of tracks but although the main destinations are marked at many of the junctions, some circuits of interest are not. It is more infuriating because of the inexplicable absence of a good park map, and visitors are advised to follow the outline in their guide books and ask detailed directions from rangers at the various gates. The main track runs directly across the top of the plateau from the eastern gates leading from Nyeri, to the Mujubio West Gate, which leads directly into the rift valley and to Naivasha.

PARK DATA

DIRECTIONS. From the east the Park can be approached from Nyeri, 154 km. (96 miles) north of Nairobi on the A2, from where there is a choice of three gates. The most direct access is via the east gate four km. (two miles) beyond the town, and the Kiandongoro gate, 22 km. (14 miles) from the town on the edge of the moorland plateau. The third gate is reached via Mweiga just north of Nyeri.

From the west the Park is approached from Naivasha, taking a right turn from the A104 highway just at the bottom of the escarpment, signposted to the Park and North Kinangop. After 14 km. (nine miles) the tarmac runs out at the top of a steep hill, when a junction left is signposted and travels 24 km. (15 miles) across grasslands to North Kinangop. Then it is a steep climb up the face of the escarpment on a series of hairpin bends to the Mujubio west gate, formerly Queen's gate.

ACCOMMODATIONS. Aberdare Country Club. Reservations: Signet Hotels, P.O.Box 48690, Nairobi (tel. 335900). Hotel tel. Mweiga 17. Wonderful country-house atmosphere, with splendid cottages.

The Ark. Reservations: Signet Hotels, P.O.Box 48690, Nairobi (tel. 335900). Located far out into the rain forest, by a waterhole. Takes its name from the unusual shape. Departure point for The Ark is at Aberdare Country Club.

Green Hills Hotel. Reservations: P.O.Box 313, Nyeri (tel. 2017, 2687). Modern hotel, with activities well to the fore. Underground disco.

Outspan Hotel. Reservations: Block Hotels, P.O.Box 47557, Nairobi (tel. 22860). Plenty of tradition and colonial character. Fishing, golf and other sports. Departure point for Treetops.

Treetops. Reservations: Block Hotels, P.O.Box 47557, Nairobi (tel. 22860). Famous mountain lodge, elevated on stilts and overlooking a waterhole in a clearing, at the southern edge of the forest. Book well in advance.

MOUNT ELGON NATIONAL PARK

The Park covers an area of only 168 sq. km. (65 sq. miles) on the eastern slopes of Mount Elgon. However it ranges in altitude from 2,000 meters (6,560 ft.) to 4,321 meters (14,178 ft.) at the crater peak of Koitoboss. It embraces a range of habitats from bamboo jungle, through forest and green woodland to alpine moor studded with giant species of plants.

The Park has a good network of tracks making it easy to explore the varied vegetation zones. In the lower parts one may see the full magnificence of the natural forest where many trees reach 30 meters (100 ft.). One of the finest is the podo tree which has a clean, straight bole, and is crowned with evergreen foliage. The Park road system climbs well into the moorland area where there are the giant heaths and heathers, groundsels and innumerable wild flowers, among which the everlasting helichrysums are particularly attractive.

There are many monkeys in the forest and bamboo, including black and white colobus—one of the most exciting animals to see on the move as it jumps from tree to tree with its long cape of fur streaming out behind it.

Elephants are also relatively numerous in the forest, although not always easy to spot. Buffalo, reedbuck, waterbuck, bushbuck, black-fronted duiker, bushpig, giant forest hog and leopard are all present in substantial numbers but can easily be missed in the forest and bamboo. The birdlife is also very rich; turacos, silvery-cheeked and red-billed hornbills, white-naped ravens and the Kenya crested guinea-fowl are of particular interest.

A unique attraction of the Park is a system of large caves, which were once inhabited by the Elgon Masai. They can easily be visited on foot, some of them being very close to the Park roads. The entrance to Kitum Cave, for example, where there is a pool used by elephants, is 50 meters (165 ft.) wide and 10 meters (33 ft.) high. Thousands of bats roost in the rear of the cave and it is an eerie and fascinating experience to explore the labyrinth with hundreds of eyes gleaming in the reflected light of a torch. The caves inspired the setting for Rider Haggard's novel, *She*.

PARK DATA

DIRECTIONS. The mountain straddles Kenya's border with Uganda, above Lake Victoria. It is reached by the main Nairobi–Uganda road, through Nakuru, Eldoret and Kitale to Endebess township. From there a left turn is signposted to the Park gate.

ACCOMMODATIONS. Mount Elgon Lodge. Reservations: African Tours and Hotels, P.O.Box 30471, Nairobi (tel. 336858). A comfortably modernized farmhouse close to the Park gate.

INDEX

GENERAL INFORMATION

223

GEOGRAPHICAL & PRACTICAL INFORMATION

Accommodations indicates hotels and/or lodges, inns, tented camps, cottages, huts, campsites. H indicates hotels only, R indicates restaurants.